Memory, Identity,
and Commemorations of World War II

Memory, Identity, and Commemorations of World War II

Anniversary Politics in Asia Pacific

Edited by Daqing Yang and Mike Mochizuki
Foreword by Akira Iriye

LEXINGTON BOOKS
Lanham • Boulder • New York • London

Published by Lexington Books
An imprint of The Rowman & Littlefield Publishing Group, Inc.
4501 Forbes Boulevard, Suite 200, Lanham, Maryland 20706
www.rowman.com

Unit A, Whitacre Mews, 26-34 Stannary Street, London SE11 4AB

British Library Cataloguing in Publication Information Available

Library of Congress Cataloging-in-Publication Data

ISBN: 978-1-4985-6769-5 (cloth)
ISBN: 978-1-4985-6771-8 (pbk.)
ISBN: 978-1-4985-6770-1 (electronic)

To our Mothers, Mochizuki Toshiko (1919–2009) and Chen Yunxiao (1922–2017). Their memories of war inspired our commitment to reconciliation.

Contents

Editors' Note

All East Asian names throughout this book follow East Asian practice with family names listed before first names.

Foreword

Commemorating 1945 in Transnational History

Akira Iriye

On August 15, 1945, the Second World War in Asia and the Pacific came to an end, Japan having surrendered to the allied powers, including the United States, Britain, and China. It had been a long and brutal war, going back to Japan's invasion of Manchuria in 1931 and ending within days after the dropping of atomic bombs on Japanese soil.

At that time I was ten years old, having been born in Tokyo in October 1934. My father, who worked for the Domei Press, the national news service, and spent most of the war years in China, urged me to start keeping a diary, undoubtedly believing that a young child should write down in his own words his observations and impressions of what he was witnessing. I did so, starting on August 19, and have kept the habit ever since. More than seventy years have passed, and I occasionally re-read my diary entries to refresh my memory about personal as well as public affairs.

The first entry in my diary, four days after the end of the war, merely noted, "My grandfather, father, sister, and I took a walk after getting up early in the morning." There is nothing about the ending of the war in the diary till August 28, when I wrote, "Today is the day when the allied forces are to start occupying the country. I noticed U.S. aircraft flying low and nonchalantly. I felt awful, but there was nothing I could do except study." This seems to have been how I "commemorated" Japan's surrender and occupation by U.S. forces. My diary does not convey any sense that I was witnessing a series of momentous developments.

And yet there is little doubt that these events were major landmarks in my life as well in the lives of hundreds of millions of Japanese, Americans,

Chinese, and so many other people. August 1945 changed their lives and serves as a major turning point in history.

Of course, it is possible to point to other dates as key turning points in history. In the European context, May 1945 when Germany surrendered would probably be considered more appropriate as a commemorative landmark, while for the Soviet Union the victory in the Battle of Stalingrad in 1943 might be viewed as having been even more important. For China, 1945 may be seen just as a way station toward the more momentous landmark year of 1949, when the Communists came to power. For the bulk of humanity in the colonial regions of Asia and Africa, historic events such as decolonization, independence, and nation-building lay even further in the future.

Nevertheless, we need some periodizing scheme to help us make sense of the past, both for individuals and for communities of people. They commemorate certain dates so as to understand where they have been, and are, and to relate themselves to historical phenomena. This essay will consider the significance of 1945 in transnational history.

Transnational history is to be distinguished from international history. The latter is a record of relations among nations, whereas the former focuses on movements and connections across national boundaries. Here the key framework is not the nation but individuals and non-national entities that cut across national boundaries, such as races, religions, age categories, and classes with which people identify themselves. They exist in all countries, and in that sense they are transnational categories. They interact with one another irrespective of diplomatic, inter-state affairs. In this sense their existence precedes that of separate states. Transnational phenomena, then, are far more extensive than international relations.

The year 1945 is susceptible of commemoration in many transnational ways. For instance, we may consider gender, race, and religious relationships. Profound changes marked these relationships around 1945, changes that were recognized by the newly established United Nations and led its member states to sponsor a Universal Declaration on Human Rights, which it adopted in 1948. Here was an unequivocal enunciation of the principle of equality not merely among nations but also among races, religions, and ways of life as well as between men and women.

It is well to recall that the first decades of the twentieth century had been a heyday of "scientific racism," the period when racial distinctions were considered to be scientifically proven and, moreover, fundamentally unchangeable. The white race was seen as being superior to others, and interracial marriages, especially between white Westerners and colored people were considered undesirable. The United States, Canada, Australia, and other "white" countries strictly limited the immigration of Asians and Africans, and even those who somehow entered and lived in these lands were not given equal treatment to whites. In many parts of the United States, for instance,

Asian children were sent to their own schools and prohibited from marrying whites. Interracial marriages were outlawed in southern states as well as elsewhere. The "scientific" basis for such restrictiveness was provided by eugenics, which popularized the notion that "race mixing" was destined to produce less intelligent, less healthy humans.

Given this background at the beginning of the twentieth century, it was a remarkable historical phenomenon that during the Great War, the governments of Great Britain, France, and Russia should denounce the Ottoman Empire's treatment of Armenians as a violation of human rights. Hundreds of thousands of Armenians were fleeing Turkey to enter Russia, many of them eager to join its armed forces to fight against the Ottomans. And when many of them lost their lives in the process, Russia and its allies castigated the Empire as having violated human rights. The Ottoman Empire was an easy target because throughout the nineteenth century its Christian subjects— Greeks, Macedonians, Armenians, and many others—had suffered from discrimination and even persecution. Of course, human rights violations had existed in Russia and its allies, the long history of slavery and serfdom providing obvious instances. But the key is that human rights violations were now chronicled and commemorated as major historical events by some of the great powers.

Ironically, the League of Nations Covenant failed to include any reference to human rights. The idea of "universal" rights might have seemed incongruent with the principle of nationalism that was enshrined in the Covenant. Each nation was to deal with its own affairs in the name of national sovereignty, and an international community of sovereign nations would establish a new world order. Internationalism was the key to the postwar world order, not transnationalism, so an insertion of transnational principles might have seemed out of place. Still, it is important to recall that the League established a committee on intellectual cooperation, designed to promote exchanges among scholars, artists, journalists, and others across national boundaries. The committee would, after the Second World War, resurrect itself as UNESCO. For the first time, transnationalism was added to nationalism and internationalism as providing a key to understanding, and periodizing, history. Commemorative events now would have to include transnational, as well as national and international, affairs.

The history of human rights may be understood in such a framework. Historical commemorations, indeed, include just as many transnational as national or international events. Or, it may be more accurate to say that even events taking place in a national or international context could have transnational significance. The abolition of slavery in the United States, to take an obvious example, was a key landmark in U.S. history, but it was also a defining moment in transnational history. It would, therefore, make sense to commemorate historical developments that hold global, not just local or na-

tional, significance. To do so, however, would require that we identify historical events that go beyond the national framework. Nations, after all, are but
one among many communities of people, the majority of whom have identities besides their nationality, including their gender, age, religion, medical
conditions, occupations, or levels of education. To commemorate only national events, therefore, would be a very narrow view of the past. It would be
important to go beyond commemorations of national landmarks if we are to
gain a fuller understanding of humankind's rich and varied legacy.

To go back to human rights, the commemoration of this principle would
have to include different chronologies, for the emancipation of slaves in
various parts of the world, for instance, did not coincide with the emancipation of women, nor did racial equality become a major principle simultaneously throughout the globe.

Nevertheless, it seems possible to commemorate the development of the
idea and practice of human rights in history. To go back to the example of
racism, the UN declaration of 1948 explicitly repudiated racial discrimination as contrary to the principle of human rights. That is why world history
may be said to have entered a new era after the Second World War. Human
affairs would not just play out in national frameworks or in the context of
international affairs. Rather, transnational principles would now form one
key element for commemorating historical events.

Instead, therefore, of commemorating post-1945 history as a continuation
of the preceding history consisting of national and international affairs, we
should consider this, the most recent phase of modern history, a new era in
transnational history. In other words, what we should commemorate in post-
1945 history is not the Cold War, decolonization, or nation-building, but the
growth of human rights.

That history would have a different chronology from the chronologies
that privilege national or international affairs. The immediate post-1945
years, for instance, would no longer be seen merely in the framework of the
origins of the Cold War but also as a milestone in the growth of human
rights. To be sure, the development of human rights was not uniform
throughout the world, but that is no reason not to commemorate this history.

To commemorate human rights as a key ingredient of post-1945 history
would enable us to look to religions, the sexes, races, and many other categories besides nations as definers of history. And post-1945 history would have
a different chronology from the ones that are determined by national or
international affairs.

If, for instance, if we were to commemorate the liberation of women as a
key feature of human affairs, developments in China after 1949 would take
on greater significance than domestic politics in the United States or the
Soviet Union. If the growth of racial equality were to be seen as the key to
recent history, then the 1960s would have to be seen as having been the

crucial moment in recent history. If such principles of human rights as freedom of thought and expression were to be commemorated, the 1970s might emerge in retrospect as having been a major turning point. If, finally, a clean environment were to be the key commemorative principle, the 1980s might be of even greater importance. The point is that depending on what is being commemorated, we might have a different chronology. That, after all, is what history is about. There can be as many chronologies as there are human communities and groups, each of whom may have its own events to commemorate.

To go back to human rights, even my modest, personal diary seems to suggest that 1945 was an important year to commemorate. A ten-year-old boy in Tokyo, would never have heard of human rights. To him and virtually to all his contemporaries, national rights had been everything, and universal human rights would have meant nothing. When this began to change is an interesting question. Sometime during my middle school years (1946–1949), I remember we were given a freshly printed copy of the new constitution, and I eagerly read its Preamble and Article Nine, both of which stressed peace as the overriding principle for which the country was now to stand. These clauses were so important that when, in March 1953, we graduated from high school and I served as valedictorian, my father urged me to focus on that theme. I do not recall that either my father or my teachers spoke about human rights as another important value for which the country was to stand. Indeed, I may never have heard of human rights till I came to the United States in 1953.

Even in the United States, however, I am not sure if the term was as widespread as it is today. The early 1950s were a heyday of McCarthyism, and the rights of many academics, artists, and others were violated as they were randomly accused of having been Communists or Communist sympathizers. Many of my teachers at Haverford and Harvard where I studied were appalled by McCarthyism and its assault upon innocent scholars and journalists, but I do not think these accusations were criticized as violations of the principle of human rights. Even during the 1960s, when protest movements became much more commonplace, both in the context of the protection of civil rights or of the opposition to the war in Vietnam, one rarely heard about violations of human rights. Public discussions were conducted either within the context of the Cold War, so that many argued that the war in Southeast Asia would be counter-productive to the more important goal of winning the contest with the Soviet Union or the People's Republic of China, or else in the framework of the Vietnamese people's right of self-determination.

It was only in the 1970s, when the Vietnam War was already waning, that human rights entered the vocabulary of daily discussions on national or international affairs. This is something scholars like Sarah Snyder and Barbara Keys have discussed in detail. In terms of the chronology of transnational history, therefore, the 1970s emerge as a decade of pivotal importance. We may add to human rights another significant global development, the movement to protect the natural environment, which also gained momentum in the decade.

Commemorations, therefore, imply as many chronologies as there are national, international, and transnational events, not to mention personal lives. It would be interesting to examine if personal and transnational commemorations may overlap. As noted above, in my own case, the commemoration of human rights has been a key, indeed the key, to personal life. Starting in 1945 and then most momentously in the 1970s, my life has been inseparable from the history of human rights. This history not only contains the 1948 Universal Declaration of Human Rights but such other instances as the civil rights legislation passed by the U.S. Congress as well as the immigration law of 1965 and the Americans with Disabilities Act of 1990.

I first came to the United States in 1953 to study at Haverford College. I was a beneficiary of American generosity in two crucial ways; the Joseph C. Grew Foundation, established shortly after the war to honor the prewar U.S. ambassador to Japan who was eager to restore friendly relations between the two countries, chose me as one of its first recipients, and Haverford, the Quaker college outside Philadelphia, admitted me without even interviewing me. I do not think that the term "human rights" was commonly used at that time, but quite clearly the rights of all students regardless of their backgrounds were respected. The early 1950s were a heyday of the Cold War, with an uneasy truce in the Korean Peninsula but with incipient conflicts in Southeast Asia, the Middle East, and elsewhere. Domestically, McCarthyism had not yet abated. But on campus, we read Marx as part of our assignments. There was complete freedom in expressing ourselves, and every teacher treated me and all other students as individuals potentially capable of achieving scholarly successes. The immigration law of 1965 eliminated racial quotas that had severely restricted the number of non-European immigrants admitted into the country. Despite, or perhaps because of, the Cold War, students were encouraged to study Chinese and Russian history and literature. Graduate schools were eager to attract a large number of students from abroad. All these circumstances provided a most fortunate environment of which I was a beneficiary.

Another fortunate circumstance for me as well as for countless graduate students, both from the United States and from abroad, was that when we obtained our doctorates—indeed, even before we did so—many of us were invited to teach in various parts of the country. Colleges were expanding in the 1960s, and it was not difficult to find a teaching position. Foreign students completing their dissertations were as eagerly sought after as American Ph.D.'s. In my own case, I did not have to look for a job, and institutions such as the University of California, Santa Cruz, and the University of Rochester offered me teaching positions even without conducting a formal search. I taught at Santa Cruz for two years and just one year at Rochester, and in 1969 I moved to the University of Chicago. There I stayed for twenty years. I was incredibly fortunate that all these places were open to foreign nationals. Indeed, I do not remember ever being asked about my nationality or citizenship even once at any of these institutions. I did not become a U.S. citizen till 2014, long after I retired from teaching (at Harvard) at age eighty. All that these employers wanted to make sure was that I was legally in the United States, as I was. I have been in the country altogether for sixty-three years, but I can categorically state that I have experienced no discrimination on account of my background.

The year 1945 thus means so much to me and I suspect to those of my generation. I spend much time with many of them at a retirement community outside Philadelphia, where the average age is eighty-five. To those who were born into, and survived, the world of the 1930s, 1945 is clearly a key date. In that sense, too, the year is of fundamental relevance in the chronology of transnational history.

Introduction

Daqing Yang and Mike Mochizuki

Anniversary, derived from the Latin word *anniversarius*—returning yearly—is the yearly reoccurrence of the date of a past event. At the individual level, birthdays are perhaps the most common anniversaries; in the public realm, anniversaries are typically associated with important religious, regal, or national events. In many cases, important national anniversaries such as Independence Day in the United States or Bastille Day in France are not only celebrated in public ceremonies, but have also become national holidays that affect everyone in the country.

Anniversaries are not just limited to particular days of the calendar; an entire year or number of years can be marked an anniversary. In some cases, it might be more appropriate to speak of "anniversary moments" or "long anniversaries." Moreover, certain anniversary years are deemed more significant largely because of the number of years that have passed. Much of the world has adopted a system from Latin where centuries (100 years) or fractions of it—quarter, half—are considered significant. In China, where sixty years were considered a cycle (*jia-zi*), years that are multiples of sixty have retained a special meaning.

The designation of particular anniversaries is never a matter of natural cycle or even culture. It is highly political. Any date or year in the calendar must have witnessed an infinite number of events in the past. Those dates or years deemed worthy enough to be marked an anniversary in a public manner always result from political considerations. The decisions designating anniversaries, not to mention the ways of observing them, demand the consideration of political interests, be they local, national, or international. And these decisions of designating anniversaries as well as how anniversaries are observed have political consequences. We call this phenomenon "anniversary politics."

For example, 2014 marks the beginning of a four-year centennial "long anniversary" of World War I in much of western and central Europe. Ranging from 1914 to 1918, the "Great War" as it has been known in Europe, took millions of lives on both sides and produced a profound impact on the history of the twentieth-century world. This centennial commemoration has taken on new political significance given the remarkable progress as well as the recent difficulties of European integration, a process that was designed to eliminate war on the continent once and for all.[1]

The year 2015 represents another such "anniversary moment." Although the year marks many important anniversaries for different countries, by far the most significant was the 70th year after the ending of World War II. What factors make the 70th year—septuagennial in Latin counting—uniquely important? As average human life span falls between 70 and 80 in the Asia Pacific, 70th anniversary means the vast majority of those with direct experience of that war are no longer alive. While the "war generation" and their firsthand experience further recedes, the vast majority of the population today learns about the event 70 years ago overwhelmingly secondhand—from history textbooks, mass media, museums and memorials, to name just a few. In other words, 70 years after World War II, that momentous event is now firmly—though not entirely—in the realm of "collective memory."

More importantly, the 70th anniversary of the end of World War II has been featured in numerous commemorations throughout the Asia Pacific region and beyond. An anniversary of past events truly becomes significant when it is acted upon, or commemorated. How anniversaries are actually commemorated provides a crucial window to how human societies remember bygone events and individuals and view their relations with the past.[2] In his seminal work *How Societies Remember* (1989) Paul Connerton questioned the dominant practice in memory studies that focus on inscribed, or written, transmissions of memories, and instead called for a focus on incorporated, or bodily, practices. He argued that images of the past and recollected knowledge of the past are conveyed and sustained by ritual performances and that performative memory is bodily. If there is such a thing as social memories, he argues, we are likely to find it in commemorative ceremonies.[3] In an era increasingly dominated by the media, how an anniversary is commemorated in a public, visible way gives us a new angle of understanding of what is called "memory works." In other words, public commemoration of anniversaries reveals the working of memory politics.[4]

Since the end of the Cold War, the study of collective memory flourished.[5] In Europe, the termination of Soviet-American confrontation provided an opportunity for intellectuals and the broader public alike to reflect on the historical legacy of World War II. The advent of the Cold War between the two former wartime allies had swept aside many difficult issues regarding not only wartime atrocities and suffering, but also the legacy of imperialism and colonialism. Although the fall of the Berlin Wall offered a triumphal moment for some in the West, the collapse of the Soviet Union and the breakup of Yugoslavia brought to the forefront emotional questions about nationalism and national identity and their implications for geopolitics. The wave of democratization offered both the political space and motivation for people to recall the past and contributed to the reformulation of national historical narratives.

In Europe, 2015 not only brings to the forefront memories about World War II, but is also the centennial of key battles and events associated with World War I, which according to some historians had sown the seeds of World War II. Thus, in this sense the two anniversaries are in mutual reference. In Asia, it is another matter. Not only was World War I not an indispensable reference point, memory politics has its own dynamics in Asia. In the Asia Pacific, the end of the Cold War did not present as sharp of a break in international history. After all, two of the conflicts that had characterized the Cold War confrontation in East Asia did not get resolved. The divisions between China and Taiwan and between North and South Korea indeed became more problematic after 1989. Nevertheless, as in Europe, the passing of the Cold War at the global level had a profound effect on collective memory. Democratization, or at least increasing pluralization, that altered the domestic political landscape in many Asian countries unleashed societal engagement regarding the history issue and buffeted many of the state-level settlements regarding the Asia-Pacific wars that had been carefully negotiated by political elites.

As a consequence, the so-called history problem became an increasingly salient issue in both international and domestic politics. In Japan, the weakening of the political hegemony of the conservative Liberal Democratic Party facilitated an effort to address Japan's past transgressions more forthrightly and to promote reconciliation with Japan's Asian neighbors. In South Korea, civil society activism spearheaded a movement to seek more meaningful redress for victims of Japanese repression, from "comfort women" survivors to forced laborers. In China, as communism increasingly lost its luster after the country's transformative economic reforms, nationalism emerged as the key way to legitimate the regime and harness the energies and hopes of the Chinese people. But the side effect of this elite-driven campaign of patriotic education was to draw public attention, especially among those of the post-Cold War generation, to Japanese aggression and atrocities against China such as the Nanjing Massacre.[6] As Chinese and South Korean criticisms of how Japan had been addressing various history issues became sharper, a nationalistic backlash emerged in Japan against those Japanese who advocated a more explicit acknowledgment of past transgressions. Japanese domestic conflicts about history textbooks and the Yasukuni Shrine thus became internationalized.

The geographic scope of the so-called memory wars, however, has not been clear-cut. All of East Asia does not continue to harbor historical animosity toward Japan. Frictions between Japan and China and between Japan and South Korea about the history problem have been undeniably the most acrimonious. But other countries in East Asia appear more willing to put the past behind and applaud Japan's contributions to regional prosperity. Although many Southeast Asian countries suffered enormously at the hands of the Japanese during World War II, the peoples of these nations in contrast to Chinese and Koreans tend to have very positive views of the Japanese.[7] Taiwan like Korea was part of Japan's colonial empire, but the people on Taiwan in general do not hold hypercritical historical views of Japan that Koreans and mainland Chinese have. Therefore, in many respects, Japan's history problem is primarily a problem regarding mainland China and Korea rather than all of Asia.

Despite this geographic limitation, conflicts about historical memory in Northeast Asia still have major consequences for international politics. For example, territorial disputes about small islands and reefs that have little intrinsic material value are especially difficult to manage because disagreements about historical narratives intensify the emotional content of these conflicts. Moreover, history has shown that dramatic changes in the power balance among major states can provoke international suspicions and fears that magnify the danger of war. Today's rapid rise of Chinese power represents such a power transition. Dealing with structural transformations like this is challenging enough; but highly charged conflicts about history can make this task even more daunting.

A focus on war commemorations not only sheds light on collective memory in the Asia Pacific but also offers new insights on the crucial question of identity. According to Anthony Smith, a leading scholar of nationalism, one of the five key features of national identity relates to "common myths and national memories."[8] These collective myths and memories are constructed and reconstructed through social and political processes.[9] In a recent work on the "history problem" in East Asia, sociologist Hiro Sato states that "Although commemoration frequently oversimplifies and even distorts, the act of remembering the past is indispensable to social life because it enables people to articulate their collective identity." Moreover, he notes that disjunctive commemorations can become sources of controversy and even conflict between groups precisely because the foundations of their collective identities are at stake.[10]

Anniversaries and commemorations about war therefore provide powerful venues for this social and political construction of national identity. However, countries vary in terms of the actual linkage between remembrance and identity. This variance is evident in the country studies included in this volume.

In some cases, remembrance of human sacrifices for a national cause in war can not only console surviving families and friends, but also pull a country together behind a positive national narrative. For example, commemorations of World War II in the United States played a role in developing the "greatest generation" narrative, according to which countless Americans in and out of uniform contributed enormously to a victory that affirmed America's greatness and its indispensable world leadership. Even in a small country like Singapore, war anniversaries helped to consolidate a national identity based on a narrative of sacrifice and national development.

In other countries, war commemorations and anniversaries can promote a unifying national narrative by accentuating a persistent divide between one's own country and a previous adversary. This "us" versus "them" distinction during remembrance events is especially salient in countries that have not reconciled historically with their former foes. For instance, in China, anniversaries of World War II have often become occasions to call attention to Japan's aggression against China as well as the heroic Chinese effort to defeat the Japanese. Similarly in South Korea, commemorations of Korean independence remind citizens of the suffering that the Japanese inflicted on the Korean people during the colonial era.[11] In both countries, national identity is linked to a critical view of Japan that places the primary responsibility for historical reconciliation on the Japanese.

Finally, in some cases, rather than unifying a country, war anniversaries can reveal and even exacerbate domestic conflicts about national identity. For example, in Japan's case, a repentant view of Japan's militaristic past has buttressed the country's postwar identity as a "peace state." But for Japanese who would like their country to come out of its so-called "pacifist haze" and assume greater responsibility for its own defense, the hypercritical Chinese and Korean views of Japan's past behavior are an affront to national honor and impose a psychological barrier on Japan to become a more "normal country." Taiwan represents a complex case of contesting national identities. On the one hand, residents in Taiwan, especially those directly linked to Chinese Nationalists who fled mainland China in the wake of the communist revolution, may share the predominant Chinese historical narrative critical of Japan. But Taiwanese who lived under Japanese colonial rule may have a less harsh view of Japan and a more critical attitude toward the Chinese Nationalists (KMT) who governed Taiwan during the early postwar years through ruthless repression. Over time, the "Taiwanization" of Taiwan's identity became associated with historical reconciliation between Japan and Taiwan.[12]

THE BOOK AND ITS CHAPTERS

Commemorations of past events like World War II at its 70th anniversary present an unique opportunity to observe—in a synchronic manner—how it is now "remembered" in societies across the Asia Pacific and beyond. The chapters in this book were first presented at a symposium convened by the Memory and Reconciliation in the Asia Pacific program at the Elliott School of International Affairs, George Washington University, in late 2015. The passage of time since then has provided the authors with a certain amount of "hindsight" for pondering the significance of the commemorative events while offering narrative and analysis fresh enough to capture the *zeitgest* of the moment.

In his essay which was first delivered as a keynote speech at the symposium, Akira Iriye, a world-renowned pioneer in international and transnational history, ponders the meanings of turning points in global history and in his own life. Living in Tokyo as a ten-year old when World War II ended, Iriye began writing a diary to record the momentous changes around him. He embarked upon a personal transnational journey of moving to the United States less than a decade later, first as a student and later as a professional historian. Speaking in that latter role, Iriye traces the transnational development of key norms such as human rights in the postwar world. He thus views 1945 as not only a watershed in his personal life but of fundamental importance to transnational history of the whole world.

The book's chapters present case studies primarily from the Asia Pacific, but also include the United States, Russia, and Germany—major protagonists in World War II as well as important players in the memory politics of war. The chapters are organized nationally, largely for reasons of consistency, clarity, and convenience. Each author goes deep into the national roots while keeping a close eye on transnational trends. To heed Iriye's plea for a transnational approach, we strongly encourage the reader to view them comparatively and interactively.

As the chapter by Daqing Yang demonstrates, commemoration of the Chinese victory in World War II took on new significance in 2015 as the government under Xi Jingping used the opportunity to project national solidarity and a "great rejuvenation of the Chinese nation." For the first time in PRC history, a military parade—the biggest ever—was staged on an occasion not related to the founding of the PRC (October 1). This was as much a show of strength to the world as a demonstration of Xi's supreme command of the domestic situation. While still preserving the narrative of the Communist leadership in the War of Resistance, Beijing has carefully cultivated the image of "all-Chinese national struggle" by including veterans and political leaders from the KMT side. International participation in such a military-centered celebration was less than overwhelming, however, due to concerns by the United States and its allies about the rise of Chinese power and its growing assertiveness.

Robert Sutter's chapter on Taiwan shows how Taipei resisted Beijing's pressure to endorse China's strident treatment of Japan and its depiction of Chinese Communist forces as Chinese liberators against Japan. Engaging in a complicated balancing act between Beijing and Tokyo, Taipei was reluctant to commemorate World War II in a way that would antagonize Japan. Taiwan has a strategic interest in fostering good relations with Japan. Furthermore, older Taiwan residents have relatively positive memories of Japanese colonial rule; and young Taiwanese have highly favorable views of contemporary Japan. They showed little interest in joining their counterparts in mainland China to commemorate the historical defeat of Japan. Therefore, in observing the end of World War II in a multiplicity of events, Taiwan leaders were careful to avoid gestures and props that would offend Japan.

Mike Mochizuki's chapter on Japan discusses how the 70th anniversary of the end of World War II served as an occasion for political divisions about history and post-World War II identity to resurface and sharpen. The focal point became Prime Minister Abe's anticipated statement about the war because he sought to supersede the 1995 Murayama statement and reorient Japan's foreign policy in a future-oriented direction by ending the need to repeat apologies. Although Abe ultimately sought to find common ground between contending views of history and avoid a diplomatic crisis, this delicate balancing papered over differences rather than resolving this historical debate. Emperor Akihito transcended domestic divisions about history by continuing his practice of visiting the sites of major battles and urging the Japanese people to study and learn from history. And despite Abe's effort to end "apology diplomacy" and the nationalist right's opposition to compensation for wartime victims, Japan did issue apologies and offer compensation during this anniversary year, such as to wartime forced laborers and South Korean comfort women survivors.

Christine Kim's chapter on Korea offers an example of two key anniversary dates, albeit closely related. In Korea, August 15, 1945, marks not only the day on which Japanese colonial rule came to an end, but also the beginning of a painful and enduring national division. The concurrence of these two historical processes has long defined, but also complicated, commemorations of the occasion in South Korea. A wide range of expressions in the various forms of official ceremony, government policies, legal decisions, and civic activism reflected not only the tumultuous year of 2015, but indeed the complexity and contradictions of South Korea's memory politics. While both regimes seek legitimacy through their commemorative acts, Seoul's approach is to tweak the national myth in the name of boosting global competitiveness, while Pyongyang's angle is to promote self-reliance by thumbing its nose at the world.

Ricardo Jose's chapter offers a sweeping survey of the war commemorations in the Philippines, one of the countries most devastated by World War II. He offers an overview of the range of war memorials and selected commemorations through time, with a detailed account of those related to the 70th anniversary. Organized by the central government and local communities, they often center on two themes—triumph and tragedy. According to Jose, one of the main objectives of commemorations is strengthening the national identity and instilling greater pride, just as the memorials to Bataan, Corregidor, the guerrillas, and the liberation sites all add to national or local identity. On the other hand, the more complicated legacies—comfort women, collaboration, and Filipino atrocities—would not become part of the mainstream ceremonies.

Tze Loo's analysis of Singapore shows that commemoration events in Singapore were limited in scope. The 70th anniversary events contrasted with the much larger scale commemorations of the 50th and 60th anniversaries of the end of World War II. Moreover, in 2015, the 50th anniversary of Singapore's independence and the passing of Lee Kuan Yew overshadowed the World War II commemoration. Singapore has deliberately deployed the history of Japanese occupation to suit its nation-state building agendas. What matters more for Singapore is the war's beginning and experience during the occupation rather than the end of the war. The critical lessons of history are therefore the following: the bankruptcy of any attempt by another country to legitimize their rule over Singapore with claims to innate superiority, no matter how benevolent that rule might seem; never to depend on others for Singapore's defense and security; and local communities coming together to help each other survive the war despite their differences. At the same time, in its relationship with Japan, Singapore has refused to let the past be an obstacle to Singapore's present and future.

According to Marc Gallicchio, Americans commemorated the 70th anniversary in a variety of ceremonies, most of which were characterized by a solemn, somber tone, and a tinge of nostalgia. In contrast to some countries in Asia where political officials were concerned about rhetorical miscues and signs of resurgent militarism, the atmosphere in the United States was subdued and the messaging nonconfrontational. Animosity toward Japan was absent from most local ceremonies, and commemorations sponsored by federal government entities celebrated the victory of freedom over tyranny with hardly any explicit mention of Japan as the enemy in the Asia-Pacific war. Prime Minister Abe's April 2015 visit to the United States and his speech to Congress provided American leaders an opportunity to remember the war by highlighting the current U.S.-Japan alliance.

Just as the Soviet Union was a crucial player in the global World War II, its successor state Russia is an indispensable player when it comes to anniversary politics of that war. Marlene Laruelle analyzes the 2015 Russian commemoration, which featured the largest-ever military parade, through the Kremlin's need for domestic support and loyalty as well as the longer tradition dating to the Soviet times. Equally important, she situates Russia's commemoration in the new memory politics about World War II in east and central Europe. Due to this heavy European focus and due to its relations with China and Japan, she notes, Russia's commemoration of its Asia theater was much more subdued and ambivalent. While Russia may move closer to China's narrative of war, it also tried to avoid the risk of putting its prospect of improving relations with Japan in jeopardy.

Even though its scope of action was largely limited to Europe and North Africa during World War II, Germany's record of dealing with the legacies of that war has become increasingly of global relevance. Drawing from Germany's rich and distinctive "culture of remembrance" in connection to the Third Reich, World War II and the Holocaust, Lily Gardner Feldman compares German and Japanese commemorations along four themes: scope, content, purpose, and context. While noting sharp differences, she emphasizes the commonalities in both countries—the generation change with the imminent disappearance of the witness generation and the challenge faced by the young generation in a transformed international world.

A few themes emerge from these chapters. One is that even when anniversary dates are fixed, their commemoration can change from year to year. In other words, as other studies have pointed out, "memory has its history." In this regard, the book goes a long way to overcome the static view of memory politics in the Asia Pacific by examining the changing external and internal dynamics behind commemorations. Moreover, there can be competing anniversaries and indeed competing agendas for public attention.

As codirectors of the Memory and Reconciliation in the Asia Pacific Program and coconveners of the symposium in 2015, we would like to express our gratitude to the institutions and individuals who have made this book possible. The U.S. Institute of Peace contributed to the establishment of the program in 2003 through a seed grant. Over the following years, George Washington University has provided generous financial support in a variety of forms, including a recent SOAR grant awarded to one of the editors. We would like to thank Bruce Dickson, then director of the Center for Asian Studies at the Elliott School of International Affairs, as well as the center's staff and graduate assistant, Mike Bouffard and Haruka Akahi, for making the symposium a success. We are also indebted to colleagues who served as discussants at our symposium: Jordan Sand (Georgetown), Katharine Moon (Wellesley College/Brookings), as well as Bruce Dickson, Alastair Bowie, Shawn McHale, and Ronald Spector (all GWU).

NOTES

1. The U.S. Congress passed World War I Centennial Commission Act on January 16, 2013, setting up the commission responsible for planning, developing, and executing programs, projects, and activities to commemorate the centennial of World War I. For scholarly anaysis of the World War I centennial in Europe, see Romain Fathi, "Symposium French commemoration: The centenary effect and the (re)discovery of 14–18," *Australian Journal of Political Science*, 50, no. 3 (2015): 545–552.

2. For a stimulating discussion concerning European history, see a forum on Anniversaries, in *German History*, 32, no. 1 (2014): 79–100.

3. Paul Connerton, *How Society Remembers* (Cambridge: Cambridge University Press, 1989) 4–5.

4. See, for example, Philip L. Kohl, Mara Kozelsky, and Nachman Ben-Yehuda, eds., *Selective Remembrances: Archaeology In the Construction, Commemoration, and Consecration Of National Pasts* (Chicago: University of Chicago Press, 2007); Jeffrey Lee Meriwether and Laura Mattoon D'Amore, eds., *We Are What We Remember: The American Past through Commemoration* (Newcastle upon Tyne, UK: Cambridge Scholars Publishing, 2012); Michael R. Dolski, Sam Edwards, and John Buckley, eds., *D-Day In History And Memory: The Normandy Landings In International Remembrance and Commemoration* (Denton: University of North Texas Press, 2014).

5. Patrick Finney, "The Ubiquitous Presence of the Past? Collective Memory and International History," *International History Review* 36, no. 3 (2014): 443–472.

6. Zheng Wang, "National Humiliation, History Education, and the Politics of Historical Memory: Patriotic Education Campaign in China," *International Studies Quarterly* 52 (2008): 783–806.

7. Lam Peng Er, "Japan's Postwar Reconciliation with Southeast Asia," *Asian Journal of Peacebuilding* 3, no. 1 (2015): 43–63.

8. Anthony Smith, *National Identity* (Reno: University of Nevada Press, 1991), 14. The other four essential elements in Smith's conceptualization of national identity are (1) a historic territory or homeland, (2) a common mass culture, (3) common legal rights and duties for all members, and (4) a common economy and territorial mobility for members.

9. John R. Gillis (ed.), *Commemorations: the Politics of National Identity* (Princeton: Princeton University Press, 1994).

10. Hiro Saito, "Competing Logics of Commemoration: Cosmopolitanism and Nationalism in East Asia's History Problem," *Sociological Perspectives* 57, no. 2 (2014): 167–185; see also his *The History Problem: The Politics of War Commemoration in East Asia* (Honolulu: University of Hawaii Press, 2017).

11. Jerry Won Lee, "Legacies of Japanese Colonialism in the Rhetorical Constitution of South Korean National Identity," *National Identities* 16, no. 1 (2014): 1–13.

12. Barak Kushner, "Nationality and Nostalgia: The Manipulation of Memory in Japan, Taiwan, and China since 1990," *International History Review* 29, no. 4 (December 2007): 793–820.

Chapter One

China

Meanings and Contradictions of Victory

Daqing Yang

Of all the countries in the Asia Pacific that commemorated the 70th anniversary of the end of World War II, China stands out for several reasons. To begin with, not only had China previously fought a war with Japan at the end of the nineteenth century, it had been involved in a military conflict with Japan since the early 1930s, well before the worldwide war began. Moreover, the current People's Republic of China (hereafter PRC or China) was founded by the Chinese Communists four years after World War II had ended after defeating the Nationalist government in a civil war. Finally, World War II, now officially termed the War of Resistance against Japanese Aggression and World Anti-fascist War (hereafter War of Resistance or Resistance War), has been enjoying something of a boom in China for more than two decades that shows no signs of abating. In the anniversary year of 2015, the Chinese government not only organized a wide range of commemorative events, but also put on perhaps the most extravagant of all—the country's largest-ever military parade on the newly revived Victory Day.

China's commemoration of World War II in 2015 thus raises important questions about memory culture and identity formation in the world's most populous country. How did China's war commemoration in 2015 compare with those in previous decades? What factors contributed to the unprecedented level of emphasis on World War II and China's victory in particular? How was the 2015 war commemoration actually implemented? Are these commemorative events harbingers of a new Chinese identity in the making? This chapter addresses these questions by situating the 2015 commemoration in both domestic and international context and by exploring its multifaceted implications in both spheres.

WWII IN PRC MEMORY CULTURE: THEMES AND VARIATIONS

Though founded four years after the war with Japan, the People's Republic of China has always accorded that war a key place in the pantheon of its revolutionary history. In the past seven decades, however, the official narratives of that war have undergone modifications and even drastic changes due to the shifting political circumstances at home and abroad.

There is no better place to start than the Monument to the People's Heroes in the center of the vast Tiananmen Square in Beijing. Built in the first decade of PRC, it epitomizes the new regime's self-identity as well as its claim to historical legitimacy. The base of the obelisk-shaped monument featured eight panels of marble relief, each portraying a key episode of "people's struggle" in recent history, beginning with the Opium War of 1840 against the British and culminating in the defeat of the Nationalists in the late 1940s. One of these eight panels featured the War of Resistance against Japan, depicting determined Communist-led soldiers and guerrillas ready to charge the enemy positions.[1] The new PRC also designated the *March of the Volunteers*, a famous song from the mid-1930s calling for resistance against the Japanese aggression, as its national anthem. In such ways, the Chinese Communists have located the War of Resistance squarely in this century-long struggle by the Chinese people against both internal and external enemies while identified themselves as their legitimate representative.

From 1949 till the late 1970s, with Chairman Mao Zedong at the helm, China identified itself as a revolutionary state founded on the Marxist-Leninist ideology of class struggle. The slogan "Never Forget the Hardship of Class (Oppression), Firmly Remember the Hatred in Blood and Tears," targeted the class enemies—*Chinese* landlords and capitalists as well as foreign imperialists—and remained the dominant leitmotif of China's memory culture during those decades. The meaning of the Resistance War against Japan was framed accordingly: it was a struggle by the Chinese people against Japanese militarists. The Chinese Nationalists under Chiang Kai-shek, branded "the enemy of the people," were not only missing completely from this resistance; worse, they were accused of collaborating with Japanese aggressors while attempting to strangulate the Communists during the war. Internationally, China pursued a "leaning to one side" foreign policy in the 1950s by forging a close alliance with the Soviet Union, and faced containment by the United States and its allies during the Cold War. The Soviet role in defeating Japan received much emphasis while that of the United States and others was all but silenced.

On September 3, 1955, the party mouthpiece *People's Daily* celebrated the first ten-year anniversary of World War II with an editorial that attributed the victory to the "long and heroic resistance of the peoples in China and other Asian countries" as well as the "strong and massive offensive by the

Soviet army." Beijing highlighted three elements: First, the Resistance War ended with the defeat of Japanese imperialism, marking the great turning point in the anti-imperialist struggle by the Chinese people for over a hundred years. Second, it was largely due to the effort of the Chinese people and the Soviet Union that Japan was defeated. Third, American imperialism is the mortal enemy of the Chinese people today.[2] On the anniversary day of September 3, Chinese and Soviet leaders would exchange greetings and congratulations, while the Chinese paid tribute at the war cemetery of Soviet soldiers in China. Such a practice continued until the two countries descended into their own bitter conflict in the early 1960s.

China's commemoration of the 20th anniversary in 1965 reflected the country's growing tilt toward ideological radicalization. In a widely read editorial in the *People's Daily*, Marshall Lin Biao emphasized the importance of "people's war" in defeating Japan, foreshadowing the bottom-up political violence unleashed during the upcoming Cultural Revolution. The Soviet Union was not even mentioned. Worse, Soviet war cemeteries and monuments to Soviet pilots were vandalized in the late 1960s as the two countries veered toward armed conflict. This situation changed somewhat at the 30th anniversary in 1975, not long after China and the Soviet Union pulled back from the brink of war. Although China still described the Soviet Union as "hegemony-seeking socialist imperialism," the Chinese government nonetheless acknowledged the contribution and sacrifice of the Soviet Union during the war and laid wreaths at the Soviet war cemeteries in China.

The beginning of the Reform and Openness period under Deng Xiaoping at the end of the 1970s coincided with the waning of the global Cold War. It also ushered in what historians have termed the "new remembering" of World War II that has largely continued till this day.[3] As the Chinese Communist Party (CCP) abandoned the ideology of revolutionary class struggle, it has increasingly placed greater emphasis on modernizing the economy and cultivating patriotic sentiment while pursuing international engagement. Beijing also began reaching out to the Nationalist regime in Taiwan in an attempt to bring about a "third CCP-KMT cooperation," following their second cooperation during the war against Japan. Furthermore, Deng's far-reaching reform brought about more openness at home, allowing greater voices from the society on many issues including the war with Japan. Last but not least, China's frictions with Japan over "history issues" such as textbook revision and official visits to the Yasukuni Shrine began in the early 1980s. Against such significant changes the War of Resistance took on new importance as well as meanings on several fronts.

First, as China opened up and joined the world community, Beijing once again emphasized the War of Resistance as part of the "worldwide anti-Fascist war." This international theme reached a peak on the 50th and the 60th anniversaries under the leadership of Jiang Zemin and Hu Jingtao, and would include Western allies for the first time. In his speech marking the 50th anniversary of the end of the war in 1995, for instance, Jiang noted that "China's War of Resistance received support from people around the world. I would like to mention in particular the human and material support provided by anti-fascist allies such as the Soviet Union, America and Britain." In an emotional turn, Jiang described how the "red flag of victory of China's War of Resistance is soaked with the blood of friends from different countries."[4]

Second, China has also come to highlight different aspects of the war. Whereas heroic resistance was what the Monument to the People's Heroes projected, greater emphasis is now placed on China's sacrifice and suffering during the War. Largely as a response to perceived denials in Japan, the Nanjing Massacre emerged out of long oblivion and was given its first-ever national museum in 1985, the 40th anniversary of the end of the war.[5] In 1995, Jiang added this new theme to his speech that has become a standard refrain ever since: China had paid a huge price in both human and material terms in that war. Based on a study by the Chinese Academy of Military Science, Jiang claimed that China suffered 35 million casualties in total, in addition to direct economic loss of 100 billion U.S. dollars and indirect loss of 500 billion dollars. In the meantime, he described China as the "main theater in the East" (*dongfang zhuzhanchan*) in World War II which made an important contribution to the global war against the Axis powers: China tied down millions of Japanese troops, preventing Japan from attacking the Soviet Union and delaying Japan's move into the Pacific. Jiang also claimed that 70 percent of the Japanese army's casualties were in the China theater.[6]

Perhaps the greatest change in the official narrative is when Beijing began to portray the War as a struggle by the entire Chinese nation against Japanese invasion. Reiterating that Japanese invasion constituted the last episode in China's "century of humiliation" at the hands of foreign aggressors in modern times, Beijing now gives public recognition to the contribution by the Nationalist government and its armed forces during the War for the first time. In 1985, the 40th anniversary of the end of the War, the official Xinhua News Agency and *People's Daily* published influential pieces such as "The Great All-Nation War of Resistance" and "China's War of Resistance is a War of Resistance by the Entire Nation against Aggression." They claimed that the War was carried out under the banner of the All Chinese National United Front of Resistance, proposed by the CCP and centered on the cooperation between KMT and CCP. The CCP, operating the main battlefront in the rear area, cooperated with the KMT that was responsible for the battle lines in the front. Publicizing this wartime cooperation in order to facilitate the reunification of the two sides of the Taiwan Strait was considered "the most important theme" of ideological work of the year. A series of commemorative events were organized along these lines in 1985. Among them a new exhibition on the "all-nation war of resistance" opened in Beijing, and brought together former generals of both the Communists and Nationalists involved in the War.[7] The national and local governments began to repair Nationalist-built war cemeteries and monuments that had been vandalized after 1949.

Such a change was the result of an ideological shift away from class struggle as well as Beijing's effort to improve relations with Nationalist-ruled Taiwan. Old contradictions persist, however. This narrative of "all-nation resistance" glosses over the fact that not a small number of Chinese collaborated with the Japanese. More importantly, the more positive evaluation of the Nationalist government during the War has produced concerns that it diminished the role of the Communists and led to pushbacks from the ideological die-hards against perceived threats to the legitimacy of the CCP in the present. As a result, there is a renewed effort to fortify the pivotal role of the Chinese Communist Party during the war. For example, an opinion piece by a retired PLA officer published in the *People's Daily* in 2015 railed against what it called "historical nihilists" for their alleged exaggeration of the role of the Nationalists at the expense of the Communists. Linguistic gymnastics has to be deployed, with the CCP now being described as "the steady column in the midst of dangerous currents" [*zhong-liu di-zhu*] before and during the War, "playing the role of forging a national united front against Japanese aggression."[8]

Following his predecessors, current Chinese leader Xi Jinping has emphasized, since coming to power in late 2012, both China's sacrifice during the war and its contribution to the final victory. Xi introduced new vocabulary and themes. In a speech entitled "History Cannot Be Distorted," Xi not only took aim at alleged distortions but also focused on "the spirit of the Resistance War [*kangzhan jingshen*]" for China's domestic audience. Although he was not the first to use the term, Xi stated that as the Chinese Communist Party provided crucial leadership during the war, it shall go on to lead the Chinese nation into the Great Rejuvenation of the Chinese Civilization.[9] He also called on the Nationalist government in Taiwan to "jointly study and write the history of Chinese national resistance against Japan."[10]

Under Xi, the Chinese government further expanded the patriotic education that has been in high gear for at least two decades. In August 2014, the Chinese government designated eighty National Memorial Sites of the War throughout the country, and added another one hundred sites a year later. While the vast majority of these historic sites were connected with the Communist forces, a few of them were related to the Nationalist war effort as well as foreign allies. Beijing instructed local authorities to "strengthen the protection and management of memorial sites and remnants related to the War of Resistance, and to deepen the understanding of the historical meaning and current significance." Through mass pilgrimage, visits and large-scale commemorative activities, they were to serve the following objectives:

to fully recognize the crimes of Japanese fascist invaders, to firmly remember the history of the Chinese nation in resisting aggression through brave struggles, as well as China's enormous sacrifice during the worldwide anti-fascist war and undeniable historic contribution to its victory. To learn and publicize the heroic deeds of anti-Japanese martyrs, to greatly cultivate and spread the great patriotic spirit, further strengthen cohesiveness and solidarity of the nation, and to provide great driving force for the realization of the Chinese Dream of the Great Rejuvenation of the Chinese Nation.[11]

As if to respond to this new emphasis on commemoration, China's new set of commemorative stamps on the 70th anniversary of the Resistance War differed from all those from previous anniversaries not only in quantity but also in the subject. Totaling fourteen—the largest ever—they all depict history museums and memorial sites related to the war instead of scenes from the war itself.[12] They not only closely mirror the official narrative of the war; in a symbolic way, they also suggest that memory has taken over history, thus making 2015 a new starting point in China's memory culture.

MARKING ANNIVERSARIES

If Xi did not deviate greatly from his predecessors in messages concerning World War II, China's commemoration of the War would differ considerably in form. In February 2014, the Chinese National People's Congress adopted two resolutions concerning anniversaries of World War II. First, a resolution declared September 3 to be Victory over Japan Day (V-J Day). Another resolution called for a National Commemoration of the Nanjing Massacre, to be held on December 13.[13]

The Day of National Commemoration of the Nanjing Massacre was a completely new designation, underscoring the importance attached to this most publicized instance of Chinese wartime suffering.[14] The Chinese V-J Day, on the other hand, has a long history dating to the immediate postwar era. In April 1946, the Nationalist government designated Sept. 3, the day after Japan signed the Instrument of Surrender aboard the USS *Missouri*, as Victory Day, and simultaneously rescinded other anniversaries of September 18 and July 7, marking the Japanese invasion of Manchuria in 1931 and the beginning of the full-scale war in 1937 respectively. On September 3 that year, China held its first national celebration of Victory Day. After its founding in 1949, the PRC commemorated the War of Resistance on August 15 but also on September 3 in order to synchronize with the V-J Day in the Soviet Union. The People's Congress in 2014 thus revived a date that was first established by the previous regime and largely forgotten after the 1950s.[15]

Interestingly, the initiatives for the new anniversaries did not always start with the top. In March 2005 a Hong Kong delegate to the Chinese People's

Congress submitted a proposal calling for a major commemoration on the 60th anniversary of the war. He proposed that China hold national commemorations on both Sept. 3 and Sept. 18, with attendance from the top Chinese leaders as well as invited foreign leaders. Moreover, China should establish national sites of commemoration, similar to the Tomb of the Unknown Soldier in Russia or the Arlington National Cemetery in America. Although his proposal was not adopted, it was widely reported in the Chinese media.[16]

There is also an international dimension to this decision. At the Sochi Winter Olympics in early 2014, President Xi Jinping agreed with his Russian counterpart Vladimir Putin to hold a joint commemoration of the 70th anniversary of the ending of World War II in Europe and Asia the following year. The crisis in Ukraine in the ensuing months did not affect their plan. When President Putin visited China in May 2014, the two governments reaffirmed in their joint communiqué "to continue firmly opposing the distortion of history and undermining of the postwar international order" through such joint commemorations. The two countries also carried out other joint programs including exchanging artists and arranging mutual visits by war veterans.[17]

In late January 2015, a Chinese newspaper in Hong Kong reported—later confirmed by the Beijing government—the decision to hold a military parade in front of the Tiananmen on September 3 that year. Immediately after the news broke, the press and internet chat rooms in China and overseas went abuzz about the significance of this ground-breaking decision to hold a military parade on the newly revived Victory Day. *Cankao Xiaoxi*, the largest newspaper by circulation in China and published by the official Xinhua News Agency, quoted the Japanese daily *Tokyo Shimbun* attributing the decision to desire to demonstrate Xi`s command of China`s military to the Chinese people, and to warn the Abe government of Japan to exercise self-restraint on issues of historical understanding and Yasukuni Shrine visits. A Chinese blogger named Zhanhao listed four major reasons: first, to demonstrate China`s military capabilities; second, to "shake Japan and warn the United States" and to show the world China's determination to defend the postwar world order; third, to increase the self-confidence and pride of all Chinese, and fourth, to show corrupted elements (in China) an additional "knife" beside disciplinary and legal forces. He specifically accused Japan under Abe for being "unrepentant about history and seeking to become militarily active again." His piece was widely reprinted in the Chinese media and was even featured on the official *People's Daily* website.[18]

Military parades in the PRC are not new. Under the influence of the Soviet Union, its then international Communist elder brother, China conducted an annual military parade celebrating the founding of the PRC in front of the Tiananmen from 1949 and 1959. Much of the style was also adopted from the Soviet model. As the Sino-Soviet alliance collapsed, China stopped the practice after the 1950s until it was revived in the 1980s. In 1984, on the 35th National Day, Deng personally inspected the military parade in front of Tiananmen. Since then, China has conducted similar military parades on the 50th and 60th National Day, presided over by Deng's successors Jiang Zemin and Hu Jingtao respectively.

In 1995, then Chinese leader Jiang Zemin began the practice of attending the Victory Parade in post-Soviet Russia as the two countries gradually and steadily strengthened their "strategic cooperation." On May 9, Jiang attended the 50th anniversary celebration of the victory of World War II in Moscow. A fluent Russian speaker thanks to his early years spent in the Soviet Union as a trainee, Jiang allegedly personally asked his host, President Boris Yeltsin, for an opportunity to address the guests that included the U.S. president and other Western leaders. After returning to China, Jiang made plans to make the September 3 commemoration a large event, though mainly for the domestic audience. Hu Jingtao followed suit in 2005, the 60th anniversary. On both occasions, the military parade in Moscow was broadcast live on Chinese television, drawing a large audience.

In any event, World War II-related anniversaries began to dominate Chinese headlines in late 2014. The country's first National Commemoration of the Nanjing Massacre took place on December 13 and was attended by President Xi himself. After mourning the most celebrated symbol of China's wartime suffering, China ushered in a year of celebrations of hard-won victory. In early May 2015 Xi and his wife traveled to Moscow for Russia's 70th Victory Day parade. They were received as the most important guests, in no small part due to the boycott of the ceremony by Western leaders in the wake of the conflict over Ukraine. In contrast to 2005 when Russia's military parade was broadcast in full in China on two separate TV channels, the main CCTV channels did not carry a live broadcast this year, as if to avoid stealing the wind from China's own a few months later.[19] On July 7, the anniversary of the outbreak of the full-scale war, a large ceremony was held at the Memorial Hall of the War of Resistance against Japanese Aggression outside Beijing. Xi delivered a speech and unveiled a statue named "Medal of Freedom." He was flanked on each side by a Communist veteran and a Nationalist veteran as well as two teenagers.

Dubbed in China as the Great Military Parade (*da yuebin*), the military parade scheduled for the Victory Day of September 3 was no doubt the climactic event in China's year of commemoration. In months leading to it, Chinese media began reporting in often minute detail about the three-month-long training and rehearsals of participating troops and their general-grade parade leaders. Emphasis was on the new record-setting number of personnel (12,000), new weaponry (84 percent for the first time, 100 percent domestic made) as well as foreign troops participating in the parade for the first time ever. The Chinese public was hungry for a spectacle, which Beijing duly delivered.

On Victory Day itself, the pageantry began before the parade itself. Staring at 9 o'clock in the morning, foreign leaders and government representatives lined up to be received by President Xi and his wife inside the Forbidden City. Each leader (and their companion) walked close to a hundred meters on the red carpet for a handshake with Xi and his wife, a brief exchange of greetings and a quick joint photo. The whole process lasted close to thirty minutes and was broadcast live on national TV and watched by the entire country. The image of China as a "great nation" (*da guo*) is unmistakable. After posing for a group photo with all the foreign dignitaries, Xi led the crowd to ascend the Tiananmen Gate for the formal celebration and the parade.

At 10 o'clock, Premier Li Keqiang announced the start of the victory celebration. After the singing of the Chinese national anthem, Xi delivered a speech. Dressed in the modern Chinese *zhongshan* suit, Xi spoke above all in his capacity as the head of the Military Commission of the Chinese Communist Party, a subtle but important reminder of the role of the Party both past and present. After repeating many of the similar themes heard over recent years about the war and the spirit of resistance, he abruptly announced the reduction of 300,000 personnel in the Chinese armed forces. Then Xi came down from the viewing deck and re-emerged in a Chinese-made Red Flag sedan to begin the inspection of Chinese troops. For the next 15 minutes, Xi rode down the vast Chang'an Avenue, exchanging greetings with the troops.[20]

After Xi returned to the viewing deck, the military parade itself began. The first groups passing the podium were war veterans and descendants of deceased veterans. They sat in open deck buses decorated with familiar battle scenes from the war. Following the veterans were eleven large formations of goose-stepping Chinese soldiers including women. To emphasize the Communist role in the war, units that traced their lineage to Communist-led forces in northeast, north, central, and south parts of China marched first. All infantry formations were each led by two senior officers of major general rank. Following the Chinese formations were foreign participants from seventeen countries. Marching in alphabetical order, Afghanistan was the first, with a column of three. Former Soviet countries like Belarus and central Asian states had relatively large formations. The Russian formation, seventy-six-men strong, came last. Then came twenty-seven equipment formations of the Chinese armed forces, together featuring over 500 pieces of forty types of military equipment. Flying overhead were ten air force formations, totalling almost 200 airplanes of two dozen types. For journalists and military analysts as well as "military fans" (*junmi*), this was a bonanza. Among the new weapons displayed were missiles that were dubbed by military wonks as "carrier killer" or even "Guam killer,"[21] although not all China's missiles were on display. Appearing for the first time were amphibious landing vehicles giving rise to various speculations. All in all, this largest military parade ever in PRC history was watched by hundreds of millions of TV viewers in China and beyond.

As part of the victory commemoration, on the day before the parade, President Xi awarded medals to a select group of Chinese war veterans as well as foreigners (or their descendants) who had contributed to China's war effort.[22] Among the latter were American, Japanese, Indian and others. The ceremony took place inside the Great Hall of the People in Tiananmen Square, and was broadcast on Chinese television. A few days before, Xi signed an order offering amnesty to several categories of prisoners including those who had fought in World War II or the "external wars" after 1949.

CHINA AS A GREAT, UNIFIED NATION:
EXTERNAL AND INTERNAL IMPLICATIONS

In March 2015, a Chinese Foreign Ministry spokeswoman indicated that China would extend invitations to leaders of all concerned countries as well as international organizations. Chinese foreign minister Wang Yi likewise insisted anyone with "sincerity" was welcome to come. The Chinese initiative was met with ambivalence on the part of the United States and its Western allies, out of suspicion that China was trying to isolate Japan in the international community, as well as weariness about giving the appearance of approving China's flexing of its military muscle, especially at the sensitive location of Tiananmen Square. In the Chinese official media as well as online discussions, the absence of many Western leaders including wartime allies like the United States was shrugged off or ignored. There was reportedly a leaked internal memo mandating so. Private discussion, however, reveals resentment against "Western countries siding with Japan and denying China's fair place."[23]

In the end, a total of thirty heads of states showed up for China's victory parade. Only one came from an EU country (Czech Republic) as other Western countries sent cabinet-level representatives or ambassadors. China's guest list included leaders of several allies such as Pakistan as well as a number of small island countries, but controversially also included the Sudanese president who is on the ICC's wanted list (a fact highlighted in the foreign press). Also present were UN Secretary General Ban Ki-moon and the Director-General of UNESCO. Moreover, a total of seventeen countries sent soldiers to march with the Chinese—either in formation or as flag-bearing representatives. Another fourteen countries sent military observers.[24]

Of these foreign guests, two received special attention. The presence of Russian president Vladimir Putin did not surprise anyone. Russia's special status at the Victory Day commemoration was obvious: Putin was the last foreign leader to shake Xi's hand before the parade, and remained at Xi's right side throughout the event. The Russian formation was placed at the end of all foreign formations, again indicating a special relationship. Immediately after the parade, Xi and Putin held talks as well as a joint press conference, an arrangement not repeated. Putin was accompanied by several high-ranking officials including Sergei Ivanov and Dmitry Rogozin, while Defense Minister Sergei Shoigu headed the Russian military observer group.[25]

If the Russian president's attendance was never in doubt, the other guest of importance had an element of surprise. Until the day of the parade there was speculation that although President Park Geun-hye of South Korea would go to China for the celebration, she might not take part in viewing the parade. (Japanese press had reported that the U.S. Government had tried to dissuade Park from going, a claim denied by the State Department spokesperson.) Park was given almost an equal place of honor, walking up the Tiananmen viewing deck on Xi's left side and seated immediately after Mr. Putin. Korean press emphasized that of all the visiting foreign leaders, only Ms. Park was treated to a one-on-one lunch with Mr. Xi the day before the parade where some of her favorite tunes were reportedly played in the background. Park's visit to Beijing was followed by her attending a reopening ceremony at the museum in Shanghai that used to be the Korean Provisional Government after 1919. In contrast, North Korea, still considered China's erstwhile ally, sent a second-ranked official who was seated rather far away from the center at the parade.[26]

Japanese prime minister Abe Shinzō had reportedly considered visiting Beijing in early September for a summit with Xi (though probably not attending the military parade, similarly to Chancellor Merkel in Moscow in May). It was not until August 24 that he publicly indicated he would not make the trip after all.[27] China was not pleased. The next day, Xinhua's official news portal carried a commentary suggesting that the current Japanese emperor should make an apology to China. Predictably, this caused considerable consternation in Japan. No Japanese official representatives were present at the ceremony; moreover, the Japanese government expressed displeasure at UN Secretary General Ban's appearance, which sparked a brief but spirited exchange.

In perhaps a less noticeable way, China's continued de facto division since shortly after World War II was on display. Although Beijing had high hopes for Taiwan to send official representatives to participate in the victory celebration, in the end only Lien Chan, former chairman of the KMT, came in a private capacity despite warnings not to go from President Ma Ying-jeou. Having visited mainland China numerous times before and allegedly with business interests there, Lien was vilified in Taiwan for his appearance. When he returned to Taiwan, a protester threw a shoe at his entourage at the airport.

The Chinese government sought to allay concerns about China's flexing its muscle through the military parade. In press conferences and public discussions leading to the Victory Day, Chinese officials as well as academics strove to justify the military parade by citing international precedents. In his short speech on September 3, Xi referred to "peace" repeatedly (eighteen times) and announced the reduction of the armed forces by 300,000.[28] All this seems to have had little effect. If international coverage and analysis were any indication, China's war commemoration raised further alarm about China's intentions since most seem to equate the victory parade as further evidence of China's turn toward hyper-nationalism and aggressiveness. Indeed, one Western analyst went so far as to characterize the military parade as a strategic miscalculation on China's part by calling it "*goose-walking into isolation.*" In his assessment of China in 2015, David Shambaugh likewise considered the military parade "another instance in which China seemingly miscalculated in terms of the image it projects abroad."[29]

It is perhaps inevitable that such a massive display of military might as well as its style would produce concerns and even negative reactions in the West and elsewhere. Indeed, U.S. (or Japanese) military intelligence need not see the parade to assess China's new weapons, but public opinion is another matter. Moreover, nearly coinciding with the military parade in Beijing, a flotilla of five Chinese navy ships were spotted in the Bering Strait for the first time. They had taken part in a joint exercise with the Russian navy in the Sea of Japan. Although the U.S. military did not sound alarmed, admitting that Chinese ships were exercising "innocent passage," its coincidence with the parade and the last day of President Obama's visit to Alaska was too perfect for the media and analysts to ignore. Tensions continued to simmer over China's island reclamation in the South China Sea, which had been going on for some time. The U.S. military conducted Freedom of Navigation (FON) flights near those artificial islands whereas Vietnam and the Philippines upgraded their own defenses or sought external help to do so. China's show of military strength at the massive parade seemed not to have deterred these countries but solicited a pushback.

However, there is no doubt that China's victory parade was first and foremost designed for domestic consumption. Twenty fourteen was a year and a half into the "Xi Jinping era." Xi is widely considered to have consolidated power much faster than his predecessors like Jiang and Hu. Since taking office in late 2012, he introduced new keywords into the Chinese political vocabulary, like his predecessors. "Chinese Dream" and "Great Rejuvenation of the Chinese Nation," came to mark the tone of the Xi era. Perhaps the most important program was anti-corruption. Xi took down several big fish in 2014 and all the way through the summer of 2015: they broke recent precedent to include an immediate past member of the Politburo Standing Committee (Zhou Yongkang), top military brass (General Xu Zehou and General Guo Boxiong), and a right-hand man of former leader Hu (Ling Jihua). The two newly established national World War II anniversary events with great public appeal no doubt would place Xi in the limelight as an assertive leader.

As it turned out, 2015 opened with a series of large human disasters in the country. The stampede in Shanghai on New Year's Day, killing dozens of youngsters, was followed a few months later by the sinking of a passenger ship in the Yangtze River during a storm, resulting in the death of upwards of 500 people, many of them retirees. In August, the port of Tianjin, one of China's largest, was shaken by spectacular explosions, killing close to 200 people and causing great material damage. As if these disasters were not enough, the Chinese economy entered a period of apparent slow-downs and turbulence by springtime. Owing to both domestic and external factors, the export and manufacturing began falling. China's nascent stock market, after experiencing an upsurge in late 2014, underwent huge sell-offs in late summer, losing as much as 30 percent of its value. The precarious real estate market was on the brink of collapse, as many in China predicted. Although the victory commemoration was decided on prior to such catastrophic events, there is no doubt it served as a welcome distraction and helped lift the mood of the nation.

The grand military parade was a carefully choreographed event, particularly for the hundreds of millions of television viewers. To ensure maximum security as well as visual effort, the Beijing government issued a number of regulations in the leading months, controlling the air quality as well as residents in the downtown area. While those spectators on the scene were relatively small at 40,000 (as compared to the 12,000–plus participants and many more mobilized to support the parade including some 850,000 residents), the visual effect for the national audience was largely achieved.

By many measures, the victory parade seemed a success. To begin with, it went without a glitch notwithstanding its unprecedented scale. It certainly drew massive attention to the carefully orchestrated display of national strength and produced considerable pride among the Chinese public. Moreover, the fact that China's two former top leaders—Jiang Zemin and Hu Jingtao, as well as all but one Politiburo Standing Committee members— stood in line with Xi projects a powerful image of the unity among the leadership under Xi. Subsequently, Xi launched a massive military reorganization (which included his promised troop reduction by 300,000) while continuing to pursue his signature anti-corruption campaign. The fortified position of Xi as the supreme leader is certainly crucial to this ambitious endeavor.

Not surprisingly, the Chinese government went to great lengths to ensure the image of pride and unity would prevail. The sky of Beijing was clear and blue thanks to closure of factories and even certain restaurants. Internet censors were busy at work making sure comments contrary to the government's goals were quickly deleted, according to a leaked internal directive as reported in the *Guardian* newspaper. Even a photo of an old lady holding an umbrella and waving a fan in front of a TV screen showing Xi during the troops inspection fell under this category. Complaints about the cost, tight security restrictions in Beijing, and the like were likewise eliminated, according to a Japan-based analyst. In subsequent months, China Central Television released a five-part television documentary, detailing the successful preparations and execution of the parade. No doubt it is the perfectly staged parade rather than the messy, popular anti-Japanese protests that turned violent in 2005 and 2012 that Beijing would like to be remembered. Together with museums and memorial sites, print and electronic media, the government-sponsored commemoration reached a new level in 2015.

It would be wrong, however, to assume the state propaganda was omnipotent. For instance, when the state media released posters promoting a big documentary on the 1943 Cairo Conference, Chinese internet went abuzz ridiculing one flagrant distortion: Mao Zedong should not have been on it since it was Chiang Kai-shek who represented China in 1943! Many Chinese critics have complained Chinese TV dramas on the war have become "magical drama" [*sheng ju*] for entertainment where heroic Chinese subdue inept Japanese invaders with almost supernatural powers.[30] On the other hand, others jumped on the bandwagon, turning World War II into populism or consumption. A locality in Henan Province created 13 Class–A Japanese War Criminals made of straw for face-slapping by locals and visitors, while an ice cream bar with the face of Gen. Tōjō Hideki went on sale in Shanghai. As 2015 drew to a close, the economic "new normal" of slower growth continued to experience turbulence. It is not clear how much pride and confidence inspired by the anniversary celebration are sufficient to weather this.

Even if the public enthusiasm for spectacles like the "great military parade" might be short-lived, one element of the official commemoration seems to have struck a chord in Chinese society and thus produced a lasting effect. The official elevation of World War II veterans regardless of wartime political affiliation seemed to enjoy a great outpouring of genuine popular support. Many Chinese saw the 70th anniversary as an occasion to remember the sacrifice of a dying generation who had been largely forgotten before. This was especially true with former Nationalist veterans, who had suffered during Mao's time for the wrong political affiliation. In the wake of the parade, Chinese Central TV launched a nation-wide online campaign "I Salute the Veterans." Within days, it received over 700 million hits, with over a million comments and 15 million re-posts. Over 98.77 percent of comments were positive. Many including 130 celebrities reportedly sent their own shots of saluting.[31] In fact, grassroots efforts to locate, interview and offer financial assistance to World War II veterans have been going on for several years in China. The privately-funded Museum of the War of Resistance in Nanjing, for instance, invited veterans of the war to watch the ceremony and gave each a monetary gift. Given their advanced age, the museum in Nanjing launched an effort to collect oral history of the war from these surviving veterans across the country.

CONCLUSION

As with most anniversary dates and years, 2015 provided the Chinese government with a special opportunity—a calendrical megaphone so to speak—to broadcast messages to both domestic and external audiences through a variety of commemorative activities. At home it sought to further construct the identity of patriotic citizens imbued with "the spirit of the Resistance War," to demonstrate the firm command of China's modern military by the Communist Party and its leader Xi, as well as to showcase China's status as a "great nation" respected by the world community. For the audience abroad these commemorative events were also meant to project the image of China as a great power and a responsible, peace-loving country.

China's World War II commemoration consisted of old contradictions and new departures. They produced mixed results. The absence of leaders from major Western ally countries as well as Japan and Taiwan is certainly among them.[32] The wide perception gap between domestic and foreign media covering the parade is another one: whereas most Chinese, at least judged by statements permitted in print or social media, seemed to support the state-sponsored commemorations, Western media and observers were overwhelmingly critical about them. In this sense, the anniversary commemoration failed to resolve the old contradictions, and instead produced new ones.

In spite of this it is all but certain that World War II will continue to outshine other recent wars and conflicts in China's memory culture in the coming years, if not decades. In 2016 the Chinese government decreed that school textbooks would describe the War as a "fourteen-year war" starting from the Japanese invasion of Manchuria in 1931.[33] The War of Resistance will continue to be enshrined and commemorated as the sacred struggle by the Chinese nation in modern history that led to ultimate victory. As such, it serves as a powerful and useful platform to orient the nation toward a collective purpose despite its inherent contradictions. Moreover, China's new international status harks back to the victory in World War II, which is a clear reminder of its role as a postwar Big Power on the world stage. Last but not least, there is a genuine popular interest in many issues related to that war. As this chapter goes to press, preparation is afoot in China to mark the 80th anniversary of the beginning of the full-scale war with Japan as well as the Nanjing Massacre. In this way, anniversaries associated with World War II will continue to be called upon to mark China's multifaceted roles in that war: as victims as well as a rising nation that overcame decades of weakness and humiliation to claim a bitter-sweet victory and indeed its place in the world.

NOTES

1. For the best analysis of this monument as well as the entire Tiananmen Square, see Wu Hung, "Tiananmen Square: A Political History of Monuments," *Representations* 35 (Summer 1991): 84–117.

2. "Weida de shinian" [Ten great years] *Renmin ribao* (September 3, 1955) (hereafter as RMRB). See also "Jiyi: 65nian kangzhan ji'nian shi" [Memory: 65 years of commemorating the War of Resistance], http://news.qq.com/zt2010/kzjn_tskz/.

3. Parks Coble, "China's 'New Remembering' of the Anti-Japanese War," *China Quarterly* 190 (June 2007): 394–410. There are many studies of history museums in the PRC. See, notably, Rana Mitter, "Behind the Scenes at the Museum: Nationalism, History and Memory in the Beijing War of Resistance Museum," *China Quarterly* (March 2000): 279–93; Kirk Denton, "Horror and Atrocity: Memory of Japanese Imperialism in Chinese Museums," in Ching Kwan Lee and Guobin Yang, eds., *Re-envisioning the Chinese Revolution: The Politics and Poetics of Collective Memories in Reform China* (Washington, DC: Woodrow Wilson Center Press, 2007), 245–86. For a study that emphasizes 1989 as a new turning point in China's remembrance of the war, see Lu Xijun, "Kō-Nichi sensō shi wo meguru Chūgoku no rekishi ninshiki mondai" [Issues in China's Historical Understanding Regarding the History of the "War of Resisting Japan"], *Kokusai seiji* 187 (April 2017): 62–79.

4. "Jiang Zemin dongzhi zai shoudu kejie jinian kang-Ri zhanzheng shengli 50 zhounian dahui shangde jianghua" [Speech by Comrade Jiang Zemin at the Assembly Commemorating the 50th Anniversary of the Victory of the War of Resistance against Japan], September 3, 1995. http://politics.people.com.cn/GB/8198/46867/46869/3380530.html.

5. This is not entirely a Communist invention. Many have written about Chinese narratives of national humiliation before as well as after 1949. See William A. Callahan, "National Insecurities: Humiliation, Salvation, and Chinese Nationalism," *Alternatives: Global, Local, Political*, Vol. 29, No. 2 (Mar.-May 2004): 199–218; Wang Zheng, *Never Forget National Humiliation: Historical Memory in Chinese Politics and Foreign Relations* (New York: Columbia University Press, 2012).

6. "Jiang Zemin tongzhi," op. cit.

7. "Weida de quanmin kangzhan" [The great all-nation war of resistance], *Xinhua*, and "Zhongguo kangri zhanzheng shi quanminzu de fan qinlue zhanzheng" [China's War of Resisting Japan is a war against aggression by the entire nation], RMRB, August 23, 1985.

8. "Jianjue pibo lishi xuwuzhuyi xu gongchandang lingdao de kangzhanshi" [Resolutely refute the nihilist history that negates the Communist-led Resistance War], August 26, 2015, http://opinion.people.com.cn/n/2015/0826/c1003–27521330.html and "Zhongguo gongzhandang wukui zhongliu dizhu" [The Chinese Communist Party was nothing less than the steady column in the midst of dangerous currents], August 26, 2015, http://opinion.people.com.cn/n/2015/0826/c1003–27521332.html.

9. "Rang kangzhan jinsheng youzhu minzu jiyi" [Make the spirit of the Resistance War a permanent part of the national memory], July 8, 2015, http://opinion.people.com.cn/n/2015/0708/c1003–27268818.html. For example, Nationalist general He Yinqing used this term in a major speech shortly after the war.

10. "Xi Jinping zhishi liang'an gongtong xie kangzhanshi ju sanda yiyi" [Three major significances in Xi Jinping's directive for jointly writing the history of the Resistance War by

both sides of the Taiwan Strait], August 4, 2015, http://www.taiwan.cn/plzhx/zhjzhl/zhjlw/201508/t20150804_10396736.htm.

11. "Guowuyuan guanyu gongbu diyipi guojiaji kangzhan jinian sheshi, yizhi minglu de tongzhi" [The State Council notice concerning the announcement of the first group of national-level memorials and remnants of the Resistance War], September 1, 2014, http://www.gov.cn/zhengce/content/2014–09/01/content_9058.htm.

12. Three were museums commemorating war efforts by the Nationalist forces whereas eight were devoted to those by the Communist forces. One was the National Museum of the War of Chinese People's Resistance, at the Marco Polo Bridge outside Beijing. Two remaining museums were sites of Japanese aggression and atrocities—in Shenyang and Nanjing respectively.

13. *Quanguo renmin daibiao dahui changwu weiyuanhui gongbao* [Gazette of the standing committee of the National People's Congress], February 2014. For analysis of factors leading to the national commemoration, see my forthcoming article "Construction of Victimhood in Contemporary China: Toward a Post-Heroic Representation of History?"

14. Since about 2000, various proposals had been made to hold an annual national commemoration on various subjects ranging from the mythical Yellow Emperor, the ancestor of all Chinese people, to Revolutionary Martyrs. Li Xiangping, "Guojia gongji yu guojia xiandaixing zhonggou de queshi" [National public memorialization and shortcomings of restructuring national modernity], *Zhongguo minzu bao*, April 3, 2009.

15. The *Journal of Asian Studies* Forum, "Looking Back on the Seventieth Anniversary of Japan's Surrender," erroneously stated 2015 was the first time the September date was commemorated in the PRC.

16. To this day, there is no national site of commemoration except museums devoted to the war in the Hunan Province. The only large World War II cemetery/memorial is the one built by the Nationalist government in 1943. It was damaged in 1944 by the invading Japanese and again before and during the Cultural Revolution.

17. See, for example, Yao Youchao, "Chinese and Russian Artists Commemorate 70th Anniversary of Victory of World Anti-Fascist War," *Voice of Friendship* No. 181 (September 2015): 11–12.

18. "Zhongguo jinnian weihe daxuebing" [Why is China having a grand military parade this year?], RMRB (January 26, 2015) http://news.timedg.com/2015–01/26/20048418.shtml.

19. One Chinese internet blogger speculated, after reviewing different explanations, that the most likely cause was disputes over potential unflattering images sourced from a Western media company, http://blog.sina.com.cn/qianlinxyz (May 12, 2015). I personally find it unconvincing.

20. Xi was seen to salute the troops with his left hand, a gesture that raised doubts about its appropriateness.

21. Andrew S. Erickson, "Missile March: China Parade Projects Patriotism at Home, Aims for Awe Abroad," China Real Time Report, *Wall Street Journal*, September 3, 2015. When DF-31A missiles were rolled out, according to the *Guardian* newspaper, on state television a presenter struggled to contain his excitement. "Look at this missile, it can hit Hawaii." This comment was likely not made on the main official channel CCTV watched by this author.

22. Nationalist veterans who fought in the war against Japan and joined the Communist side afterwards were eligible for the medal.

23. Chinese Foreign Ministry spokeswoman on March 3, 2015. Of the fifty-one invitations reportedly sent out, only two invitees failed to show up: Japan and the Philippines. Based on this, it seems no formal invitations were ever sent to leaders from other Western countries including President Barack Obama. See also the analysis http://news.ifeng.com/opinion/bigstory/special/militaryparade2015/.

24. China's official response concerning Sudanese president was China was not a signatory of the Rome Convention. Several former state leaders from Europe, including Tony Blair and Gerhard Schroeder, attended, as did Filipino former president Joseph Estrada who attended in his capacity as the current mayor of Manila. Former Japanese prime minister Murayama Tomiichi became ill and was not able to view the parade. Those seventeen countries are Belarus, Cuba, Kazakhstan, Kirgizstan, Mexico, Mongolia, Pakistan, Serbia, Tajikistan, and Russia as

well as Afghanistan, Cambodia, Fiji, Laos, Vanuatu, and Venezuela, which sent official representatives. Military observers are from Ethiopia, Tonga, Papua New Guinea, Iran, France, Sudan, Poland, Vietnam, Thailand, Malaysia, Singapore, Myanmar, and North Korea. China reportedly had invited both Koreas to send honor guards. According to a Korean source, President Park's decision depended on whether North Korean honor guards would take part in the parade. See "China Invites Koreas' Militaries to Parade Marking End of WWII," *Yonhap News*, July 1, 2017.

25. Putin and company left Beijing that same evening for Vladivostok where he opened a forum for economic development of the Russian Far East. Japan was expected to play a role there. For an in-depth analysis of China-Russia relations seen through the 70th anniversary year, see Maria Repnikova, "When Xi Went to Moscow and Putin Went to Beijing," *Journal of Asian Studies*, 74 no. 4 (November 2015): 809–814.

26. For an in-depth analysis of China's relations with the two Koreas, see John Delury, "Irony on Parade: Sino-Korean Friendship 1945/2015," *Journal of Asian Studies*, 74 no. 4 (November 2015): 798–802.

27. "'Abe Xi kaidan' shikirinaoshi, 9–gatsu hōchū miokuri" [Abe-Xi meeting postponed; September visit to China cancelled], *Nihon Keizai Shimbun*, August 25, 2015. See also the chapter by Mike Mochizuki in this book.

28. See for example, "V-Day parade presents collective will for peace," September 6, 2015, People's Daily Online (http://en.people.cn/n/2015/0906/c90000–8946192.html). This was the fourth troop reduction since 1985 (one million), 1997 (500,000), and 2003 (200,000).

29. See, for example, "Chinese Military Parade's Main Message is not Peace but Power," *Guardian*, September 3, 2015; David Shambaugh, "2015: China's Year of Diplomatic Highs and Domestic Lows," *South China Morning Post*, December 27, 2015.

30. "Kō-Nichi senden rekishikan wo tōsei shijutsu iddatsu no enshutsu eiyu yayu wo haijō" [Propaganda of resisting Japan, control of historical views, performance deviating from historical facts, dismissal of ridiculing heroes], *Asahi shimbun*, August 29, 2015.

31. "Yiwan wangmin sai zhipai xiang kangzhan laobing jingli" [Hundreds of millions of netizens show selfies, saluting veterans], http://shaoer.cntv.cn/2015/09/04/ARTI1441373149842346.shtml.

32. After the parade, the spokesperson of the PRC's Taiwan Affairs Office renewed the call for both sides of the Taiwan Strait to "share the sources and jointly write history in spite of the gaps that exist in assessment of the war." "Guotaiban fayanren jiu yaoqing Taiwan gejie renshi canjia kangzhan jinian huodong fabiao tanhua" [Spokesperson of State Council's Taiwan Office speaks about inviting Taiwanese from all fields to participate in commemoration of Resistance War], September 4, 2015, http://www.xinhua.net.

33. "'8–nian kangzhan' weihe gaiwei '14–nian kangzhan' de yuanyin" [Reasons for changing "Eight-year war of resistance" to "14-year war of resistance"] *Xinjingbao*, January 11, 2017.

Chapter Two

Taiwan

*Government Balancing Acts
in Commemorating World War II*

Robert Sutter

EXTERNAL AND DOMESTIC FORCES INFLUENCING
TAIWAN'S COMMEMORATION

The commemoration in Taiwan of the 70th anniversary of Japan's defeat at the end of World War II was much more modest than China's large scale commemorations focused on a September 3, 2015, military parade in Beijing.[1] Those Chinese events came against a background of years of state-sponsored efforts by the People's Republic of China (PRC) government to instill Chinese people with harshly negative views of Japan's twentieth-century aggression and with strongly positive views of the Chinese Communist Party in defeating Japan and in continuing to resolutely protect China's integrity and sovereignty.[2]

Beijing for many years has been attempting (thus far in vain) to elicit support from Taiwan in endorsing China's often strident treatment of Japan and characterization of Tokyo's defeat featuring a prominent role of the Chinese Communist forces. Also prominent in recent years have been thus far unsuccessful PRC efforts to get Taiwan to cooperate and coordinate policies with Beijing in defending Chinese sovereignty claims over disputed maritime territory in the East China Sea and the South China Sea. Both sides agree on the judgment, disputed by others, that the territories were returned to China following Japan's defeat; but in fact today the disputed Senkaku (Diaoyu) Islands in the East China Sea are under the control of Japan and many of the disputed Spratly Islands in the South China Sea are controlled by

Vietnam, the Philippines and Malaysia, despite the Chinese claim to all the islands as a result of Japan's defeat in World War II.[3]

Taiwan's government has been unwilling to join Beijing in strident opposition to Japan and its depiction of the Chinese Communist forces as Chinese liberators against Japan. It also takes a much more moderate approach in dealing with the maritime territorial disputes in the East China Sea and the South China Sea that have their roots in Japan's defeat in World War II.

The Taiwan government's stance can be understood as a complicated balancing act influenced by a variety of important and often conflicting variables, many of which have become more pronounced in recent years. Thus, Taipei's behavior is influenced by strong pressures from China to take a hard line against Japan, to cooperate with Beijing in advancing Chinese claims in disputed maritime territory, and to join with China in marking Japan's World War II defeat. These pressures run up against strong Taiwan interests in fostering good relations with Japan and in cooperating in the efforts of the United States, Taiwan's main security guarantor and close ally of Japan, to deter Beijing's coercive expansionism at the expense of Japan and other claimants in the maritime disputes.

Domestically, the Kuomintang (KMT) Party government of President Ma Ying-jeou faced divided opinion on how to deal with Japan and World War II. The Taiwan government, the Republic of China (ROC), and Ma's Kuomintang Party (KMT) trace back to Generalissimo Chiang Kai-shek whose forces bore the brunt of the fighting against Japan in China from 1937 to 1945. Chiang's ROC government was dominated by the then authoritarian KMT and represented China at various World War II events including marking Japan's surrender. To legitimate the PRC claim that the Chinese Communist forces played a major role in Japan's defeat is seen to belittle the enormous sacrifices of the ROC forces. Indeed, those sacrifices are viewed as an important reason why the ROC lost the Chinese civil war (1946–1949) to Chinese Communist forces which carefully strengthened themselves for the civil conflict and eschewed major conflict with the occupying Japanese.[4]

Meanwhile, the main Taiwan opposition party, the Democratic Progressive Party (DPP), represents perspectives of many groups in Taiwan that have little interest in glorifying historical accomplishments of the ROC and the KMT on mainland China. The Ma government's popularity declined markedly in recent years, and his Kuomintang Party was defeated by a landslide by the DPP in important island-wide elections in November 2014 and in presidential and legislative elections in January 2016. Many observers rightly foresaw the DPP candidate, party chair Tsai Ing-wen, winning the Taiwan presidential election in January 2016. As a result, the sentiment of Taiwan groups that differ from Ma's government and the KMT on Japan and its defeat was rising in importance. Even PRC specialists and media are well aware of these groups and see their impact as "worrisome" for China's interests in fostering cooperation with Taiwan on various issues.[5]

The groups include older Taiwan residents who have comparatively overall positive memories of Japanese colonial rule, especially when contrasted with the rule of the ROC in Taiwan after occupying the island in 1945. The strict Japanese colonial administration fostered rapid economic development. Its record contrasted sharply with the grossly incompetent and abusive ROC rule in the years immediately following handover in 1945 which led to the massacre of thousands at the hands of ROC military forces in 1947. That crackdown was followed by the imposition of martial law and what was seen by critics as "white terror" carried out by more competent but often grossly abusive ROC authorities for decades after that.[6] In addition, the children and grandchildren of the hundreds of thousands of Taiwan men who volunteered and fought for Japan in World War II tend to find commemoration of Japan's defeat distasteful or even repulsive.[7]

Finally, younger people in Taiwan who include those leading contemporary movements against closer Taiwan integration with China have little interest in commemorating the historical defeat of Japan, a country Taiwan people favor more than any other. Corroborated by other recent surveys, a survey sponsored by Japan's de facto embassy in Taipei found that when asked what their favorite country was in a recent survey, 43 percent said Japan, while only single digits said Singapore, the United States or China. The support for Japan was even stronger among Taiwanese aged 20–29, with 54 percent of respondents in that age group listing Japan as their favorite foreign country. By contrast, only 2 percent of respondents between the ages of 20 and 29 said China was their favorite foreign country.[8]

PURPOSE AND SCOPE OF THIS CHAPTER

The following section briefly discusses the remarkable increase since 2012 in China's strident criticism and coercive and intimidating pressures on Japan regarding disputes over maritime territory and other matters related to World War II. This provides the context for China's efforts to influence Taiwan's policy and behavior regarding Japan, territorial disputes and other matters related to World War II in the lead-up to the September 2015 commemoration.

The chapter then discusses in more detail how and why the Ma government maneuvered effectively in avoiding being seen as partnering with Beijing against Japan, while sustaining ROC interests in highlighting Taiwan's role as an independent stakeholder in the maritime disputes that is determined to sustain its claims to the disputed maritime territory. In general, the Ma government defended its territorial claims and dealt with various issues related to Japan and its negative behavior in World War II in much more moderate ways than China. It occasionally criticized assertive Chinese actions against Japan, especially when those actions had an impact on Taiwan's claims and interests. Taiwan placed much more emphasis than Beijing on seeking issues of common ground while putting aside clashing claims of sovereignty. Its behavior seemed designed to and generally succeeded in avoiding serious upset in important Taiwan relationships with the United States and Japan; it also resulted in some substantial economic and reputational benefits for Taiwan.

The maneuvering of the Ma government in the face of pressure from Beijing and major imperatives in sustaining close relations with Japan and the United States also was influenced by competing domestic views in Taiwan of Japan and its defeat in World War II. Those influences set limits and established boundaries on the Ma government's freedom of action as it balanced competing international imperatives. The section discusses those influences when they appear relevant to particular Taiwan policies and actions. It judges that the Ma government's freedom of action became more constrained with the sharp decline in recent years of public approval of the president and his party.

The most important events in cross strait relations in the year following the war anniversary were the November 7, 2015, summit meeting between President Xi Jinping and President Ma Ying-jeou and the election of DPP president Tsai Ing-wen on January 16, 2016. Those and related events are briefly assessed in a following section that among other things explains why China's posture toward a DPP-led Taiwan government hardened on cross strait issues following the January 2016 presidential and legislative elections.

The conclusion shows how and why changing international and domestic determinants support the kinds of pragmatic balancing acts we have seen in recent years by the Ma Ying-jeou and Tsai Ing-wen governments.

BEIJING SETS THE CONTEXT FOR THE WORLD WAR II COMMEMORATIONS

Marking a decennial anniversary of an important event generally declines in importance as the decades pass, though an uptick in interest is expected at the centenary. And as PRC-Japan relations have waxed and waned in recent decades, Chinese interest in pressuring Japan through commemoration of such events has similarly vacillated.[9] Unfortunately for those seeking cooperative Sino-Japanese relations, Beijing recently has seen its interests best served with high pressure, coercion and intimidation against Japan, bringing relations to their lowest point since World War II. The pressure has been supported widely by the nationalistic Chinese elite and public opinion strongly conditioned by Chinese education, media and other publicity emphasizing the very negative Chinese experiences at the hands of Japanese forces up to the end of World War II.

Earlier cooperative Sino-Japanese relations foundered notably over the increasingly contentious territorial disputes over the Senkaku (Diaoyu) Islands, which became acute when Japan arrested a Chinese fishing boat captain for ramming Japanese coast guard ships near the islands in 2010. Two years later, Democratic Party (DPJ) prime minister Noda Yoshihiko sought to limit the damage to Japan-China relations caused by Japanese right-wing politicians seeking to purchase some of the Senkaku (Diaoyu) islands and use them to antagonize China. Noda decided in September 2012 to have the Japanese government purchase the islands instead.[10]

The Chinese reaction was extraordinary. The PRC organized the largest ever Chinese demonstration against a foreign target. An intense and massive propaganda barrage, authoritative government, party, and military pronouncements, and remarks by the full range of top leaders all urged the Chinese people to register their "righteous indignation" over the Noda decision. The demonstrations in 120 Chinese cities, with associated burning and looting of Japanese properties, followed.[11]

Prime Minister Noda failed to appreciate that his seemingly pragmatic decision on purchasing the islands came amid heightened public Chinese determination to defend territorial claims along China's maritime rim; and it followed China's successful use of coercion and intimidation to force Philippine fishing boats and security forces out of the disputed Scarborough Shoal in the South China Sea in mid-2012. Chinese nationalistic assertiveness now had a much more important target than the Philippines. China used coast guard forces, legal and administrative measures, trade pressures, diplomatic threats, and other means to force Japan to reverse its actions and negotiate with China over the disputed islands. The DPJ woes contributed to the landslide election victory of the Liberal Democratic Party (LDP) under Abe Shinzō in late 2012. Abe was firm in the face of Chinese pressure; protracted tensions ensued.[12]

Coming to power amid the enormous Chinese demonstrations and nationalistic outrage against Japan's purchase of the disputed Senkaku (Diaoyu) Islands in 2012, the Xi Jinping government for two years pursued a confrontational posture over territorial disputes reflecting the higher priority Beijing gave to advancing its claims in the East China Sea and South China Sea. Strident official statements and commentary repeatedly attacked and sought to demonize Japanese prime minister Abe who had Japanese forces stand against Chinese intrusions in the Japanese controlled islands. The Chinese attacks against Abe constantly focused on his policies, practices and alleged views on Japan's negative historical record in World War II in order to discredit the prime minister at home and abroad. Trade and investment dropped sharply. Japan did not buckle under Chinese pressure. It became China's main international opponent as it built defenses at home, maneuvered for advantage in Asia and sought and received strong backing from the American government of President Barack Obama that became increasingly concerned with Chinese assertiveness and expansion.

The adverse circumstances and poorly considered aspects of the Xi Jinping government's activist and arguably overreaching Japan policy saw China avoid acknowledging mistakes or compromise; yet it bent despite its image of strength and resolve in pursuing nationalistic goals. The Chinese leader met with Prime Minister Abe in November 2014 and began a process of limited mutual accommodation amid continuing strong differences reflected in negative Chinese treatment of Japan in the World War II commemorations in September 2015.[13]

MA MANEUVERS OVER JAPAN DISPUTES AND WAR ISSUES, AVOIDS COMMON FRONT

Rising tensions over the disputed Senkaku (Diaoyu) Islands in mid 2012 saw the ROC government, with President Ma Ying-jeou playing a leading role, take steps to strengthen Taipei's own claim to the islands and to defend the many Taiwan fishing boats using the contested seas. President Ma issued in early August an "East China Sea Peace Initiative," staking out a unique position while calling attention to Taiwan's important interest in the controversy. He called on all parties to set aside disputes over sovereignty, focus on cooperative resource development and behavior that adheres to the rule of law, and rely on peaceful approaches and dialogue. Ma seemed to add to the tension over the disputes with strong vows to protect Taiwan fishermen in contested East China Sea waters; he notably backed the dispatch of ROC Coast Guard ships to escort several dozen Taiwan fishing boats which sailed within Japanese-claimed territorial waters around the islands in late September. The two sides' coast guard ships sprayed each other with water cannons while circling one another in rough seas over the course of a few hours.[14]

More constructively, the two governments agreed to resume stalled bilateral fishing talks after a three year hiatus. Facing intense pressure from China, Japan seemed anxious to make a deal with Taiwan. Ma was pleased with the agreement in April 2013 opening vast new areas to Taiwan fishermen and boosting public support of the president in Taiwan. Beijing had strong reservations and was frustrated in its efforts to get Taiwan to join with China in a common front against Japan over the territorial issues. Ma said the fishery agreement with Japan was consistent with his East China Sea peace initiative as neither side yielded on its territorial and maritime claims, and the sovereignty issue had been put to the side. The U.S. government reportedly was concerned with Taiwan adding to rising tension with the faceoff of the Taiwan-Japan coast guard ships in September and was pleased with the decline in Taiwan-Japan tensions and the conclusion of the fishing agreement.[15]

Beijing's efforts to have Taiwan collaborate with China in defending Chinese sovereignty were also in vain regarding the South China Sea, the other disputed maritime area where both Beijing and Taipei agree that Japan's World War II defeat resulted in the territory being returned to Chinese control. Keeping China at arms length, the Ma government in May 2015 offered a South China Sea peace and resource sharing initiative roughly in line with its earlier East China Sea peace initiative. The Taiwan initiative highlighted Taiwan's moderation and its status as a stakeholder in the South China Sea. It called for avoiding infringements on sovereignty while seeking ways to share resources, respecting and adhering to international law, seeking to peacefully resolve disputes, and upholding freedom of navigation and overflight.[16]

The Taiwan plan stood in favorable contrast with the Xi Jinping government's repeated use of coercion, intimidation and bold and disruptive tactics to have its way against disputants in the South China Sea and other concerned powers, notably the United States and Japan. In particular, the Xi government dismissed international complaints as it used rapid and massive dredging and building of artificial islands on Chinese controlled reefs, resulting in the expansion by 3,000 acres in 18 months of Chinese controlled territory in the South China Sea. The new territory was widely seen as the basis of a buildup of military facilities that would increase Chinese power projection and control in this critically important waterway and exacerbate international tension over the South China Sea. China's official response to the Taiwan plan came from the Chinese foreign ministry spokesperson who advised Taiwan of its "obligation" to cooperate with Beijing in protecting Chinese sovereign territorial claims. The spokesperson advised that "Chinese people across the Taiwan Straits are obliged to jointly safeguard national territorial sovereignty and maritime rights and interests, and maintain peace and stability in the South China Sea."[17]

The period leading up to the September 2015 70th anniversary featured strengthened Taiwan efforts to define positions acceptable to Japan, the United States and other powers concerned with Chinese pressure tactics against Japan, the Philippines, Vietnam and other East Asian countries in control of maritime territory that the Xi Jinping government claims belongs under its control. The Taiwan positions on the anniversary also reflected a balance among competing views on Japan and World War II in Taiwan. Those competing views were important as the Ma Ying-jeou government developed an official Taiwan stance on Japan's war responsibilities that was more moderate than those of China, North Korea and South Korea. Thus, unlike the sharp reactions from China and the Koreas that greeted Prime Minister Abe's visit to the controversial Yasukuni war memorial in Tokyo in December 2013, President Ma's delayed response briefly noted disappointment and puzzlement over the visit. He later posted remarks briefly criticizing the shrine visit in an article on his personal Facebook page where he discussed his meeting with a now aged "comfort woman" from Taiwan, noting continuing "wounds" left by Japanese forces during the war, but avoiding the kind of vitriol that characterized Chinese and Korean treatment of Japanese reprehensible behavior during World War II.[18]

Ma laid out a distinct Taiwan position on Japan and World War II in a December 1, 2013, speech marking the 70th anniversary of the Cairo declaration. The declaration came from a wartime summit in Egypt among President Franklin Roosevelt, Prime Minister Winston Churchill and Chiang Kai-shek. As Ma noted, it was at this summit that the allies said that "all the territories Japan has stolen from the Chinese . . . shall be restored to the Republic of China," thereby providing a foundation of Chinese claims in the recent maritime disputes. In referring to the war effort against Japan, Ma said the victory over Japan was "a brilliant feat for the Chinese people." He made no specific reference to the Communist forces. He said victory was due to the joint efforts of the ROC army and the general public. He also highlighted "critical international assistance," with the United States providing "the most important assistance."[19]

Showing independence from China, Ma used the speech to address at length an important contemporary crisis caused by PRC truculence over disputed territorial rights against Japan in the East China Sea. He criticized China's November 23, 2013, announcement of an East China Sea Air Defense Identification Zone (ADIZ). Ma grouped Taiwan with the United States and Japan in registering "deep concern" over the abrupt Chinese announcement, and advised that the Taiwan air force would carry out exercise and training activities as normal in the ROC's ADIZ, which overlapped substantially with China's newly announced zone.[20]

The months before the September 2015 70th anniversary date featured a military parade on July 4 that Taiwan used to commemorate the 70th anniversary of the defeat of Japan. The event was held at a military base in northern Taiwan. The military display included jet fighters, attack helicopters and air-ground integrated operations. It was big by Taiwan standards, involving 3,858 military personnel. President Ma presided, gave a speech praising the valor of the ROC military then and now, and distributed service medals to 127 veterans of the war against Japan.[21] In a small but significant sign of Taiwan's interest in not allowing the commemoration ceremonies to complicate good relations with Japan, the Taiwan military removed prior to the ceremony Japanese flags that were painted on two of the Taiwan planes that represented the number of Japanese planes shot down by an American pilot and an ROC pilot defending against the Japanese in China during World War II.[22]

A major element in China's commemoration activities was to encourage veterans from Taiwan who fought the Japanese during World War II and others from the island to come to China and participate in commemoration events there. For the occasion, Beijing modified its past view focused on Chinese Communist Party forces being responsible for Japan's defeat to one that recognized the contribution of the ROC forces, reflecting the "the ultimate victory won by all Chinese people."[23] The Taiwan government rebuffed the Chinese efforts. The Taiwan ministry of defense spokesperson on June 23 called on veterans who fought in the war against Japan not to be influenced by Beijing's "unification propaganda" and "united front campaign."[24]

Beijing commentators disapproved of such "unwise voices" in Taiwan seeking to discourage veterans from Taiwan participating in the Chinese commemoration events. They also took offense over the common practice in Taiwan to emphasize the role of the ROC forces in fighting the Japanese military without mentioning the contributions of the Communist forces, though they argued that such differences should be put aside in the interests of fostering Chinese unity in joint commemoration of the victory over Japan.[25]

In a related development, longstanding KMT leader and former vice president and premier Lien Chan accepted Beijing's invitation and participated in the anniversary celebrations in the Chinese capital. He also met with President Xi Jinping. His visit was criticized by President Ma, other KMT leaders and the political opposition.[26]

As often happens, China's insistence on using hard tactics in order to have its way with Taiwan interferes with its periodic positive blandishments to Taiwan. On the one hand, the Ma Ying-jeou government insisted on pursuing a policy of moderation and accommodation toward China despite the latter's massive military buildup and other pressures designed to coerce and intimidate Taiwan to avoid moves toward greater separatism from China and to move toward reunification sought by China. On the other hand, the Chinese pressure tactics became so egregious at times that even the accommodating Ma government could not but protest. A case in point came in July during the emphasis by Chinese officials and commentary in recognizing the ROC forces role in the war against Japan in efforts to encourage ROC veterans to participate in Chinese commemorations of the war against Japan.[27] On July 5, China Central Television featured dramatic footage of an annual military exercise in northern China highlighting infantry assaults on a mock city. The video went largely unnoticed abroad until July 23 when a media outlet in Shanghai said it showed how Beijing "would use force to solve the Taiwan issue." As a result, many Taiwan commentators angrily reacted to those segments from the newsreel that appeared to show Chinese troops advancing through an urban battleground toward a red and white structure with distinctive early twentieth-century European style architecture that closely resembled Taiwan's Presidential Office in Taipei. In response, Taiwan's defense spokesman said the implied assault on Taipei was "unacceptable." The most important resident of the office, President Ma Ying-jeou, also complained about the exercise to the *BBC* on July 27. He advised in carefully measured language that "the situation in China . . . is not very stable," the threat from China to Taiwan continues and Taiwan needs defensive measures against such threats. [28]

The period leading up to the massive September 3 Beijing commemoration saw other Taiwan events marking the anniversary and remembering aspects of the war against Japan and its implications that reflected the kinds of balancing noted above. Beijing's pressures for Taiwan to join with China in a united front harshly critical of Japan were kept at arms length. Taiwan's interests in sustaining good relations with Japan by avoiding excess in the war remembrances and disputes over related territorial issues seemed successful. The ROC president was in the lead in registering strong support for ROC claims to disputed territory, notably the Senkaku (Diaoyu) Islands now controlled by Japan. The United States, Taiwan's main security backer and Japan's sole ally, also welcomed Taiwan's constructive role in dealing with territorial disputes in the East China Sea and the South China Sea that have their roots in the territorial settlements resulting from Japan's defeat; Taiwan's position stood positively in the American view in contrast with China's overbearing and dangerously expansive policies and practices. The Taiwan commemoration of the war also carefully balanced the contrasting views of citizens in Taiwan of Japan and World War II. The achievements of the ROC forces and the sacrifices of Chinese people in the war against Japan were repeatedly recognized, but without continued animus toward Japan. The sacrifices included events dealing with reprehensible Japanese practices during the war, notably the egregious Japanese behavior in the assault and occupation of Nanjing in 1937 and the so-called "comfort women" issue involving forced Japanese mobilization of women in occupied countries as sex-slaves for Japanese servicemen. At the same time, the commemorative events also paid tribute to those in Taiwan more sensitive to the brutal rule of the early ROC occupiers in Taiwan seen notably in the crackdown and massacre of Taiwan oppositionists on February 28, 1947.

Relevant events and related developments showing Taiwan's balancing of competing imperatives in commemorating Japan's defeat included:

- Five government-produced brief videos on the role of ROC forces in the war against Japan released in July led to criticism from historians and commentators arguing that the videos lacked a "Taiwan-centered perspective" and notably omitted reference to the harsh ROC rule after 1945 including the February 28, 1947, crackdown killing thousands of Taiwan oppositionists. A government official duly defended the videos, but President Ma on August 4 seemed to respond to the critical sentiment. Ma took the occasion of a release of historical documents to deliver a speech in Taipei affirming his deep empathy for the victims of the 1947 crackdown, stressing the government's efforts over the past 20 years to right these egregious wrongs of the past, and affirming that they will "never be forgotten" to insure that "such an event never happens again."[29]

- On August 4, Taiwan media reported the re-release on a nation-wide basis later that month of an award-winning 2013 film featuring the stories of six Taiwan "comfort women." The release coincided with Taiwan's ongoing World War II commemorations and was part of activities marking International Memorial Day for Comfort Women.[30]

- On August 5, Taiwan media reported a one-day "East Asian Maritime Peace Forum" highlighting the government's East China Sea peace initiative and South China Sea peace initiative that showed Taiwan's distinctive constructive approach to the tense disputes while sustaining Taiwan's territorial claims. President Ma Ying-jeou used the opportunity of a speech at the conference to offer a long defense of the ROC government claims to the disputed territory "from the points of view of history, geography, geology and international law." He gave special emphasis to disputes with Japan over the Senkaku (Diaoyu) Islands.[31]

- On August 13, Taiwan media reported that the relatives of two of the foreign nationals who worked against great odds in protecting Chinese civilians from the brutality of the Japanese "rape of Nanjing" in 1937 were in Taipei to meet with President Ma as part of Taiwan's World War II commemorations. In contrast with commentary in China focusing on the negatives with Japan, the Taiwan media highlighted the visitors' remarks urging that remembering the past should be used to learn to "make friends with enemies" and advance peace.[32]

- President Ma and the ROC government were more measured and moderate than the Chinese and South Korean governments in response to Prime Minister Abe's statement on August 14 on the 70th anniversary of the end of World War II. In a speech at an exhibition marking the occasion, Ma said that he hopes Japan can do better and carry out more self reflection, especially on the issue of the so-called comfort women. Recalling Japanese aggression during the war he said that "although mistakes of the past can be forgiven, the truth must not be forgotten." And he underlined that "all of the people of Asian countries, including those of Japan, were "victims of militarism" and that "the firm and friendly ties between Taiwan and Japan after the war are an example of reconciliation for other Asian countries seeking to step out of the conflict's shadow."[33]

- While the KMT government of Ma Ying-jeou argued in moderate language against the visits of former vice president Lien Chan and of Taiwan World War II veterans to the anniversary celebrations in Beijing, they had a harder time opposing in a measured way interview statements by former ROC president Lee Teng-hui in July and August about his own and other strong pro-Japan sentiment in Taiwan during World War II. Lee disputed the Ma government's claims of longstanding Taiwan resistance to Japanese rule. Lee and his brother were among the over 100,000 Taiwan men serving loyally in the Japanese military at the time. Lee also said the Senkaku (Diaoyu) Islands belong to Japan and that the comfort women issue was settled in Taiwan and did not have to be raised further. KMT leaders and legislators reacted with outrage, demanding a cut-off of privileges Lee receives as a former ROC president. By contrast, DPP leader Tsai YIng-wen, who maintains strong political ties with Lee, took a much more moderate and seemingly detached stance. She argued that "Each generation and ethnic group in Taiwan has lived a different history, and therefore their memories, experience and interpretations of the past are not the same. . . . When a nation faces such a situation, we have to maintain an attitude of understanding, so that we can learn from history, instead of using what happened as a tool for manipulating rivalry and social division."[34]

OUTLOOK UNDER PRESIDENT TSAI ING-WEN

Tsai Ing-wen's remarks foreshadowed a significant shift in Taiwan government policies toward Beijing and Tokyo based on her government's well developed sense of identity in Taiwan politics very much at odds with that of Ma Ying-jeou and his KMT colleagues. Ma Ying-jeou left office with a strong affirmation of the concept of one China seen in his unprecedented summit meeting with President Xi Jinping in November 2016 where both leaders strongly affirmed the importance of the 1992 consensus. That consensus represented a vague endorsement of the concept of one China that provided the basis for Beijing to allow forward movement in cross strait agreements and other cooperation with Taiwan during Ma's tenure. Both leaders knew that Tsai Ing-wen and the DPP long opposed the consensus as infringing on Taiwan's sovereignty. In effect, they put Tsai in a spotlight during the concluding weeks of the Taiwan election campaign, forecasting deterioration of cross strait relations if she were elected and refused to endorse the 1992 consensus.[35]

The Taiwan electorate's opinion and identity seemed much more in line with Tsai than with Ma, evidenced in various public opinion polls and the landslide DPP victory in island-wide presidential and legislative elections in

January 2016. The KMT as a coherent force in Taiwan politics was called into question as a result of its drubbing. The KMT took over a year to reorganize under a somewhat more effective leadership. The KMT leader after the election strongly stressed a view of one China that Beijing supported but was backed by only a small minority in Taiwan. After reorganization, the new KMT leaders were more measured in line with prevailing opinion in Taiwan, though they strongly affirmed the 1992 consensus. They also used past KMT rhetoric critical of Japan in recalling the wartime struggles with Japan, notably in the 80th anniversary in July 2017 of the battle that started the Chinese war with Japan in 1937 that did not end until Japan's defeat in 1945.[36]

Facing ever increasing military, economic and diplomatic pressure from China to accept the 1992 consensus or encounter negative outcomes for Taiwan's interests, the Tsai government remained moderate but firm in not accepting the 1992 consensus. The DPP government's more favorable attitude toward Japan was seen in the appointment of Frank Hsieh, a former premier in the Taiwan government and a veteran DPP stalwart, as the head of Taiwan's de facto embassy in Tokyo. The Japanese-speaking Hsieh received his higher education in Kyoto University and over the years he has developed a strong network of important connections among various Japanese elites.[37] Tsai also was much less interested than Ma in engaging in high profile actions in support of the Republic of China's large claims (the same as those of the People's Republic of China in Beijing) to maritime territories in the East China Sea where Japan is a disputant and the South China Sea where Vietnam, the Philippines, Malaysia and Brunei are disputants. And whereas Ma strongly affirmed support for Taiwan comfort women claims against Japan and for the heroics of ROC resistance against Japan over half a century ago, the Tsai government's interest in such matters was much less.[38]

Showing how the Taiwan government needs to take into account unexpected developments as it preserves its interests and sense of identity amid international and domestic pressures was the Tsai Ing-wen's government's complicated reaction to the July 2016 ruling of the arbitral panel associated with the Permanent Court of Arbitration in support of the Philippines case against Beijing's wide-ranging claims in the disputed South China Sea. As noted above, Taipei as the Republic of China has basically the same large claims in the South China Sea and the East China Sea as Beijing. The KMT government of Ma Ying-jeou, while refusing to jointly stand with Beijing in defense of the traditional Chinese claims, strongly affirmed support for those longstanding claims against Japan in the East China Sea and against the South China Sea disputants. The Tsai government was less vigorous in both regards, but remained careful to avoid disavowing the claims and thereby risking strong Beijing reaction against such steps as challenging Beijing's view of one China.

Observers in Taipei said that the Taiwan government was working close-ly with the U.S. government, which supported the Philippines bringing the legal case against China's claims, in preparing to respond in measured terms to the arbitral tribunal's ruling. Taiwan sought to keep on good terms with Washington while avoiding major retreat from its traditional expansive claims to the South China Sea which mirror Beijing's. To do the latter could cause problems with Beijing at a delicate time in Taiwan-China relations by signaling that Taiwan was moving away from its support of territorial claims associated with one China.

However, the ruling had a negative impact on elite and public opinion in Taiwan. In particular, the ruling used a phrase very offensive to people in Taiwan in referring to the Taiwan government. And to the reported surprise of Taipei and Washington, the tribunal made a ruling regarding Taiping Island, the largest natural land feature in the Spratly Islands of the South China Sea which is controlled by Taipei. The ruling said that Taiping Island did not qualify as an island under terms of the UN Law of the Sea. Thus, it was not eligible for the large Exclusive Economic Zone (EEZ) given to islands as opposed to "rocks" permanently above sea level or above sea level at low tide. This development came as a significant setback to Taiwan's claims of fishing and other territorial rights in the South China Sea and prompted strong negative reaction in Taiwan that had to be accommodated by the government, according to observers in Taipei. The result was a strong statement from the Taiwan government criticizing the U.S.-backed ruling and affirming Taiwan's territorial claims.[39]

CONCLUSION: INTERESTS, IDENTITY AND CHANGING CIRCUMSTANCES

This chapter discussing Taiwan's behavior in dealing with the 70th anniver-sary of World War II reflects changing pressures and developments impact-ing Taiwan from abroad mixing with contrasting identities and divergent interests among the elites and public opinion on the island. As the results of Chinese blandishments to Taiwan in marking the 70th anniversary of Japan's defeat came to little, the unsatisfactory outcome from Beijing's perspective reinforced sentiment in the Chinese leadership that other less accommodating and tougher measures are needed in order to move cross strait relations in what Beijing sees as a positive direction. Chinese pressure has increased with the transition from Ma Ying-jeou to Tsai Ing-wen. As in many areas of U.S. foreign policy, the Donald Trump administration's stance toward Taiwan remains uncertain, sometimes supportive and sometimes not. Japan is one of the few international powers with clear leaning in support of Taiwan, and this leaning is being reciprocated by the Tsai government, but whatever is going on between the two governments is generally kept under wraps so as to avoid serious backlash from Beijing.[40]

The respective identities of the Kuomintang of the Ma Ying-jeou government and the DPP of the Tsai Ing-wen government clearly lead to differences on how to deal with pressure from and opportunities provided by Beijing. The identities have deep historical roots which also help to explain why the Ma government was much more active than Tsai Ing-wen and the DPP in support of commemorations of the war anniversary, in criticism of Japan's behavior in the war, notably regarding the so-called comfort women issue, and in support of China reclaiming the disputed territory on the East and South China Seas after World War II. Of course, veteran observers of identity formation in Taiwan often see changes over time and with the passing of generations. In many respects, identity among people and elites on the island is a work in progress; it is not fixed or unmoving.[41]

At bottom, amid the changing international circumstances and evolving definitions of identity and related interests in Taiwan, an understandable pragmatic approach of balancing various imperatives has seemed advisable for the Taiwan government. This chapter has shown the Ma Ying-jeou and the Tsai Ing-wen governments following such approaches, albeit with each also reflecting the different priorities they have on some sensitive issues, notably how they define and preserve Taiwan's sovereignty.

NOTES

1. This chapter is based on a paper for the Conference on Commemorating the 70th Anniversary of the End of WWII sponsored by the Sigur Center for Asian Studies, George Washington University, Washington DC, September 10, 2015, by Robert Sutter, George Washington University. It benefited greatly from the constructive remarks at the conference and the constructive comments of the editors.

2. Suisheng Zhao, "Chinese Nationalism and Its International Orientations." *Political Science Quarterly* 115, no. 1 (Spring 2000): 1–33.

3. Denny Roy, *Return of the Dragon*, New York: Columbia University Press, 2013, pp. 81–137.

4. Michael Schaller, *The United States and China*, New York: Oxford University Press, 2002, pp. 93–94.

5. "Both sides of Straits celebrate anti-fascist victory," *China Daily*, July 6, 2015, http://usa.chinadaily.com.cn/epaper/2015–07/06/content_21192500.htm.

6. Shelley Rigger, *Taiwan's Rising Rationalism: Generations, Politics, and Taiwanese Nationalism*, Washington, DC: East-West Center, 2006.

7. "Both sides of Straits celebrate anti-fascist victory."

8. Michael Thim and Misato Matsuoka, "The Odd Couple: Japan and Taiwan's Unlikely Friendship," *Diplomat*, May 15, 2014, http://thediplomat.com/2014/05/the-odd-couple-japan-taiwans-unlikely-friendship/.

9. Michael Yahuda, *Sino-Japanese Relations after the Cold War*, London: Routledge, 2013.

10. Adapted from Robert Sutter, *Chinese Foreign Relations: Power and Policy since the Cold War*, Fourth Edition, Lanham, MD: Rowman & Littlefield, 2016, pp. 189–192.

11. James Przystup, "Japan-China Relations," *Comparative Connections* 14, no. 3 (January 2013): 109–11.

12. Kosuke Takahashi, "Shinzo Abe's Nationalist Strategy," *Diplomat*, February 13, 2014, http://thediplomat.com/2014/02/shinzo-abes-nationalist-strategy.

13. See Zhao Shengnan, "Xi and delegates signal 'thaw,'" *China Daily*, May 25, 2015, http://www.chinadaily.com.cn/china/2015–05/25/content_20805947.htm.

14. Alan Romberg, "Shaping the Future-Part II: Cross-Strait Relations" *China Leadership Monitor*, No. 39, Hoover Institution, Stanford University, October 2012, http://media.hoover.org/sites/default/files/documents/CLM39AR.pdf.

15. Alan Romberg, "Striving for new Eqilibria," *China Leadership Monitor*, No. 41, Hoover Institution, Stanford University, June 2013, http://www.stimson.org/images/uploads/CLM41AR.PDF.

16. Shannon Tiezzi, "Taiwan's Plan for Peace in the South China Sea," *Diplomat*, May 27, 2015, http://thediplomat.com/2015/05/taiwans-plan-for-peace-in-the-south-china-sea/.

17. Tiezzi, "Taiwan's Plan for Peace in the South China Sea."

18. "Japanese leader's Yasukuni visit 'puzzles' Ma," *CNA*, January 13, 2014, http://www.taipeitimes.com/News/taiwan/archives/2014/01/13/2003581195.

19. "President Ma attends International Conference on 70th Anniversary of Cairo Declaration," Office of the President, Republic of China (Taiwan), December 1, 2013, http://english.president.gov.tw/Default.aspx?tabid=491&itemid=31367&rmid=2355.

20. Ibid.

21. "Ma presides over commemorative war victory parade," *Taiwan Today*, July 6, 2015, http://www.taiwantoday.tw/ct.asp?xitem=232229&CtNode=414.

22. "Amid Japan's Concerns, Taiwan Air Force removes 'kill' markings from jets," *CNA* June 30, 2015, http://focustaiwan.tw/news/aipl/201506300029.aspx.

23. "Commemorate joint war efforts of KMT and CCP," *China Daily*, July 8, 2015, http://www.chinadailyasia.com/opinion/2015–07/08/content_15287170.html.

24. "Taiwan urges veterans not to respond to China's united front tactic," *CNA*, June 23, 2015, http://focustaiwan.tw/news/aipl/201506230032.aspx.

25. "Commemorate joint war efforts of KMT and CCP."

26. Mai Jun, "Taiwan's Ex-premier Lien Chan arrives in Beijing for China's Victory over Japan parade," *South China Morning Post*, August 30, 2015, http://www.scmp.com/news/china/policies-politics/article/1853878/taiwans-ex-premier-lien-chan-arrives-beijing-chinas.

27. The following is taken from "Palace Intrigue: Chinese Soldiers Storm Replicas of Taiwan Presidential Office," *Wall Street Journal, China Real Time*, July 23, 2015, http://blogs.wsj.com/chinarealtime/2015/07/23/palace-intrigue-chinese-soldiers-storm-replica-of-taiwan-presidential-office/.

28. "President unhappy about China's simulated attack on Taiwan," *CNA*, July 27, 2015, http://focustaiwan.tw/news/acs/201507270014.aspx.

29. Shi Hsiu-chuan, "Experts slam ministry's WWII videos," *Taipei Times*, July 12, 2015, p. 3; "In defense of videos," *Taipei Times*, July 16, 2015, p. 8; "Ma urges February 28 Incident reconciliation," *CNA*, August 8, 2015, available at http://taiwantoday.tw/ct.asp?xItem=233345&ctNode=452.

30. "Taiwan Documentary Pays Tribute to Comfort Women," *Taiwan Today*, August 4, 2015, http://taiwantoday.tw/ct.asp?xItem=233279&ctNode=452.

31. "East Asian Maritime Peace Forum opens in Taipei," *CNA*, August 5, 2015, available at http://taiwantoday.tw/ct.asp?xItem=233359&ctNode=452; Office of the President, Republic of China (Taiwan), "President Ma attends 2015 East Asian Maritime Peace Forum," August 5, 2015.

32. "ROC honors foreign heroes in Rape of Nanjing," *CNA*, August 13, 2015, available at http://taiwantoday.tw/ct.asp?xItem=233796&ctNode=452.

33. "Ma responds to Abe's speech on end of WWII," *Taiwan Today*, August 17, 2015, http://taiwantoday.tw/ct.asp?xItem=233866&ctNode=420.

34. Loa Iok-sin and Alison Hsiao, "DPP's Tsai calls for end of muckraking over histories," *Taipei Times*, August 23, 2015, p.1; "Lee Teng-hui's benefits as ex-president may be stripped,"

CNA, August 22, 2015, http://www.wantchinatimes.com/news-subclass-cnt.aspx?id= 20150822000101&cid=1101.

35. David Brown, "A Meeting and a Campaign," *Comparative Connections*, Vol. 17, no.3 (January 2016), 73–80.

36. Adela Lin, "Taiwan's Opposition Kuomintang Elects Wu Den-yih as Chairman," *Bloomsberg*, May 20, 2017, https://www.bloomberg.com/news/articles/2017–05–20/taiwan-s-opposition-kuomintang-elects-wu-den-yih-as-chairman-j2xfiwkd; Sean Lin, "KMT Marks incident that sparked war," *Taipei Times*, July 8, 2017, http://www.taipeitimes.com/News/taiwan/print/2017/07/08/2003674128.

37. Ko Shu-ling, "Taipei's new Tokyo envoy pick has affinity for Japan, looks to strengthen ties," *Japan Times*, May 3, 2016, http://www.japantimes.co.jp/news/2016/05/03/national/politics-diplomacy/taipeis-new-tokyo-envoy-pick-has-affinity-for-japan-looks-to-strengthen-ties/#.WXCIB4jyuM8.

38. Jeff Kingston, "Complicating Taiwan love affair with Japan," *Japan Times*, September 3, 2016, http://www.japantimes.co.jp/opinion/2016/09/03/commentary/complicating-taiwans-love-affair-japan/#.WXCHoIjyuM8.

39. Robert Sutter and Satu Limaye, *Washington Asia Policy Debates: Impact of 2015–2016 Presidential Campaign and Asian Reactions*, East-West Center, Honolulu 2016, p. 24

40. David Brown, "Adrift without Dialogue," *Comparative Connections*, Vol 19, no. 1 (May 2017), pp. 61–66.

41. Sung Sheng Yvonne Chang, "Introduction" [especially pp. 8–10, "identity as a sit of reinventions"] in Sung Sheng, Yvonne Chang, Michelle Yeh, and Ming-ju Fan (eds.), *The Columbia Sourcebook of Literary Taiwan*, New York: Columbia University Press, 2014, pp. 1–10.

Chapter Three

Japan

Contested History and Identity Conflict

Mike Mochizuki

Anniversaries are artificial markers in the continuous flow of time. For most countries, war anniversaries not only provide an opportunity to reflect on the past and remember and honor the war dead, but also serve as occasions to pull a nation together. In Japan, however, recent ten-year anniversaries of the end of World War II in the Asia Pacific have caused political divisions about history and post–World War II identity to resurface and sharpen.

PREVIOUS TEN-YEAR ANNIVERSARIES

In 1985, Prime Minister Nakasone Yasuhiro used the 40-year anniversary of the end of World War II to call for a general accounting of the postwar era [*sengo sōkessan*], which meant breaking out of the shackles of the postwar order. After the December 1983 electoral setback for the ruling Liberal Democratic Party (LDP), Nakasone sought to stir populist nationalism to revive the conservatives and promote national pride. Symbolic of this effort was Nakasone's official visit as prime minister to the Yasukuni Shrine on August 15, 1985. For him, Japanese leaders should not be shy about honoring the military war dead at the national shrine established for that purpose. Although Nakasone was successful in leading the LDP to a stunning victory in the July 1986 election, he chose to refrain from further visits to Yasukuni as prime minister after China protested and he failed to get the names of the Class-A war criminals removed. In Nakasone's mind, the strategic importance of stable relations with China trumped his symbolic politics.

Ten years later, the Japanese political landscape had changed considerably. In 1993, the LDP fell out of power for the first time since its formation in 1955. Desperate to regain the reins of government, the LDP formed a coalition with its long-time adversary, the Japan Socialist Party (JSP), and agreed to have the JSP leader Murayama Tomiichi serve as prime minister in 1994. Prime Minister Murayama sought to use the 50th anniversary in 1995 to advance the process of historical reconciliation with Japan's Asian neighbors by proposing a Diet "no war" resolution. Although Murayama wanted a clear acknowledgment and unequivocal apology for Japan's past aggression and wartime atrocities, the resolution provoked an intense parliamentary debate, with conservatives in both the government and opposition questioning whether Japan's past behavior was that different from those of other imperial states. In the end, the House of Representatives passed a resolution that appeared to relativize Japan's historical transgressions. Disappointed with the result, Murayama worked with "liberal" allies in the LDP and professional diplomats to issue on August 15 a prime minister's statement with the imprimatur of the cabinet that went beyond previous government statements of remorse.[1] The Murayama statement explicitly mentioned "colonial rule" and "aggression" and the "tremendous damage and suffering to the people of many countries, particularly those of Asian countries" that Japan had caused through "its mistaken national policy." Going beyond previous statements of "deep reflection" [*fukaku hansei*], Prime Minister Murayama stated his "heartfelt apology" [*kokoro kara no owabi*].[2] Thus the Murayama statement became the gold standard of Japanese official apology for Japan's historical transgressions.

During the 2005 anniversary, Prime Minister Koizumi Junichiro's repeated visits to the Yasukuni Shrine after assuming office in 2001 raised concerns that the rise of nationalist voices might undercut the legacy of the Murayama statement. Although Koizumi had used the Yasukuni issue opportunistically to defeat former prime minister Hashimoto Ryūtarō in the race for the LDP presidency in 2001, Koizumi was careful to distance himself from the nationalist right's view of history. After his Yasukuni visits, he emphasized that he did not go to the shrine to glorify the past war or to honor war criminals, but rather to show his respect to the war dead and to pray for peace. Soon after his first pilgrimage to Yasukuni as prime minister, Koizumi went in October 2001 to the Marco Polo (Lugou) Bridge (where an armed clash triggered the Second Sino-Japanese War) and the Memorial Hall of the War of Resistance Against Japanese Aggression located in the outskirts of Beijing and placed a wreath and expressed his heartfelt apology and condolence. During his remarks at the 50th anniversary of the Bandung Conference in April 2005, he repeated the phrases in the Murayama statement. And on the 60th anniversary of the end of World War II, Prime Minister Koizumi issued a statement that paraphrased the Murayama statement: "In the past,

Japan, through its colonial rule and aggression, caused tremendous damage and suffering to the people of many countries, particularly to those of Asian nations. Sincerely facing these facts of history, I once again express my feelings of deep remorse and heartfelt apology, and also express the feelings of mourning for all victims, both at home and abroad, in the war. I am determined not to allow the lessons of that horrible war to erode, and to contribute to the peace and prosperity of the world without ever again waging a war."[3]

The focal point of Japan's 70th anniversary of the end of World War II became Prime Minister Abe Shinzō's statement precisely because he expressed a desire to issue a statement that would supersede the 1995 Murayama statement and reorient Japan's foreign policy in a future-oriented direction by ending the need to repeat apologies. This chapter examines the domestic and international context of the August 14, 2015, Abe statement and analyzes the process leading up to the statement and the reaction to it. Although the statement avoided a diplomatic disaster by not negating the prime minister statements during the 50th and 60th anniversaries, the ambiguities of Abe's phraseology prevented the 70th anniversary from becoming an occasion to propel forward the process of historical reconciliation between Japan and its neighboring countries in East Asia. As central as the Abe statement was for the 70th anniversary, other developments also shaped the Japanese discourse about war memory. Emperor Akihito played an important role through his words and travels. Anniversaries regarding the atomic bombing and the Battle of Okinawa served as poignant settings for reflecting on how the past matters for the present and future. And the controversial issues of Yasukuni and the "comfort women" demonstrated the challenges of overcoming the sharp divisions within Japan about history.

CONTEXT OF THE ABE STATEMENT

After returning to the prime ministership in December 2012, Abe repeatedly declared his intention to issue a 70th anniversary statement that would be future oriented rather than one focused on the past. This message provoked much hand-wringing domestically and internationally because of fears that Abe might undercut the previous statements by Murayama and Koizumi given his views on history. In his 2006 book entitled *Toward A Beautiful Country*, Abe had criticized the Tokyo War Crimes Tribunal and argued that Japanese prime ministers should not hesitate to go to the Yasukuni Shrine.[4] Before becoming prime minister, Abe was one of the leaders of the movement within the conservative Liberal Democratic Party to rescind the 1993 Kōno statement of apology regarding comfort women. During parliamentary interpellations, Abe stubbornly refused to admit that Japan had launched a war of aggression. On August 15, 2013, Abe ended a practice begun in 1993 by then prime minister Hosokawa Morihiro of expressing condolences to "victims throughout Asia" as well as in Japan during the Budokan ceremony to remember the war dead. In December 2013, Abe followed through on his long-standing promise to visit the Yasukuni Shrine as prime minister despite the negative effect this would have on Japan's delicate relations with China and South Korea. Abe's close ties to a number of right-wing commentators and nationalist groups added to concerns that his 70th anniversary statement might tarnish Japan's international reputation.

Abe's views on history and the 70th anniversary were part of a larger political agenda. In various speeches, he echoed Nakasone in vowing to have Japan break out of the postwar regime. He openly talked about changing the Constitution. Although the requirement of a two-thirds majority in both houses of the National Diet remained a formidable obstacle to constitutional revision, he nevertheless pushed through a national referendum bill that established the procedure for a public vote in case the National Diet at some future point did pass a constitutional amendment proposal. In July 2014, the Abe cabinet decided to reinterpret the Constitution to enable Japan to exercise to a limited extent the right of collective self-defense. Abe followed up in 2015 by submitting an ambitious package of security-related bills that altered substantially the parameters of Japanese defense policy and U.S.-Japan security cooperation.[5]

Japanese critics of Abe's intention to draft a new statement about World War II charged that the prime minister was attempting to downplay Japan's militarist past in order to chip away at the country's postwar identity as a peace state. At the same time, supporters of Abe's efforts to strengthen the U.S.-Japan alliance and to pursue a more proactive security policy were anxious that his views on history could backfire diplomatically. There was a danger that a new war anniversary statement could further complicate relations with both China and South Korea, which were already suspicious of Abe's reinterpretation of the Constitution.

In September 2012, the Japanese central government under Prime Minister Noda Yoshihiko purchased three of the Senkaku Islands (called Diaoyu Islands by China) to prevent then Tokyo governor Ishihara Shintarō from buying the islands and provoking China by following through on his promise to place personnel and structures on the islands to protect Japan's sovereignty and control over this territory.[6] Rather than accepting Noda's explanation, Beijing responded by dispatching on a regular basis Chinese coast guard vessels into the Senkaku territorial waters as well as permitting large-scale anti-Japanese demonstrations throughout China.[7] After succeeding Noda as prime minister, Abe refrained from escalating the conflict by deploying personnel or erecting structures on the disputed islands, but he used the potential security threat to justify an upgrade of Japanese defense capabilities. Moreover his December 2012 pilgrimage to Yasukuni impeded diplomatic efforts to reverse the downward spiral in Japan-China relations. Eventually, both Beijing and Tokyo recognized the economic and military risks of prolonged bilateral tensions, and the two countries finally managed to forge a joint statement in November 2014 that would open the way to brief summit meetings between Abe and his counterpart Xi Jinping as well as the resumption of bilateral dialogues in various functional areas. Therefore, as the 70th anniversary year arrived, Japan's foreign policy community did not want Abe to issue a statement that could unravel the delicate diplomatic effort during 2014 to stabilize Japan-China relations.

Also problematic were Japan's relations with the Republic of Korea (ROK). Despite the fact that Japan and South Korea shared common security and economic interests and were both democracies and allies of the United States, ROK president Park Guen-Hye who was inaugurated in February 2013 refused to hold a bilateral summit with Abe. The primary obstacle was the so-called comfort women issue. In South Korea, Abe was known for his efforts to revoke the Kōno statement before becoming prime minister the first time around in 2006. He also played a key role in blaming the liberal Japanese newspaper *Asahi Shimbun* for provoking the comfort women controversy through its misleading reports about the forced recruitment of Korean women and girls into the Japanese military system of sexual servitude. Because much of the South Korean public saw Abe and his loyal political supporters as deniers of Japanese government responsibility for the comfort women tragedy, President Park could not afford to normalize relations with Japan under Abe without some progress on this issue. As in the case of Japan's relations with China, there were concerns within Japan's foreign policy circles that a misguided Abe statement about World War II would further aggravate the Japan-South Korea relationship.

The United States was another critical factor in establishing the international context of Japan's 70th anniversary. After Abe's December 2012 visit to Yasukuni, the U.S. embassy in Tokyo issued an unprecedented statement expressing its "disappointment" with this action. Believing that Abe embraced revisionist views of history, members of the U.S. policy community were anxious that he might dilute the positive effect of the 1995 Murayama statement. The Obama Administration was aghast that relations between two critical U.S. allies in East Asia were becoming increasingly acrimonious. Fearing that this trend could become irreversible with enduring strategic consequences, President Obama made a point of bringing Prime Minister Abe and President Park together in a brief photo-op meeting in March 2014 during the Hague nuclear security summit. Washington was also concerned that further aggravation of the Senkaku/Diaoyu Island dispute could entrap the United States in a military conflict with China over several uninhabited small islands about which Washington had staked a neutral position regarding the question of sovereignty. Although the Obama Administration welcomed Abe's efforts to strengthen the bilateral security relationship, it was deeply concerned that Abe might undermine regional stability by issuing a statement about World War II that whitewashed Japan's war responsibility.

Abe therefore confronted strong cross-pressures. On the one hand, in addition to staying true to his historical beliefs, he wanted to respond to the expectations of his supporters on the nationalist right who were increasingly irritated by Japan's so-called apology diplomacy and Chinese and Korean use of history to demean Japan. On the other hand, Abe did not want his statement to damage relations with the United States and other countries in the West as well as provoke Japan's Asian neighbors. Moreover, despite his firm grip over his own Liberal Democratic Party, Abe had to be responsive to his coalition partner, the Kōmei Party, which tended to hold a more repentant view of Japanese behavior during its militarist past.

LEAD-UP TO THE ABE STATEMENT

On January 1, 2015, Emperor Akihito made a surprising and moving statement that shaped the historical discourse within Japan during the 70th anniversary year: "I think it is most important for us to take this opportunity to study and learn from the history of this war, starting with the Manchurian Incident of 1931, as we consider the future direction of our country." Through these words, the emperor did two important things. First, by emphasizing the importance of studying and learning about the history of the war, he reminded the nation that a future-oriented outlook should not cause Japanese to forget the lessons of the past. Second, the emperor's specific reference to the Manchurian Incident of 1931 implied that he himself recognized Japan's war responsibility. Although in the postwar period the emperor lost his political authority, the continuing symbolic importance of the imperial institution gave the emperor's statement a moral authority that Abe could not ignore.

Various speeches that Abe gave prior to August 2015 provided a preview of his thinking. On July 8, 2014, Abe gave a well-received address to Australia's parliament that expressed his condolences and his gratitude for Australia's magnanimous spirit of tolerance and friendship toward Japan. While acknowledging the trauma, painful memories, and evils and horrors of history, Prime Minister Abe offered no explicit recognition of Japanese war responsibility and no apology. During his April 22, 2015, speech at the 60th anniversary of the Bandung Conference, Abe expressed remorse about the past; but unlike Prime Minister Koizumi in the April 2005 Bandung anniversary meeting, he did not mention Japan's colonial rule or aggression and he did not provide an apology. In his speech to the U.S. Congress on April 29,

2015, Abe invoked the word "repentance" for the first time as well as declared his "deep remorse." Echoing his speech to the Australian parliament, he also expressed his gratitude to Americans for "reconciliation." While stating how "history is harsh," Abe shied away from giving a clear and direct acknowledgment of Japanese responsibility.

To advise him on how to address the 70th anniversary, Prime Minister Abe convened a sixteen-member advisory panel on the History of the Twentieth Century and on Japan's Role and the World Order in the Twenty-First Century, with Nishimuro Taizō (former president of Toshiba Corporation and current president of Japan Post Holdings Company) as chairman and Kitaoka Shinichi (a prominent Japanese diplomatic and political historian and president of International University of Japan) as deputy chairman. The committee encompassed scholars, journalists, and influential voices in the foreign policy community, and Abe appointed many moderates and limited the representation of those from the nationalist right. This composition provided some political cover for Abe to refrain from stridently right-wing "revisionist" views of history in his anniversary statement, especially about the 1931–1945 period. But there was also a noticeable absence of a prominent specialist on Korean affairs.

The advisory panel met seven times from February to July 2015 and discussed the following topics: the proper view of Japanese and world history in the twentieth century and the lessons of history; the path taken by Japan after World War II; Japan's pursuit of reconciliation with the United States, Australia, European countries, China, the Republic of Korea and other Asian countries; Japan's vision for Asia and the world in the twenty-first century and the contribution that Japan should make; and the "specific measures" Japan should take on the 70th anniversary. In addition to some of the committee members, a few outside experts were also invited to present on the above topics to stimulate discussion.

The most controversial issue within the committee was the question of Japan's aggression.[8] The panel's report, which was released on August 6, contained the following statement: "[After] the Manchurian Incident, Japan expanded its aggression against the continent, deviated from the post-World War I shift toward self-determination, outlawry of war, democratization, and an emphasis on economic development, lost sight of global trends, and caused much harm to various countries, largely in Asia, through a reckless war."[9] A few members of the committee, however, disagreed with the characterization of Japan's behavior as "aggression." The three reasons for their dissent regarding the use of the term "aggression" were included in the following footnote in the report: "The reasons for this [dissent] were (1) the definition of 'aggression' has not been established under international law; (2) there is objection from a historical perspective to stating that the series of events from the Manchurian Incident onward constituted 'aggression'; and

(3) there is a sense of reluctance toward stating that only the actions of Japan constituted 'aggression' while other countries were taking similar action." This reluctance to apply the term "aggression" to Japanese actions during the 1930s converged with Prime Minister Abe's own hesitation to do so when questioned in the National Diet.

The advisory panel's recommendations addressed four broad areas: (1) deepening the understanding of history, (2) supporting the international order, (3) contributing to peace and development, and (4) opening up Japan. Regarding the first area about history, the committee report focused on the following concrete tasks. First, to address the inadequacy of Japanese education regarding modern and contemporary history, the panel proposed that this subject be part of the "compulsory curriculum" in high schools. Second, the group recommended expanding joint historical studies on "wars, colonial rule, and revolutions in the twentieth century" to many other countries beyond China and the Republic of Korea with which there have already been such joint studies. A third recommendation called for an upgrading of the Japan Center for Asian Historical Records so that the collection and public availability of materials will cover the postwar as well as the pre-World War II periods.[10] Finally, the committee argued that "the government must strengthen efforts to tackle such issues of the war dead as gathering their remains." Although the report offered a generally critical interpretation of Japanese foreign policy in the 1930s and rejected the view "that Japan fought to liberate Asia as a matter of national policy," the advisory panel shied away from making any explicit recommendation about what Prime Minister Abe should include in his 70th anniversary statement.

Concerned that Abe might issue a statement that would diminish the effect of the 1995 Murayama statement, a group of 74 Japanese scholars of history, international law, and international politics led by Mitani Taiichirō (professor emeritus at the University of Tokyo) and Ōnuma Yasuaki (distinguished professor at Meiji University) issued a joint statement on July 17, a few weeks before the release of the advisory panel report.[11] These scholars argued that Abe's statement in the Diet to the effect that "the definition of aggression has yet to be established" is "not necessarily correct from an academic perspective." They insisted that Japan's wars of aggression in the 1931–1945 period violated international law and constituted a "grave and inexcusable mistake." Their statement pointed out that Japanese postwar rehabilitation and prosperity were "based on deep self-reflection with regard to Japan's earlier behavior," including "the recognition that colonizing Taiwan and Korea and the wars of 1931–1945 had been grievous mistakes, as well as the deep remorse that more than three million Japanese and several times as many Chinese and other foreign citizens were killed." In commenting on Abe's forthcoming 70th anniversary statement, the scholars noted that "wording matters." If the Abe statement did not incorporate key phrases such as "feelings of deep remorse" and "heartfelt apology" regarding "colonial rule" and "aggression" that were first included in the Murayama statement and later repeated in the Koizumi statement of 2005, they warned that this shortcoming would provoke a harsh judgment from the international community.

CONTENT OF AND REACTION TO THE ABE STATEMENT

After much anticipation and debate, Prime Minister Abe issued his 70th anniversary statement at a press conference on August 14, one day before the August 15 anniversary date.[12] The statement received the imprimatur of a Cabinet decision and therefore represented a compromise between two main parties in the ruling coalition: the Liberal Demoratic Party and the Kōmei Party. While seeking to find common ground between the contending views of history in Japan, Abe engaged in a delicate balancing act that papered over differences rather than resolving this historical debate.

Echoing the January 1 comments of the emperor and the view expressed in his advisory panel, the prime minister declared: "With the Manchurian Incident, followed by the withdrawal from the League of Nations, Japan gradually transformed itself into a challenger to the new international order that the international community sought to establish after tremendous sacrifices. Japan took the wrong course and advanced along the road to war." Abe incorporated the emotional language that he had used in his April speech to the U.S. Congress by saying how he finds himself "speechless" and how his "heart is rent with utmost grief" when recalling the "immeasurable damage and suffering" that Japan inflicted on "innocent people." He also appeared to consider the joint statement of the 74 Japanese scholars which emphasized the importance of wording when he included the so-called keywords "aggression," "colonial rule," "deep remorse," and "heartfelt apology" that were the hallmarks of the 1995 Murayama statement:

> Incident, aggression, war –we shall never again resort to any form of the threat or use of force as a means of settling international disputes. We shall abandon colonial rule forever and respect the right of self-determination of all peoples throughout the world. . . . Japan has repeatedly expressed the feelings of deep remorse and heartfelt apology for its actions during the war.

But in contrast to the Murayama statement, the Abe statement did not explicitly declare that Japan had committed "aggression" and that "colonial rule" was a mistaken policy. And although he mentions that Japan had already expressed "feelings of deep remorse and heartfelt apology," Abe left ambiguous his own personal attitude regarding those apologies.

The Abe statement, however, went beyond the Murayama statement by referring to specific countries by name (Indonesia, the Philippines, Taiwan, the Republic of Korea and China) when referring to the "suffering of the people in Asia." Similarly to his speeches in Canberra and Washington, D.C., Abe raised the theme of reconciliation by expressing his thanks for the "tolerance" and the "effort of reconciliation" among the nations and peoples who had suffered. Although he did not refer directly to the "comfort women" issue, his statement did allude to the "women behind the battlefields whose honor and dignity were severely injured during wars in the twentieth century." He declared that "Japan wishes to be a country always at the side of such women's injured hearts. Japan will lead the world in making the twenty-first century an era in which women's human rights are not infringed upon."

Finally, the statement reflected Abe's desire to bring to an end the need for Japan to keep apologizing: "We must not let our children, grandchildren, and even further generations to come, who have nothing to do with that war, be predestined to apologize." At the same time, Abe noted that "we, Japanese, across generations, must squarely face the history of the past" and that Japanese "have the responsibility to inherit the past, in all humbleness, and pass it on to the future." But he stopped short of explicitly mentioning the importance of educating future generations about the past.

Japanese commentary regarding the Abe statement was mixed. Former prime minister Murayama criticized the statement as a retreat from his 1995 statement. He declared that Abe "trivialized" and "left ambiguous" the use of the term apology and "diluted the weight of such words as colonial rule and aggression."[13] Professor Mitani, one of the leaders behind the 74 scholars joint statement, noted that while referring to "colonial rule," the Abe statement failed to express any self-criticism about Japan's colonial rule over Taiwan and Korea. Moreover, according to Mitani, Abe did not clearly mention which country committed aggression, thereby avoiding the issue of war responsibility.[14] While generally supporting the Abe statement, Professor Kitaoka who served as deputy chairman of Abe's advisory panel expressed disappointment that Abe did not personally acknowledge Japan's aggression.[15] On the other hand, commentators on the nationalist right, such as Takubo Tadae, leader of the Nihon Kaigi (Japan Conference), praised Abe for not stating that Japan had committed aggression, thereby countering the so-called Tokyo war crimes trial view of history. However, Professor Tanaka Akihiko, an influential international politics scholar at the University of Tokyo and former president of the Japan International Cooperation Agency, summed up the views of centrists. In an op-ed in the conservative-leaning *Yomiuri Shimbun*, Tanaka gave this assessment: "Critics say Abe's August 14 statement satisfied nobody perfectly, but this criticism was off the mark because what was important was that the statement leaves no one extremely dissatisfied."[16]

Editorials of the major Japanese newspapers also reflected a diversity of opinion.[17] Liberal papers like *Asahi, Mainichi,* and *Tokyo Shimbun* faulted Abe for equivocating on the issue of Japan's aggression and for offering no apology for colonial rule. The conservative newspaper *Yomiuri* felt that Abe did recognize aggression by including this term in the statement and praised Abe for stating that future generations should not have to keep apologizing for what Japan did in the past. The more nationalistic *Sankei Shimbun* echoed this point about ending apologies and criticized the 1995 Murayama statement for going against Japan's national interest by making the country vulnerable to foreign demands for compensation.

Public opinion surveys conducted by Japanese media organizations showed that while the public was generally supportive of the Abe statement, a significant portion of the people had negative views, suggesting that the public remains divided regarding the history issue. Four months before Abe issued his statement, according to an opinion survey conducted by the *Asahi Shimbun,* 74 percent felt that the statements issued on the 50th and 60th anniversaries were "appropriate," while only 13 percent believed that those of 1995 and 2005 were "inappropriate."[18] A week after Abe's August 14 statement, the *Asahi* conducted another survey to gauge public views. The newspaper found that 40 percent regarded the statement favorably while 31 percent did not.[19] Opinion polls conducted by other Japanese media organizations yielded similar results. Kyodo News found 44.2 percent to have positive views of the Abe statement, while 37 percent were negative. The surveys conducted by more conservative newspapers showed a higher positive public reaction to the statement. For example, 48 percent of the respondents to the *Yomiuri* survey viewed the Abe statement favorably; and 57.8 percent of those polled by the nationalistic *Sankei Shimbun* were positive about the statement.

Opinion surveys conducted by Japanese newspapers also asked about Japanese apologies. In a *Mainichi Shimbun* survey conducted a week before Abe's August 14 statement, 13 percent stated that there was no need for Japan to apologize to neighboring countries regarding the "previous war" and 44 percent believed that Japan had already apologized sufficiently, while 31 percent felt that Japan had not apologized sufficiently.[20] The *Asahi Shimbun* also asked about specific points in the statement. For example, the survey inquired about the following sentence: "We must not let our children, grandchildren, and even further generations to come, who have nothing to do with that war, be predestined to apologize." Sixty-three percent agreed with Abe's view that future generations should not have to apologize, while 21 percent disagreed.[21]

REMEMBERING THE WAR DEAD
AND COMPENSATING VICTIMS

Although much of the national and international attention focused on Prime Minister Abe's statement, there were other notable events in the 70th anniversary year which revealed the persistent divisions within Japanese society. In June 2015, Prime Minister Abe went to Okinawa to attend a ceremony to remember the Battle of Okinawa. Each year, the Japanese prime minister makes this pilgrimage to remember those who died in the largest battle on Japanese territory during the Pacific War. Although Abe did recognize the sacrifices of Okinawans during the war and its aftermath, some attendees of the ceremony heckled the prime minister by shouting "What are you doing here?" and "Go home," reflecting the local anger about the large number of U.S. military personnel and bases that remain on this island prefecture.[22]

On August 6, like other prime ministers before, Abe went to Hiroshima to participate in the annual ceremony to remember the atomic bombing. When Abe went in 2013 and 2014, he reiterated his commitment to the three non-nuclear principles just as his predecessors had done.[23] But during the 2015 Hiroshima ceremony, Abe broke a tradition since 1994 and refrained from mentioning these principles, which sparked immediate criticism from atomic bomb survivors and Japan's anti-nuclear movement. Perhaps in response to this criticism, however, Abe did give explicit support to the three non-nuclear principles when he attended the memorial ceremony at Nagasaki on August 9.

While Abe was stirring controversy because of his historical views, the emperor transcended political divisions by continuing his practice of visiting the sites of major battles. In 2005, the emperor had visited Saipan. Ten years later on April 2015, he went to Peleliu Island of Palau, the scene of a fierce three-month battle in 1944 that killed about 100,000 Japanese and 1,700 American soldiers.[24] Then in January 2016, the emperor followed up with a historic visit to the Philippines. Prior to his departure to Manila, he made the following statement: "Many Filipinos, Americans and Japanese lost their lives in the Philippines during the war. Especially in the battle in Manila, a tremendously large number of innocent Filipino civilians were victims. Upon making this visit, we need to bear this in mind at all times."[25]

Despite Abe's effort to end the so-called "apology diplomacy" and the nationalist right's opposition to providing compensation to wartime victims, during the 70th anniversary year, Japan did issue apologies and offer compensation. In July 2015, Mitsubishi Materials Corporation formally apologized for using U.S. prisoners of war as slave laborers.[26] Former Japanese diplomat Okamoto Yukio, who served on Abe's advisory panel on history and was an external director of Mitsubishi, joined the press conference at which this apology was announced. In a subsequent interview, Okamoto stated that he "entered with a heavy heart, seeking forgiveness" and that "we also have to apologize for not apologizing earlier." According to Okamoto, the Japanese Foreign Ministry was moving away from its previous legalistic stance that all compensation issues had been settled by the San Francisco Peace Treaty.[27] Then in August, Mitsubishi Materials revealed that it would issue an apology and pay compensation for wartime forced labor in China. Each of the Chinese plaintiffs of the forced workers and their families would receive 2 million yen in compensation.[28]

Finally, as the 70th anniversary year was coming to a close, Japan and South Korea reached an agreement to overcome the diplomatic impasse regarding the comfort women issue on December 28. Although the Japanese government did not admit to legal responsibility or offer legal reparations, the Abe government went a bit further than the Asian Women's Fund (AWF) initiative, which was inaugurated by Japan in 1995. Under the AWF program, Japanese prime ministers sent letters to former comfort women that extended their "most sincere apologies and remorse" and acknowledged Japan's "moral responsibilities" as well as "an involvement of the Japanese military authorities." According to the December agreement, however, Prime Minister Abe not only reiterated the language of the previous apology and acknowledgment of Japanese military involvement, but also declared "the Government of Japan is painfully aware of responsibilities from this perspective." While the Japanese statement of December 28 refrained from referring to *legal* responsibility, it was explicit about the *government's* awareness of responsibilities. By not using the modifier "moral," which was included in the prime minister apology letters under the AWF, Abe's apology implied that the government's responsibilities were not just moral in nature.

In the AWF program, state funds had been allocated to provide medical and welfare support (3 million yen per person, or about $25,000) to Korean comfort women survivors, and private contributions were to be used for "atonement" money (2 million yen per person, or about $16,667). Arguing that this amounted to charity rather than legal reparations, many Korean comfort women survivors with the encouragement of the Korean Council refused this Japanese contribution.[29] This time around, the Japanese government agreed to make "a one-time contribution" of one billion yen from the public budget to a foundation established by the South Korean government to provide support to the comfort women and engage in Japan-ROK cooperative projects "for recovering the honor and dignity and healing the psychological wounds of all former comfort women." During the negotiations with South Korea, the Abe government sought an agreement that would be final, that would commit South Korea to remove the statue of a girl depicting a comfort woman which is located across the street from the Japanese embassy in Seoul, and that would stop criticisms of Japan in the United Nations and other international organizations regarding the comfort women issue.

The political reception in Japan to the "comfort women" agreement was generally positive. Even liberal and leftist leaders who had been critical of Abe expressed their support of the agreement. Most of the grumbling came from the conservative camp. Several prominent Liberal Democratic Party politicians insisted that the comfort woman statue near the Japanese embassy in Seoul must be removed expeditiously, and a few complained that the agreement did not mention the comfort women statues and memorials in the United States or that Abe did not need to apologize and compromise since South Korea was entirely to blame for the deterioration in bilateral relations. Despite this discontent, however, Abe managed and deflected intra-LDP opposition given his own nationalist credentials. Although the South Korean government did not make progress in removing the comfort woman statue near the Japanese embassy, the Japanese government went ahead and deposited the promised one billion yen (about $8.7 million) to the Reconciliation and Healing Foundation that was established in South Korea to implement the December 2015 agreement.[30]

THE LONG ANNIVERSARY AND FUTURE PROSPECTS

The 70th anniversary of the end of the Pacific War evolved into a "long anniversary" when U.S. president Barack Obama made his historic visit to Hiroshima in May 2016. Previous American presidents had refrained from going to the site of the first atomic bombing because of opposition from U.S. veterans who had felt that the bombing had been necessary to save lives and because of concerns that a presidential visit might be interpreted as an apology. Prior to Obama's Hiroshima visit, however, an interview survey of 115 survivors of the Hiroshima and Nagasaki atomic bombings showed that about 80 percent did not seek an apology from the U.S. president.[31] President Obama, who had received the Nobel Peace Prize for his vision of a world free of nuclear weapons, managed to rise above the apology question by calling for "the start of our own moral awakening." Prime Minister Abe responded by noting that he and the president had offered their "deepest condolences for all those who lost their lives during World War II and also by the atomic bombings." He praised Obama by noting that his decision and courage to visit Hiroshima had opened "a new chapter to the reconciliation of Japan and the United States."[32]

Obama's visit to Hiroshima cleared the path for Abe to make his journey to the USS *Arizona* Memorial at Pearl Harbor on December 27, 2016. Seventy-five years after the Japanese attack initiated the Pacific War, Prime Minister Abe expressed his "sincere and everlasting condolences," but refrained from offering an apology. Instead he echoed the themes of his April 2015 address to the U.S. Congress. He thanked the United States and the world for "the tolerance extended to Japan" and repeatedly mentioned "the power of reconciliation."[33]

Although Prime Minister Abe may have succeeded in ending an era of Japanese apologies, he did not bring an end to debates about history within Japan. Abe had engaged in a shrewd balancing act and crafted a statement about which no one was extremely dissatisfied, as Tanaka Akihiko observed. But by blurring the divisions about history, the Abe statement did not resolve the contentious debates, which are as much about national identity as about historical interpretation. These divisions are likely to surface again as Japanese address questions about history education in the schools, the legitimacy of the Yasukuni Shrine as a memorial to honor the war dead, the demands for acknowledgment and compensation from other wartime victims, and of course constitutional revision. In the final month of 2015, Inada Tomomi, a close political ally of Prime Minister Abe who was later appointed in summer 2016 to become defense minister, called for the establishment of a panel to re-examine the Tokyo war crimes trial as well as the postwar occupation of Japan. In her view, Japan must correct the historical distortions of the Tokyo trial if the nation is to restore its "Japaneseness" and tackle the task of constitutional revision.[34]

Just before Prime Minister Abe issued his 70th anniversary statement, he announced from his home constituency of Yamaguchi Prefecture that he would like to see a politician from Yamaguchi be the prime minister when Japan celebrates the 150th anniversary of the Meiji Restoration in 2018.[35] Journalists speculated that Abe was suggesting his desire to remain as prime minister for at least another three years. This possibility indeed became more likely after the LDP's impressive victory in the October 2017 House of Representatives election. Chōshu, one of the key domains that spearheaded the Meiji Restoration and governed the Meiji State, was located in present-day Yamaguchi. This region produced some of the most celebrated political leaders of modern Japan. By alluding to the upcoming 150th anniversary of the Meiji Restoration, Abe perhaps wants to cast the eyes of Japan and the world on what he may view as Japan's glorious past, in contrast to the dark period of the early Shōwa era. The question of national identity is again likely to be intertwined with Japanese anniversary politics.

NOTES

1. Murayama Tomiichi and Sataka Makoto, *"Murayama Danwa" to ha nani ka* [What Is the "Murayama Statement"?] (Tokyo: Kadokawa Shoten, 2009), 47–52.

2. Statement by Prime Minister Murayama Tomiichi "On the occasion of the 50th anniversary of the war's end" (August 15, 1995), http://www.mofa.go.jp/announce/press/pm/murayama/9508.html.

3. Statement by Prime Minister Koizumi Junichirō, August 15, 2005, http://www.mofa.go.jp/announce/announce/2005/8/0815.html.

4. Abe Shinzō, *Utsukushii kuni e* [Toward a beautiful country] (Tokyo: Bungei Shunju, 2006), 66–74.

5. Jeffrey W. Hornung and Mike M. Mochizuki, "Japan: Still An Exceptional U.S. Ally," *Washington Quarterly* 39, no. 1 (Spring 2016), 95–116.

6. Sunohara Tsuyoshi, *Antō: Senkaku Kokuyūka* [Secret Feud: Nationalization of the Senkakus] (Tokyo: Shinchosha, 2013): 51–242.

7. James Reilly, "A Wave to Worry About? Public opinion, foreign policy and China's anti-Japan protests," *Journal of Contemporary China* 23, Issue 86 (2014): 197–215.

8. "Panel on war anniversary statement have heated debate on word 'aggression,'" *Japan Times*, March 24, 2015.

9. The English translation of this report is available at the following link: http://www.kantei.go.jp/jp/singi/21c_koso/pdf/report_en.pdf. The substantive presentations and deliberations in the various panel sessions can be found in the following: 21 Seiki Kōsō Konwa Kai (ed.), *Sengo 70–nen danwa no ronten* [Issues about the Postwar 70th Year Statement] (Tokyo: Nihon Keizai Shimbun Shuppansha, 2015).

10. In 1994, then prime minister Murayama in preparation for the following year's 50th anniversary of the end of World War II proposed the creation of an Asian Historical Document Center to support historical research by collecting and cataloging historical documents. Following this initiative, a 1999 cabinet decision formally established the Japan Center for Asian Historical Records, https://www.jacar.go.jp/english/index.html.

11. The English translation of this statement by the 74 Japanese scholars can be accessed at the following link: https://justiceglobale.files.wordpress.com/2015/03/english_joint-statement-by-74–japanese-scholars-20150801.pdf.

12. The full text of Prime Minister Abe's August 14 statement can be accessed at the following link: http://japan.kantei.go.jp/97_abe/statement/201508/0814statement.html.

13. "Ex-PM Murayama slams Abe's war anniversary statement," *Mainichi Daily News*, August 15, 2015.

14. "Sengo 70–nen no Abe danwa–Mitani Taiichirō Tōdai Meiyō Kyōju ni kiku" [Abe Statement of the Postwar 70th Year: Interview with Mitani Taiichirō, Tokyo University professor emeritus], *Asahi Shimbun*, August 15, 2015.

15. "Abe danwa ni Kitaoka Shinichi 'Shinryaku, ichi-ninshō de itte hoshikatta," [In the Abe Statement, Kitaoka Shinichi wished that "aggression had been said in a first-person sentence"], *Asahi Shimbun*, August 31, 2015.

16. Tanaka Akihiko, "Abe Well-Suited to Uplift Japan's Asia Diplomacy," *Daily Yomiuri*, October 26, 2015.

17. "Abe Danwa: Kaku shi no shasetsu wareru" [Abe Statement: Newspaper Editorial Divided], *Asahi Shimbun*, August 18, 2015, p. 3.

18. "Survey: 74% view past apologies to Asian neighbors as 'appropriate,'" *Asahi Shimbun Asia Japan Watch*, April 14, 2015.

19. "Asahi poll: Abe's war anniversary statement resonated more favorably than not," *Asahi Shimbun Japan Watch*, August 25, 2015.

20. "Mainichi Shimbun Seron Chōsa: Heiwa Kōken '9 jō' 5 wari" [Mainichi Shimbun Public Opinion Survey: Contribution to Peace "Article 9" 50 percent], *Mainichi Shimbun*, August 14, 2015, p. 9.

21. "Asahi poll: Abe's war anniversary statement resonated more favorably than not," *Asahi Shimbun Japan Watch*, August 25, 2015.

22. "Japan Marks 70th Anniversary of WWII Battle of Okinawa," *New York Times*, June 23, 2015.

23. Reiji Yoshida, "Exclusion of nonnuclear principles from Abe's Hiroshima speech causes stir," *Japan Times*, August 6, 2015.

24. "Japan's Emperor Prays at WWII Battleground on Pacific Island," *New York Times*, April 8, 2015.

25. "Imperial Couple arrive in Philippines," *Japan Times*, January 26, 2016.

26. "Mitsubishi Materials apologizes for using U.S. POWs as slave labor," *Asahi Shimbun Asia & Japan Watch*, July 20, 2015.

27. "Yukio Okamoto: 'POWs, Chinese laborers subjected to inhuman conditions,'" *Dispatch Japan*, August 9, 2015, http://www.dispatchjapan.com/blog/2015/08/yukio-okamoto-pows-chinese-laborers-subjected-to-inhuman-conditions.html.

28. "Insight: Mitsubishi Materials moving to settle wartime forced labor issue with China," *Asahi Shimbun Asia & Japan Watch*, August 4, 2015.

29. C. Sarah Soh, "Japan's National/Asian Women's Fund for 'Comfort Women,'" *Pacific Affairs* 76, no. 2 (Summer 2003): 209–233. The Korean Council is an umbrella organization of activist groups working on the comfort women issue in South Korea; and its full name is the Korean Council for Women Drafted for Military Sexual Slavery by Japan.

30. "Japan completes transfer of ¥1 billion to South Korean 'comfort women' fund," *Japan Times*, September 1, 2016.

31. "80% of hibakusha in poll not seeking Obama A-bomb apology during Hiroshima visit," *Japan Times*, May 23, 2016.

32. "Remarks by President Obama and Prime Minister Abe of Japan at Hiroshima Peace Memorial," May 27, 2016, https://obamawhitehouse.archives.gov/the-press-office/2016/05/27/remarks-president-obama-and-prime-minister-abe-japan-hiroshima-peace.

33. "The Power of Reconciliation: Address of Prime Minister Shinzō Abe," December 27, 2016, Pearl Harbor, http://japan.kantei.go.jp/97_abe/statement/201612/1220678_11021.html.

34. "LDP takes aim at modern history," *Japan Times*, December 29, 2015.

35. "Abe wants Yamaguchi politician to be PM in 2018, 150th anniversary of Meiji Restoration," *Mainichi Daily News*, August 13, 2015.

Chapter Four

South Korea

Commemorations, Revision, and Reckoning

Christine Kim

The end of World War II is noted in South Korea with a national holiday known as "Kwangbokchŏl."[1] Although commonly translated as National Liberation Day, the noun marking the occasion is a metaphor whose literal meaning refers to "light" (*kwang*) and "recovery" or "restoration" (*pok*), the implied darkness alluding not just to the war, but to the 35 years of Japanese occupation. The term thus carries the connotation of reclaiming sovereignty, exercising self-determination, and seeking new beginnings.

Historically, the notion of *kwangbok* was closely tied to nationalist projects of the early twentieth century when Korea was besieged by Japanese imperialist design, from secret societies formed in the countryside (Taehan kwangboktan, est. 1913) to the Korean Liberation Army (Han'guk kwangbokkun, 1940) that served as the armed force of the Provisional Government in Chongqing, the Chinese wartime capital. Yet although frequently conflated with the more prosaic terms "liberation" (*haebang*) and "independence" (*tongnip*), the term's metaphor of light allows it to transcend the specific context of colonialism. South Korean official commemorations have often utilized the anniversary to articulate a vision of Korea's autonomous and brilliant future, seeking, as it were, its place in the sun. It is in this spirit that the nationalist leader Kim Ku (1876–1949) proclaimed in 1946, on the first anniversary of Japan's surrender: "Today our nation sets foot on the world stage."[2]

In many ways, this official predilection for facing the future was born of political exigencies. For all the talk of new beginnings, 1945 was hardly a "Year Zero"—a clean slate onto which could be inscribed the narrative of a new order. The archival photographs of jubilant crowds throughout the pe-

55

ninsula cheering the news of Japan's defeat notwithstanding, the euphoria of the war's end was fleeting, and did not result in a complete overhaul of the established colonial system. The American occupation of the southern half that immediately followed, whereby political authority was transferred from the Japanese administration to the U.S. armed forces for three years, retained many of the colonial institutions and personnel of social control, including, for a while, both Japanese officials and colonial collaborators, even members of the detested police force. In this manner, American authorities limited Korean agency not just in terms of shaping its postwar destiny, but also the ability to come to terms with its complicated past colonial history.

As Ian Buruma has observed, the heroic narrative that renders the end of World War II in 1945 a sort of foundation myth for much of the world requires careful editing, entailing both an exaggerated focus upon, and deliberate elision of, aspects of the past.[3] The process of selective remembering is readily apparent in Korea, where the division of the peninsula, and subsequently the Korean War, preordained what would emerge as South Korea's (conservative) post-World War II narrative: the story of a fledgling new nation transformed over time into a formidable middle power, achieving democracy and prosperity through its alliance with America. The rags-to-riches story serves to reinforce the Cold War fairy tale: the powers of capitalism, democracy, and globalization culminating in the happy ending of South Korea's triumph over the Communist North. In doing so, it papers over the multiple grey zones of history during the colonial period (the extensive levels of collaboration; the emergence of communism); as well as the Cold War contexts of the post-liberation occupation (the de facto civil war conditions between U.S.-backed conservatives and left-leaning partisans) and since the Korean War (military dictatorships; the rise of anti-American sentiment).

With so much history redacted from the tableau of national myth, South Korean leadership has frequently used National Liberation Day as a platform to promote unity and nation-building for the sake of establishing legitimacy. Two years after Kim Ku spoke of Korea's global aspirations, his political rival Syngman Rhee (1875–1965, in office 1948–1960) stood at the very same podium and delivered his inaugural address as the republic's first president. A lifelong freedom fighter who had spent the previous four decades promoting independence from abroad, Rhee had secured his leadership by forming an alliance of convenience with the old colonial elite. In an effort to bring an end to the American military occupation (1945–1948), Rhee formalized the peninsula's division through a separate election held solely in the south. Somewhat surprisingly, given Rhee's well-established antagonism toward Japan, his inauguration address kept references to the former empire to a minimum. Instead, in a speech brimming with Western political ideals and configured to appeal to the departing American authorities, Rhee identified democracy, civil rights, liberalism, national unity, and world peace as the "strong foundations" upon which Koreans would build a "new nation" (sae-nara kŏnsŏl).[4]

Both Rhee's articulation of future goals, as well as his unwillingness to engage with the past, were harbingers of an official approach that persisted into the 1990s. In a broad survey of presidential addresses delivered on National Independence Day over five decades, Kim Hyeon-Seon observes a recurring theme of nation-building—couched variously as "national reconstruction" (Park Chung-hee, 1962), "new Korea" (Kim Young Sam, 1993), or "second nation building" (Kim Dae Jung, 1998). These rhetorical flourishes, with their focus on revitalization and the future, allowed leaders to keep discussions of early twentieth-century history to a minimum, whether it involved Japanese colonial rule, Koreans' participation in that imperial project, or their own role in sustaining the peninsula's division. Not only did the imposed amnesia limit proper postcolonial reckoning; it also delayed the emergence of apology politics for successive administrations.[5]

The observance of the fiftieth anniversary of World War II's end, just at the moment of what Carol Gluck has called "global memory culture" was gathering momentum in Asia, represents a major disruption by drawing explicit attention to Japan. In 1991, Korean "comfort woman" Kim Hak-sun's public revelations of her experiences and demands to the Japanese government for accountability—the press event was scheduled for the eve of National Independence Day—initiated a wave of nationalistic outrage that continues to this day. In 1995, continuing frustrations over the shape and tenor of Japanese actions culminated in an act of monumental destruction. In a striking departure from the commemorations of August 15 of yore, which had largely eschewed explicit criticism of Japan, the government of Kim Young-sam (1993–1998) marked the occasion with the demolition of the former colonial administration building. As if to exorcise demons of the colonial past, the wrecking was carried out before crowds in a festival-like setting complete with beating drums, flags, and firecrackers. In a new iteration of nation-building, Kim described the colonial past as "a vestige of history that remains in our consciousness" that necessitated erasure.[6] The edifice, which had since 1945 been used as a government administrative building—in front of which Kim Ku and Syngman Rhee had made their historic addresses—and then as the national museum, was nonetheless viewed as a symbol of "the material negation of Korea's autonomy." Stripped of its post-colonial historical contexts, the building was anachronistically recast as an obstacle to national autonomy. To emphasize the connection to Korea's dynastic past, the resulting open space from the building's removal was allocated to the reconstruction of the old Chosŏn palace, thereby affirming the greatness of Korea's past.[7]

The Kim government may have expected the destruction of a controversial historical monument to win favor with the public. But the newly democ-

ratized society proved to be unwieldy when it came to grappling with issues
of historical memory. In coordinated acts of protest, student activists demonstrated that they understood the true meaning of *kwangbok* to be tied to
national reunification. This notion had gained traction during the 1980s,
embraced by students and the *minjung* movement, at times exhibiting an anti-
American bent.[8] In 1995, an emboldened younger generation, successors to
the so-called "386 generation" that had been instrumental in realizing South
Korea's political liberalization, questioned the enduring Cold War political
system that had sustained the peninsula's division for five decades. Their
convictions led to violent physical confrontations with the state, just as Kim
was addressing the crowds in front of the Governor-General's building; protests erupted in downtown Seoul and along the road to the Demilitarized
Zone, as students clashed with hundreds of riot police blocking their way to
the border—and, in their minds, prevented Koreans from reclaiming their
true sovereignty.

YEAR 70: REVISING HISTORY IN 2015

Kwangbokchŏl in 2015 appeared, in many ways, a throwback to an earlier
time. Once again a conservative administration dictated government policies
focused on economic growth and a hardline approach to North Korea; the
American alliance remained solid; and historical memory issues that now
included, in addition to the "comfort women," textbook revisionism, occasional visits by high-ranking officials to the Yasukuni Shrine and a maritime
border dispute, had stirred up anti-Japanese sentiment to its highest levels.
Despite these continuities, there were significant differences in Korea's domestic and international politics that shaped the event's observances.

The 70th anniversary came at a time when South Korea was particularly
demoralized over recent political and social crises. Foremost among them
was the Sewol Ferry Disaster of 2014, which had claimed nearly 300 lives,
most of them high school students. In the spring, an outbreak of the Middle
East Respiratory Syndrome (MERS) virus raised anxiety levels and strained
the economy. The government's handling of these crises—the obfuscation of
facts, exposure of corruption, and callous treatment of the afflicted— undermined its authority and legitimacy. A pervasive sense of malaise exacerbated
divisions in the nation's culture, economy and social fabric that had come to
the fore during the 2012 presidential election, polarizing society along ideological and generational lines. An incident involving North Korean land
mines ten days before the historic date only added to the tensions.

Under the circumstances, the Park administration might have opted to
make use of Japan's intransigence to redirect the public's attention away
from its missteps. That it did not speaks to both the enormous diplomatic

pressure applied by the United States upon its two main Pacific allies to resolve their differences. During a visit to Seoul in April 2014, even President Obama had weighed in on the matter, exhorting both sides to push forward to make progress through coordinated efforts.[9] The restraint shown by Seoul was all the more remarkable in the context of Japan's cat-and-mouse responses to Korean demands that it offer a satisfactory political apology.

From the Korean perspective, there had been several opportunities to do so throughout the year. During a highly anticipated address to the joint session of the U.S. Congress in April 2015, Prime Minister Abe Shinzō failed to allude to Japan's prewar expansionism or acknowledge colonial rule of Korea in any meaningful way. Yet even then, much of Korean society appeared to expect that mounting external pressures in the form of North Korea's provocations, China's maritime expansionism, and above all American political influence would yield some form a bilateral breakthrough. In the run-up to August 15, a handful of Japanese overtures intimated that some gesture of reconciliation might be forthcoming. In July, a former senior diplomat and advisor to Prime Minister Abe, Okamoto Yukio, referred to Japan's annexation of Korea as "the greatest sin" and expressed regret over the forced assimilation policies enacted during wartime. Then, just days before August 15, former prime minister Hatoyama Yukio (in office 2009–2010) traveled to Seoul to visit the Sŏdaemun Prison History Hall, and mirroring West German chancellor Willy Brandt's 1970 visit to the Warsaw Ghetto Uprising memorial, fell to his knees and apologized to those who had experienced harsh treatment under Japanese colonial rule. Yet these preliminary acts of contrition soon became a source of disappointment for those who had hoped that Abe's anniversary address would offer a recantation or at least moderation of the previous Japanese stance. South Korean media outlets across the political spectrum were uniformly critical, variously lambasting the speech as "insincere" and "disingenuous" (*Han'guk ilbo*), "regretful" and "shirking responsibility" (*Minjung ŭi sori*), and "insulting" (*Hankyŏre*).

In her own address on the following day, South Korean president Park Geun-hye chose not to belabor the issue. While acknowledging that the Japanese statement "did not quite live up to our expectations," much of her address in fact downplayed the momentous significance of the 70th anniversary and the anticipated reckoning, and simply called upon the Japanese government to "uphold the view of history articulated by previous administrations" and refrain from revisionism. The request to "resolve the 'comfort women' issue," too, was submitted gingerly, couched in terms of improving regional ties. Redirecting the focus to the realm of economics, Park, echoing the relentless pursuit of economic development undertaken by her father Park Chung-hee during the 1960s and 1970s, instead linked colonial struggles to national traits of perseverance and ingenuity that would lay the groundwork for yet another cycle of industrial innovation.

ECONOMIC DEVELOPMENT PLANNING

Park's economic pitch was by then already a familiar refrain. Months earlier, the president delivered an address to commemorate the anniversary of the March 1 Movement, a milestone event in the nation's history that inspired millions of Koreans in 1919 to protest Japanese colonial rule. Along with National Liberation Day, March 1 is a national holiday that is most inextricably linked to colonial resistance; it is celebrated equally for its high-minded expressions of peaceful demonstration and for promoting national unity. Park paid homage to the occasion by connecting "the spirit of the Independence Movement" to "[laying] the groundwork for our history of miracles—the accomplishment of democracy and economic prosperity . . . in just half a century."[10] The speech then made the jump from abstraction to concrete policy, inserting a plug for the government's recently announced Three-year Plan for Economic Innovation to establish "an ecosystem for a creative economy." Park even invited Japan to join as a critical partner in generating regional prosperity. Citing the bilateral trade volume, people-to-people exchanges, and the two countries' shared values of liberal democracy and a market economy, she called on Japan to "open a new era of cooperation in the twenty-first century." The sole reference to the two countries' difficult past appeared almost in passing, when she made reference to the Japanese government's redress of the "human rights violations against comfort women victims" as the precondition for engagement.

Beyond the presidential address, the Park administration's preoccupation with stimulating the economy was fully evident in a number of political gestures. The government declared August 14 a one-time public holiday, the resulting long weekend to serve as an antidote to the low morale and loss of economic profits spurred by the MERS outbreak that had been proclaimed over less than three weeks earlier. The add-on holiday was an unprecedented act, unthinkable during South Korea's go-go years of the 1960s and 1970s; indeed, the number of extraordinary holidays in South Korea can be counted on one hand, usually instituted to mark milestones such as the opening day of the Seoul Olympics in 1988 or the country's success in the World Cup tournament in 2002. In a cabinet meeting, Park explained the decision in terms of expectations that "the 70th Liberation Day would serve as a turning point to boost the public sense of pride, revive the depressed atmosphere and boost consumers' confidence"—to the tune of 1.3 trillion won in domestic revenue and 46,000 new jobs, by one government estimate. In an effort to stimulate the tourism industry, government and private industries unleashed a host of incentives for foreign and domestic tourists alike: motorway tolls, discounted rail fares, free admission to national heritage sites and parks, even theme parks.

Park further applied the economic imperative to justify granting a presidential pardon to a prominent corporate leader (Chey Tae-won, chairman of the SK Group). Chey's inclusion in the special amnesty, an annual tradition to commemorate the national holiday, predictably provoked a backlash from the left, who pointed to Park's campaign promise to get tough on chaebŏl corruption; business interests conversely lodged their own complaints that the scale of pardons was smaller than expected, and argued that "sweeping pardons on business people were necessary for national unity and economic rebound." Yet few seem to have taken issue with the administration's wider preoccupation with stimulating the economy, whose connection to commemorating the war's end was tenuous at best.

Other government agencies honored the memory of Korea's colonial and postwar struggles, on lesser stages. At the An Chung-gŭn Memorial Hall in downtown Seoul, the Ministry of Justice conferred citizenship upon 11 descendants of independence fighters—an ad hoc naturalization process initiated in 2006 that simultaneously gave a nod both to the nation's history of resistance and its rising global position. The National Museum for Korean Contemporary History organized two exhibitions of the nation's 70 years' history using photographs and quotidian objects chosen to represent the astounding improvements in Koreans' everyday lives. Like the blockbuster film of 2014, *Ode to My Father* (Kukche sijang), criticized for idealizing South Korea's authoritarian past, the micro-historical approach allows viewers to appreciate the notion of material progress outside the contexts of geopolitics or domestic factors. Much like the president's address, the ceremony and curated shows endeavored to define Korean achievements in economic terms.

THE QUIET AMERICA

Just as she had steered away from placing inordinate attention upon Japan during the 70th anniversary address, Park's commemorative speech notably made scant mention of the United States; the sole reference to its erstwhile benefactor was made in the context of the United States's recent rapprochement with Cuba as a possible model for future inter-Korean relations. Yet in no way did this indicate a cooling of relations between the two allies. On a trip to Washington made two months later, Park spoke with admiration of the United States and the United Nations as inspirations for South Korea's values and ideals; she specifically credited the U.S.-Korea alliance as "a steadfast buttress" that had shaped Korea's transformation into a modern nation, the linchpin that had "defended the values of democracy, the free market system and human rights on the Korean Peninsula" from "the ashes of war."[11]

No doubt unintentionally, Park's statement highlighted the significance of the Korean War in raising South Korea's strategic importance to American geopolitical interests. It also deliberately minimized the American role in Korean affairs after 1945: the partition, military occupation, and support of authoritarian regimes during the Cold War. It was these issues that compelled a group of 300 activists to congregate just outside the U.S. ambassador's residence on August 15. Comprised of members of a left-leaning civic group and labor union, the protestors shouted anti-American slogans such as "Oppose the War!" and "Oppose the U.S.!" for roughly 10 minutes before the police forced them to disband. The demonstration, on the whole peaceful, was an attempt to refocus the spotlight on inter-Korean relations, and to challenge the continuing American involvement in the peninsula's security. The demonstration failed to garner much public support, illustrating in no small measure the general and uncritical acceptance of the American alliance by mainstream society that had developed over the decades. Paradoxically, the main thrust of the demonstrators echoed in sentiment the president's address in which she proclaimed: "For Koreans, true liberation will only come when we become a reunited people."

Reunification has been a familiar refrain of South Korean leaders marking the anniversary of the war's end. On rare occasions, August 15 has served as a platform for a breakthrough in inter-Korean relations, such as the Red Cross talks of 1971–1972 and divided family reunions since 2000. But public sentiment was decidedly against North Korea in 2015, as earlier in August land mines in the demilitarized zone had wounded two South Korean soldiers. In her speech Park included overtures to Pyongyang, but also delivered a series of reprimands for the repeated provocations and its nuclear development program. And although she made a number of proposals for improving relations, such as resuming the family reunions, promoting cultural events, and cooperating on environmental projects, these olive branch gestures were undermined by the recent order to reactivate, after an 11-year hiatus, the loudspeakers along the demilitarized zone border to broadcast propaganda messages into North Korea. Pyongyang responded to this punitive measure by threatening "strong military action," elevating tensions to a level that limited the scope of possible actions.

PARK'S PIVOT TO CHINA

Korean commemorations of the end of the war in 2015 were at once conventional and muted, practically anticlimactic after the built-up anticipation of some sort of momentous change. Indeed, the most emphatic observance unfolded not in the nation's capital but beyond the peninsula's borders, weeks after August 15, when Park traveled to Beijing to participate in China's victory parade. On September 3, she stood alongside Chinese president Xi Jinping and Russian president Vladimir Putin to review a massive procession involving thousands of Chinese troops and an arsenal of tanks, planes and missiles in a tightly choreographed march across Tiananmen Square. Park's trip to China, which included a second leg to Shanghai, can be regarded as an effort to fulfill multiple Korean global aspirations: bolster ties with China, signal implicit criticism of Japan, and marginalize North Korea. The Beijing appearance was faulted by many as damaging to South Korea's democratic stature and its alliance with the United States. Yet it largely succeeded in achieving its goals and enhancing South Koreans' confidence on the world stage, in part by drawing upon the historical memory of Koreans' colonial struggles in China.

Park's appearance at the Victory Day Parade marked her third visit to China (and sixth meeting with Xi) since assuming office in 2013, and it reflected South Korea's intense courtship of its powerful neighbor. China's importance to Korea may have been fundamentally rooted in issues of economics and security, but history was never far off. When the two countries normalized relations in 1992, both sides had to bury memories of fighting on opposite sides during the Korean War, as well as China's support of North Korea into the 1980s. In the early 2000s, relations were severely tested over competing claims to sixth-century mural paintings excavated near the Sino-Korean border, as UNESCO world heritage designation threatened to complicate each country's connection to its ancient national history. South Korea's promotion of Korean nationals fighting the Japanese empire in the early twentieth century thus served as a welcome diversion in spite of the adverse historical context, as it recalibrated the Sino-Korean dynamic to accentuate the common ground in the two nations' past. Over the course of her multiple visits, Park skillfully parlayed her influence into establishing two shrines to Korean anti-colonial nationalism on Chinese soil: the An Chung-gŭn Memorial in Harbin and the Korean Provisional Government building in Shanghai.

The memorial to the Korean nationalist An Chung-gŭn (1879–1910) was opened at Park's behest in 2014, in what might be considered part of an early and expansive commemoration of the war's end. An is one of the preeminent figures in Korea's pantheon of nationalist heroes, famous for his 1909 assassination of the Meiji statesman Itō Hirobumi who is regarded as the principal architect of Japan's imperialist designs on Korea. Although An's writings reflect a dabbling in Pan-Asian thought, his political act has rendered him, somewhat anachronistically, the face of the Korean independence movement. So closely tied is he to the nationalist ethos that in 2017 the South Korean government branded his celebrated handprint, which features a broken finger

used to sign a blood oath, as an emoji to commemorate National Independence Day. Yet for all of his renown today, An's apotheosis as a patriotic
icon began in earnest in 1970 under the direction of Park's father, President
Park Chung-hee, with the opening of a commemorative museum in the heart
of Seoul.[12] (It is at this site that the naturalization ceremony of the independence fighters' offspring is held on August 15.) Ironically, it was in Republican China that An had attained posthumous renown for having defied the
Japanese empire; his story was recounted extensively in Chinese literature,
biographies, and journalism, even forming the basis of a commercial film.[13]
The Harbin memorial to An thus served a number of political objectives; it
promoted Sino-Korean ties, bolstered each country's historical memory of
Japanese aggression, and boosted Park's own nationalist credentials.

   The dedication of the building that had once housed colonial Korea's
government-in-exile went one step further. Although it had failed to gain
official recognition from world powers even at the height of World War II,
the provisional government has long served as a source of political legitimacy for the Republic of Korea; all South Korean presidents since 1992 have
made a pilgrimage to the site. Park's journey to Shanghai immediately following the Victory Day Parade once again emphasized the two countries'
shared history; in addition to Chinese central and municipal governments'
financial contributions to the building's renovations, the mayor of Shanghai
pronounced the site of Korean nationalist activity as "a joint historical as-
set."[14] This Chinese recognition of the site considered by South Korea as its
ideological birthplace united the two countries against what they perceived as
an unrepentant Japan. Equally important to Seoul was the Chinese legitima-
tion of its colonial history, which by validating the colonial struggles by
South Korea's founding fathers, placed it on par with the North's. South
Korean media repeatedly pointed out that Park, reviewing the military parade
in Beijing, was standing in the front row alongside Xi and his wife while the
North Korean envoy Choi Ryong Hae was placed in a far corner two rows
back, the point being that South Korea had managed to gain the upper hand
in the contest for China's good will. Park's September trip thus yielded
tremendous gains in terms of domestic political capital—her approval rating
rose to its highest since the Sewol Ferry incident—and allowed the leader to
overcome provisionally her personal liabilities.

"COMFORT WOMEN" CONTROVERSIES IN 2015

As the daughter of the leader who led South Korea's transformation into an
economic powerhouse, Park had long been burdened with a singular patrimo-
ny. Although she was able to ride a wave of nostalgia for the Park Chung-hee
era through successive parliamentary victories and ultimately to the Blue

House,[15] Park also had to grapple with various criticisms stemming from this familial association. Arguably the most personal among them was the label of "pro-Japanese collaborator" attached to the elder Park—a reference both to his colonial career as an officer in the Japanese imperial army, and his later role as president who concluded the Korea-Japan normalization treaty in 1965. Park Geun-hye's much-criticized attempts to regulate government-issued history textbooks so that they promoted a conservative outlook—that is, one that downplayed issues of colonial collaboration and subsequent authoritarian politics—were in effect a response to this charge. Similarly, when Park declared that 2015 would be the year that the "comfort women" issue would be dealt with once and for all, she may have been seeking not only to resolve a long-standing diplomatic imbroglio between South Korea and Japan, but also to rectify her personal reputation as well.

The "comfort women" issue has been a constant flashpoint in Korean-Japanese relations since it first emerged in the early 1990s, with no signs of abating 25 years later. Weekly demonstrations staged in front of the Japanese embassy in Seoul and various statues have maintained the issue's longevity in public consciousness in Korea (and now increasingly in Korean-American communities). These efforts are roughly coordinated by a government-sponsored office, the Korean Council for Women Drafted for Military Sexual Slavery by Japan, which has devoted resources to building commemorative sites both in Seoul (War and Women's Human Rights Museum) and in the provinces to shape historical memory. The memorials are funded from private sources, but both the national and provincial governments lend financial support to prepare the facility.[16] In 2015 one of these memorials, in Taegu, North Kyŏngsang Province, added a "history hall" (yŏksagwan) to display the personal effects of some twenty-odd victims from the area.

In February 2015, the South Korean judicial branch stepped into the arena of memory politics when it handed down a guilty verdict in a libel case against an academic offering a revisionist interpretation. In her book *Comfort Women of the Empire* (*Cheguk ŭi wianbu*), the scholar Park Yu-ha presents the women not just as casualties of war, but as victims of deeply engrained transnational systems of gender, class, and ethnic discrimination. Park's argument is based on extensive use of testimonies collected by the Korean Council, the very organization that has been the main advocate on behalf of the victims. But in spite of the book's reliance on vetted primary sources, the court found the interpretations made selective use of the material and thus "distorted" the experiences and memories of the wartime victims; it ordered the author to redact passages and pay reparations to the nine women who filed suit. (Park subsequently lost a civil lawsuit in 2016, but later won the criminal case of defamation in 2017.) Park's legal troubles illustrate how the public memory concerning "comfort women" has claimed the subject as sacrosanct and "inviolable," rendering even academic debate as beyond the pale.[17]

The landmark agreement on the "comfort women" reached by the Korean and Japanese governments during the final days of December 2015 thus represented a departure from state-society agreement on the issue. Although it offered to the 46 surviving women an official apology and $8.3 million in care assistance funded by the Japanese government, the terms of the agreement allowed Japan to skirt the issue of legal responsibility and formal reparations. As various episodes prior to the agreement attest, a large segment of the South Korean public had come to regard the "comfort women" issue as epitomizing the injustices of its colonial experience, such that the administration's promise not to seek future claims from Japan was unacceptable. Park appealed to the nation to accept the agreement by stressing Japan's importance as an economic and strategic partner, the administration once again taking a pragmatic approach that paid little heed to the demands of the activists, opposition leaders, and many of the surviving victims themselves. Park's promise to seek a resolution to the "comfort women" issue by the year's end thus managed to meet the self-imposed deadline, but failed to deliver satisfactory closure for the many parties involved.

70TH ANNIVERSARY OF *KWANGBOK* IN HISTORICAL PERSPECTIVE

Commemorating the end of World War II in South Korea has historically been complicated by the convergence of two equally enduring processes: the end of colonial rule on the one hand, and the beginning of national division on the other. Whereas for more than four decades a succession of authoritarian regimes chose to project onto the future rather than look back, since the late 1980s there has been far more engagement with the past that has sought to capitalize on emerging public memory. The completion of Korea's Independence Hall in 1987, the demolition of the former colonial administration building in 1995, and the reunion of families separated by the North-South Korean border in 2000 were each milestone events scheduled for August 15, intended as celebrations of the indomitable Korean spirit that had variously overcome colonial rule and persevered in spite of a vast ideological divide.

National commemorations are invariably linked to promoting state legitimacy, and in that regard the commemorations of the war's end in 2015 are notable for how that goal was projected. On the actual date itself, the commemorations were distinctly lacking in pomp—an extra day off, along with routine, top-down business stimulation measures, all of which seemed to reflect deep-seated anxieties over the country's ability to devise new strategies for economic growth. Park's invitation to Japan to become a part of

South Korea's "creative economy" may have been intended as an iteration of *kwangbok*, a magnanimous gesture asserting the country's parity with the former colonizer, with no hard feelings. But it also echoed the entrenched political economy system that had flourished during the 1970s, the heyday of the elder Park's economic push. When at the year's end the "comfort women" agreement was announced, negotiated amidst great secrecy between the governments of Seoul and Tokyo, it was difficult not to note the business-as-usual manner in which a matter of tremendous historical and emotional importance to many Koreans was determined without their input or knowledge.

Arguably the more distinctive commemoration took place in Beijing, when Park played a supporting role in China's end of war celebrations. While the Victory Day Parade in Beijing itself had very little to do with South Korea, or Sino-Korean relations in 1945 for that matter, it marked a triumphant moment for South Korea in 2015—for edging out North Korea as the favored Korean neighbor, and creating a mini-regional alliance that took silent aim at Japan's erroneous past. Park had used the year skillfully to connect South Korea's anti-colonial history to that of China's, thereby reinforcing the nation's political myth. However poorly this maneuver reflected upon South Korea internationally, it provided Koreans with a sense of historical validation, and buoyed Park's political approval ratings to an all-time high in the process.

All of the political staging underscores South Korea's predicament as it seeks to commemorate the past and look toward the future. Government efforts to open a new chapter in Korea-Japan relations appear to have underestimated the deep reserves of anti-Japanese public sentiment on the one hand, and possibly succumbed to geopolitical pressure on the other. At the same time, South Korea's political gains from embracing China illustrate that national division continues to define how it chooses to think about the colonial past and conduct diplomacy. Thus it is that 70 years after the end of the war, despite taking enormous strides in development in democracy, South Korea has yet to move out of the long shadow of its past.

NOTES

1. North Korea uses a different term, the Fatherland Liberation Day (Choguk haebang ŭi nal), to commemorate the date.

2. "Haebang idŭmhae ch'ŏt kwangbokchŏl mosŭp ipsu. . . 'mungk'ŭl,'" SBS News, August 12, 2015, http://news.sbs.co.kr/news/endPage.do?news_id=N1003119908.

3. Ian Buruma, *Year Zero: A History of 1945* (New York: Penguin, 2013); see also Delury's comments in John Delury, Sheila A. Smith, Maria Repnikova and Srinath Raghaven, "Looking Back on the Seventieth Anniversary of Japan's Surrender," *Journal of Asian Studies* 74, no. 4 (2015): 801.

4. "President Syngman Rhee's Inaugural Address, 15 August 1948," in *Sources of Korean Tradition*, vol. 2, ed. Peter H. Lee et al. (New York: Columbia University Press, 1997), 348–51.

5. Kim Hyeon-seon, "State Rituals, Symbolic Space, and Korean National Identity," in *The Review of Korean Studies* 8, no. 2 (2005): 96–97.

6. Kim Yŏngsam, "Che 50 chunyŏn kwangbokchŏl kyŏngch'uksa," August 15, 1995.

7. Koen de Ceuster, "The Changing Nature of National Icons in the Seoul Landscape," in *Review of Korean Studies* 3, no. 2 (2000): 75.

8. Kwŏn Hyŏkt'ae, "8–15 nŭn ŏttŏke kiŏk/haesŏk toeŏ wannŭn'ga: Taejung munhwa rŭl t'onghae pon Han'guk ŭi Ilbon insik," in *Han-Chung-Il samguk ŭi 8–15 kiŏk* (Seoul: Yŏksa pip'yŏngsa, 2005), pp. 187–88.

9. The White House, "Press Conference with President Obama and President Park of the Republic of Korea," April 25, 2014.

10. "Address by President Park Geun-hye on the 96th March 1 Independence Movement Day," Seoul, March 1, 2015.

11. "Her Excellency President Park Geun-hye: Statesmen's Forum Address at the Center for Strategic and International Studies," Center for Strategic and International Studies, Washington, DC, October 15, 2015.

12. "Guide to the memorial museum," Ahn Jung Geun Memorial Museum, www.thomasahn.org.

13. Inhye Han, "The Afterlives of Korean An Chunggŭn in Republican China: From Sino-centric Appropriation to a Rupture in Nationalism," in *Cross-Currents E-journal* 17 (December 2015).

14. "Park Visits Shanghai Site of Korea's Exiled Provisional Government," *China Daily*, September 4, 2015.

15. On the Park Chung-hee "nostalgia boom," see Carter J. Eckert, "South Korea's Break with the Past: The End of the Long Park Chung-hee Era," *Foreign Affairs* Snapshot, May 11, 2017.

16. "'Comfort women' museum opens in South Korea," *Japan Times*, December 6, 2015.

17. Jordan Sand, "A Year of Memory Politics in East Asia: Looking Back on the 'Open Letter in Support of Historians in Japan,'" *Japan Focus*, 14, Issue 9, No. 3 (May 1, 2016).

Chapter Five

The Philippines

Memorials and Ceremonies over 70 Years

Ricardo T. Jose

The Philippines was one of the most devastated countries in Southeast Asia as a result of World War II. As such, memories of the war's tragedies are inescapable. With most of its major cities seriously damaged by aerial or naval bombardment, or destroyed deliberately by Japanese forces, and over one million dead (out of a population of seventeen million), World War II was a traumatic event that would be hard to forget. Physical reminders of the tragedy of war were visible all over the country, and surplus military equipment (stockpiled for the invasion of Japan that was cancelled because of the atomic bombs) was part and parcel of everyday life for years after the war.

But the war also produced heroes, who showed that Filipino patriotism was very much alive and was something to be proud of. The Philippines was, after all, on the side of the victors, and Filipino soldiers had as much right as any to share in the honors of victory. Those who had fought for the defense of the country in 1941 and 1942, although they were forced to surrender, were credited with upsetting the Japanese timetable and buying valuable time for the Allied counterattack. Guerrillas had never yielded to the Japanese occupiers and tied down Japanese forces which could have been used in other battlefronts; the information gathered by guerrilla agents proved crucial in hastening Japan's defeat. Furthermore, Filipinos had survived what was probably the worst situation that could ever be dealt: they had showed strength.

On the other hand, there were other incidents from the war years that were not as palatable. Collaboration with the Japanese—politically, economically, militarily and even culturally—was controversial and divided the country after the war. Guerrilla leaders led the campaign to try and imprison those who had worked with the Japanese. Not all had collaborated voluntarily, however, and key political leaders from the pre-war government rebutted their critics by saying they had the country's interests above all, and had merely been carrying out President Manuel L. Quezon's orders as he went into exile in the United States.

Even more controversial were tortures and killings committed by Filipinos. Japanese atrocities against Filipinos were clear-cut and many were tried by military tribunals. But Filipino guerrillas—or those posing as guerrillas— had also inflicted losses on the civilian population. Opportunists took advantage of the situation and looted and cheated. Post-war trials proved controversial and opened old wounds.

World War II in the Philippines thus left several mixed and sometimes clashing memories: a legacy of courage and patriotism—through its heroes and the courageous battles fought, in defending against the Japanese invasion; in resisting the Japanese occupation; and in fighting, with the Americans, to liberate the country from the Japanese. It also left a legacy of tragedy, which painful as it was, had to be remembered. These two themes— triumph and tragedy—would become the mainstay of commemorations of World War II in the Philippines. The more complicated legacies—collaboration and Filipino atrocities—would not become part of the mainstream ceremonies, although they would be discussed in textbooks and remained in the popular memory.

This chapter intends to provide an overview of the range of World War II memorials and selected commemorations through time. Filipino (government and non-government) and American memorials will be discussed, but not the Japanese memorials as they are best left for discussion in another paper.[1] Particular attention will be paid to the activities of 2015, marking the 70th anniversary of the end of the war.

FROM UNIT MEMORIALS TO STATE COMMEMORATIONS

The end of World War II was bittersweet. While the Philippines were part of the victorious Allies, it had suffered much during the period 1941 to 1945. The sense of triumph was tempered by the heaviness of the cost.

The first memorials constructed combined celebrating victory with honoring dead fighting men. These were constructed by the U.S. Army divisions to commemorate their battles, and remember their dead. Among those put up in 1945, just as the war ended, were the 33rd Infantry Divisions markers in Baguio, marking where and when the division liberated the city. Other U.S. Army divisions also put up their own memorials before they left the Philippines.[2] Members of the Mexican 201st Fighter Squadron, which flew combat sorties over Luzon and Taiwan from May 1945, built a small cement memorial prior to returning home after the war, to remember members of the squadron who died performing their duties.[3]

Victory celebrations were held in various towns in 1945 and the years immediately after. But the war was still so near, its events common knowledge that state sponsored commemorations were not held regularly. It was time to count the cost and in this regard the many military cemeteries were consolidated. The U.S. and Philippine governments worked to exhume remains and bring them to more central locations for more permanent war cemeteries which would, in the case of the Americans, also serve as a war memorial, under the American Battle Monuments Commission.

Many of the Philippine war dead had been buried in very shallow graves in Camp O'Donnell in central Luzon. The camp had served as a prisoner of war camp following the Bataan Death March and tens of thousands of Filipinos died due to disease, malnutrition and maltreatment. It was in these grounds that Philippine president Manuel Roxas (who had served as an officer in the Philippine Army under MacArthur in 1942) officially remembered the war dead on November 30, 1946—four months after the Philippines had become independent. This was a national holiday, National Heroes Day, which honored Filipino heroes from the revolution against Spain and beyond. In honoring the war dead, Roxas recognized their sacrifice and promised to strengthen and protect the nation. Thus while the tragedy of war was remembered, the occasion was also one to promote nation building.[4]

The late 1940s and 1950s continued with the themes of not forgetting the terrible cost with the aim of not repeating the tragedy—"We shall never forget" was a common phrase in the speeches and memorials of that time. Apart from the painful sacrifice, the glory of victory, other themes in the memorials and speeches were the strong alliance with the United States, and the devotion to peace. Corregidor, guarding the mouth of Manila Bay and heavily fought over in 1942 and again in 1945, was turned over to the Philippines in 1947 (it had remained under the U.S. Army until then), and in the turnover ceremonies, the shared sacrifice of the Philippines and the United States was highlighted, and how this close relationship would remain strong.[5]

The first state-sponsored historical markers were put up in the late 1940s and early 1950s. The National Historical Committee, which had been in existence prior to World War II, selected World War II sites. Corregidor, which had held up against the Japanese until May 6, 1942, and had been taken by a joint paratroop and amphibious assault in 1945, was one obvious choice. It symbolized Philippine-American unity, steadfastness and love of freedom. Gen. Douglas MacArthur, commanding the Philippine defense forces, had his headquarters there during the siege, and the Philippine Commonwealth government, headed by President Manuel L. Quezon, had transferred to the island fortress after Manila was declared an Open City in December 1941. (Quezon would later leave for the United States to set up a government in exile[6]).

Bataan Province was equally important, since Bataan and Corregidor stood together in the defense of the Philippines against the Japanese in 1942. Bataan, in fact, was more of a Filipino fight since over 80 percent of the soldiers defending the peninsula were Filipino, coming from all parts of the Philippines. Bataan fell on April 9, 1942, after a ferocious Japanese on-slaught with fresh reinforcements. The defenders had been on the peninsula since January and were exhausted, sick and hungry at the time of the Japanese push. The Japanese onslaught could not be stopped and Gen. King decided to surrender the forces under him to prevent further loss of life.[7]

After Bataan surrendered, the Japanese forced the prisoners of war to march to San Fernando in the province of Pampanga; most prisoners were jam-packed into enclosed boxcars and transported to Capas town in Tarlac Province, from where they were forced to march to Camp O'Donnell. The march became known as the Death March, with hundreds dying along the way. Tens of thousands died in prison camp in the months following.

The suffering was, it was said, not in vain, as the prolonged defense had disrupted the Japanese timetable, enabled MacArthur (who had been evacuated to Australia) to build up forces for the counterattack, and had shown the world how the Filipinos fought for freedom. Perhaps the earliest historical marker to recognize the importance of Bataan, placed by the Philippine Historical Committee in the late 1940s, quoted U.S. president Franklin D. Roosevelt's tribute: "The little mountainous peninsula of Bataan saved democracy and the whole world from the evil hands of the devil."[8]

In 1956, fifteen years after the start of the war, President Ramon Magsaysay presided over anniversary ceremonies in Balanga, capital of Bataan Province. Five years later, Congress passed a law declaring April 9 of every year a national holiday—Bataan Day.[9] Twenty years after the fall, large-scale state ceremonies were held in Manila and Bataan and Corregidor. When Ferdinand Marcos became president in 1966, Bataan Day became an important national holiday. Marcos had served in Bataan during the war, and his fellow veterans occupied important positions in government and in the armed forces. He laid the cornerstone for a huge memorial complex on top of Mount Samat shortly after he took office; the shrine was completed in 1970. Mount Samat had a commanding view of the entire peninsula and was stiffly fought for. The complex—Shrine of Valor (Dambana ng Kagitingan)—a towering cross near the peak, and a shrine with a museum a few meters below, provides the venue for annual ceremonies to this day.[10]

During this period, at the height of the Cold War, the Philippines was a very close ally of the United States, and the government had a strong anti-Communist stance. The ceremonies on Bataan and Corregidor highlighted this special relationship between the two countries. Two of the largest U.S.

bases in Southeast Asia—Clark Field and Subic Naval Base—were in the country, and ideally provided defense against external threats. Philippine-American solidarity was always the centerpiece of the commemorations, and American dignitaries and veterans were in attendance alongside Filipinos.

If the Philippine government's main World War II shrine was on top of Mount Samat, in Bataan, the Americans pledged to put up the Pacific War Memorial on Corregidor. The structure was patterned after a parachute—commemorating the paratroop assault in 1945—with a circular tablet directly below a hole at the top of the roof. The hole and altar were aligned so that the sun would shine directly on the altar at noon on May 6, the exact time when the firing stopped. A museum and steel eternal flame sculpture designed by a Filipino artist completed the memorial complex, set amidst the ruins of head-quarters and other buildings.[11]

Large-scale ceremonies were conducted on special anniversaries: the 20th anniversary of the surrender in 1962; the 25th anniversary (1967); 1970, when the Mount Samat shrine was completed, 1977 (the 35th anniversary), 1982 (40 years after the surrender), 1992, and 2002. The 1967 rites were an extravaganza with many American and Filipino veterans returning to the sites of combat, a large exhibit of weaponry and models in the National Library, and a grand parade. Historical markers were placed at significant battlefields in Bataan, and every kilometer of the Death March was marked by signs along the road. An illustration by Cesar Legaspi, a renowned Filipi-no artist later declared National Artist, depicted the shared suffering among Filipino and American soldiers in every kilometer marker. The 1982 ceremo-nies—the 40th (Ruby) anniversary—were perhaps the largest, and one of the last, in which actual veterans of the campaign were actively involved. Mu-seum exhibits were opened, special trips not only to Bataan and Corregidor, but also to the sites of the former prisoner of war camps in Camp O'Donnell and in Cabanatuan were organized, and new memorials completed.

Marcos had proclaimed martial law in 1972, and thus these state-spon-sored ceremonies were supported by the full resources of the government. During this period, Marcos had opened the Philippines to Japan and actively invited Japanese veterans to return and perform their own commemorations. Thus, while the formal ceremonies still extolled Philippine-American friend-ship, courage and gallantry, peace and co-existence were also highlighted. In 1977, Marcos launched the Reunion for Peace program, inviting veterans from all countries to return to their former battlefields and also see the gains the Philippines had made. The Japanese, in particular, were invited to return and put up memorials to their war dead.[12]

The state commemorations of Bataan Day were criticized, however. In 1963, prolific writer Quijano de Manila (pseudonym of National Artist Nick Joaquin) published a cynical appraisal, purporting to show how the founda-tions of Bataan Day were empty and propagandistic. He alleged that the

Japanese had not outnumbered the Filipino-American forces and that they were not that well trained. The Filipino defenders of Bataan challenged his claims, citing official American sources. But as the 1960s wore on, so did cynicism of Bataan Day, and the U.S.-Philippine friendship it endorsed. This was the era of anti-American and pro-nationalist movements among intellectuals and students; anti-Vietnam War rallies and criticism of American intervention in Philippine affairs were rife. Filipino nationalists decried the continuing reliance on the United States, which had after all not been able to defend the Philippines in 1942. Furthermore, the Americans had not recognized many Filipino veterans, denying them benefits they rightly deserved; and the United States had not paid for all of the damages caused by the war. A growing skepticism by Filipinos of their heroes, for that matter, had been eating away at the previously unquestioned patriotism of established heroes. Other critics asked why a defeat should be celebrated and urged that Philippine military history be rewritten, focusing on victories instead. [13]

Partly in reaction to this criticism, Marcos moved the commemoration of World War II from Bataan Day, April 9, to May 6, to be known as Day of Valor (Araw ng Kagitingan). This day would now encompass the anniversary of the fall of Bataan, the fall of Corregidor, as well as the Filipino victory over the Japanese in Bessang Pass on June 14, 1945. The sacrifice and importance of Bataan and Corregidor, which were inextricably linked, was balanced by the significant Filipino victory in 1945. (Marcos claimed he had fought there.) A more positive and Filipino slant was thus given the date. But it was an artificial move, and later administrations returned to April 9.

In addition to issues raised against the choice of Bataan Day, questions were raised about the veracity of Marcos' war record. Challenges to his claims to heroism were published in the United States, but when reprinted in the Philippines, a government counterattack tried to mute the damage. The Manila newspaper that published the American articles was closed down. But discontent with the Marcos regime grew and his authority to rule was further undermined when an American historian publicized official U.S. documents exposing that Marcos' exploits were largely invented. Marcos was overthrown in 1986. The revelation of Marcos' exaggerated World War II claims tainted the image of Filipino veterans and the generally accepted narratives of World War II. [14]

Following the overthrow of Marcos, the commemorations of Bataan Day—now officially known as Day of Valor but restored to April 9 by President Corazon Aquino—were more subdued. This was partly so because of more immediate problems that had to be faced—coup attempts, rebuilding the Philippine economy. President Aquino did give more attention to the veterans, but the potentially important 50th anniversary of Bataan was relatively quiet given that it was an election year and more pressing issues had to be dealt with.

Succeeding presidents, depending on their demeanor, gave the Day of Valor uneven treatment. President Aquino's successor, Fidel V. Ramos, was a military man and took over in time for the 50th anniversaries of the battles for the liberation of the Philippines, but he further strengthened the commemoration of the Day of Valor by also declaring the week of April 9 as Veterans Week, bringing in more ceremonies and honoring all other Filipino veterans. By this time the Bataan survivors were fewer in number, and less able to endure the long trip to Bataan. Other veterans took over in the ceremonies.

While Mount Samat and Corregidor were developed, the former prisoner of war camp in Capas, Tarlac, had been forgotten. A simple concrete marker had been erected in 1942. Through the years that had been the only reminder of the thousands who died there. The Defenders of Bataan and Corregidor worked to have the site declared a national shrine, and pushed to have an appropriate memorial built. The law was passed during President Ramos' term, but progress was slow. The complex was finished in 2003, providing an alternative venue for commemorating the Day of Valor. The law setting the land aside as a shrine also provided that a tree should be planted in memory of all those who did not survive the camp—some 25,000 Filipinos and 6,000 Americans in all.[15]

President Gloria Macapagal-Arroyo made the holiday flexible, in her policy of what was called holiday economics—moving national holidays to the nearest Monday to allow people to enjoy longer weekends and thus spend more—in malls, in domestic tourism—and help spur the Philippine economy. It was during her time that the developments in Capas Shrine were finished, and for the first time the Day of Valor was commemorated, in 2003, in the former prisoner of war camp. The survivors of Bataan, the Death March and the camp attended, but were made to wait under the sun because of the president's late arrival. Instead of recognizing their sacrifices and feats, President Arroyo spoke on the need to fight the war on terror.

Elsewhere in Bataan were local or private memorials and markers. A large monument was built in Layac Junction—critical to the defense in January 1942, and where a fierce delaying action was fought. Unfortunately, the local authorities did not give much attention to accuracy and the monument (which also displaced two other earlier markers) has been controversial. A museum has been set up in Balanga, capital of the province, in the school grounds where the formal surrender details were worked out. A life-sized rendition of the negotiations stands approximately where the event took place in 1942. Many other markers and memorials serve as their respective towns' sources of pride.

The Death March kilometer posts, mounted on steel poles, gradually diminished in number, due to accidents, road expansion projects or looting. A joint Filipino-American organization, the Filipino-American Memorial

Endowment (FAME), was created in 1986 to rehabilitate the markers. It was decided to replace all the markers with more durable concrete markers by the side of the road. Attempts have been made to educate the local people as to the importance of the markers, and how they can help preserve them and the memories of what happened.

The maintenance of Corregidor as a historical and tourist spot was transferred by President Corazon Aquino from the military to a private organization, the Corregidor Foundation. The foundation, working with the Department of Tourism and private tourist agencies, has tried to develop and maintain the more significant sites, such as the big guns and remains of barracks and headquarters buildings. The island was designated the Island of Valor, Peace and International Understanding in the 1990s, and toward that end memorials for the Japanese, the Spaniards (who controlled the island prior to the coming of the Americans) and especially for Filipino heroes, were erected. A sound-and-light presentation was opened in the tunnel complex, which housed MacArthur's headquarters and the Commonwealth government. But in order to attract tourists and bring in revenue, non-historical features were added such as camping grounds, a zip line, nature treks, ghost hunting expeditions and others.

With the shift of Bataan Day to Day of Valor and its attendant Veterans Week, the focus of attention shifted from the Bataan campaign to a wider scope. Initially several themes were highlighted: the story of valor and courage of defending the country against foreign invaders, even if ill-armed, ill-equipped and inadequately trained; the heartbreak caused by the surrender on April 9, which affected the whole country; the horror and tragedy of the Death March and subsequent prisoner of war experience. Also celebrated was the alliance between the Philippines and the United States, and a dedication to peace. With the shift to Day of Valor and Veterans Week, all other veterans were included—the guerrillas and their campaigns, and also postwar veterans of military campaigns in and outside the Philippines. Present-day heroism in other forms—in the battle against poverty, the war against terrorism and the importance of nation building—became the stress of the speeches.

COMMEMORATIONS AND AGENCIES: NATIONAL AND LOCAL

Immediately after World War II, three other sites were recognized as being important by the Philippine government. These were Palo, Leyte, where Gen. MacArthur landed on October 20, 1944, thus fulfilling his promise to return; Lingayen, Pangasinan, where U.S. forces landed on Luzon on January 9, 1945; and Kiangan, Ifugao, where Gen. Yamashita surrendered to U.S. forces on September 2, 1945.

MacArthur's landing on Leyte galvanized Filipinos who were fighting the Japanese as guerrillas and marked the beginning of what has been called the Liberation of the Philippines. Accompanying MacArthur was President Sergio Osmeña, who had succeeded President Quezon, thus reinstating the Philippine Commonwealth government on Philippine soil. The fighting for Leyte was intense, involving combat in land, air and sea. The battles became known worldwide, and MacArthur's landing is commemorated annually.

Although not a national holiday (it is a province-wide non-working holiday), the ceremonies are usually national in the sense that the president or his representative attends, along with diplomats and country representatives. As in the Bataan commemorations, the 20th, 25th, 40th, 50th and other key anniversaries have been large-scale events, with reenactments of the landing and a show of force by the Philippine armed forces, usually with American and other forces also present. Philippine-American friendship is typically a central theme. From the late 1970s, as Japan became more important as an economic partner, Japanese sacrifices were also mentioned. The role of Filipino guerrillas is also highlighted. Memorials to various battles and units are scattered over the whole island, but the center of attention is MacArthur Park in Palo, where larger than life statues of MacArthur and his entourage stand at the beach where the landing took place. During the period of martial law, it was no small help that the hometown of the First Lady, Imelda Marcos, was Tacloban.[16]

As with Bataan, criticism of the Leyte ceremonies attacked the continued reliance on the United States, colonial mentality and the unfair treatment given Filipino veterans by the United States. Nationalist historians also criticized the fact that MacArthur's return brought more destruction to the country, and that the event merely marked the reoccupation of the Philippines rather than its liberation. Thorny issues relating to the continued presence of U.S. bases on Philippine soil, and the lack of an iron-clad guarantee that the United States would defend the archipelago against foreign threats added to the anti-American feeling.

The 50th anniversary of the landing was an expensive affair, with full-scale military exercises. The American bases had just been closed, but a new military agreement had just been signed. As a result of the bases closure, American assistance to the Philippines decreased. The man playing MacArthur waded ashore, arrogant and confident, when he stumbled and fell into the water. This humiliation was seen by some Filipinos as poetic justice for the years of unequal treatment by the American government.[17]

The Leyte commemorations continue on. While the MacArthur landing is the center of attention, sites of other landings on the island are also commemorated, and the tragedy of one town—Dulag, which was shelled by warships without warning, killing many townspeople in their homes—is also remembered.

Another World War II site of importance was the beaches of Lingayen Gulf, where American forces landed in January 1945 to wrest the island from the Japanese. A large complex in front of the provincial capitol building displays war relics, maps and photographs depicting the events of that day. Other memorials mark specific landing zones, and in particular MacArthur's landing. The ceremonies are sometimes national, as when President Fidel V. Ramos attended the 50th anniversary rites (he hails from the area).

A third important commemoration is that of the surrender of General Yamashita on September 2, 1945. The school building where the initial sur-render negotiations were held has been declared a historical landmark. Close by a park celebrating the surrender—and hence the end of World War II in the Philippines—was constructed by the national government. The main structure, a shrine and museum, is built in the style of the local people's homes, serving as a tribute to the Filipino mountain peoples who fought as hard as their lowland brothers.

While Yamashita had turned himself in in Kiangan, the formal surrender rites were held in Camp John Hay, in Baguio City, the next day. The building where the surrender documents were signed—the summer residence of the U.S. ambassador to the Philippines (in 1945, the residence of the American High Commissioner)—still stands, and the table on which the documents were inked is as it was in 1945. Due to security concerns, however, access to this site is very limited and thus the rites commemorating the end of the war are held at Kiangan. No Filipino attended the formal surrender, in Baguio, although Filipino guerrillas surrounded the place.

The national commemorations ideally strengthen the state and provide foundations for its being. They ideally inspire the youth and provide a sense of identity. They also serve to situate the present with past events, making the current generation aware of the sacrifices of the veterans who fought the war, and the value of freedom and democracy. The national ceremonies also are dedicated to peace and friendship, toward a world of no more war. At least those are the motives publicly enunciated in the speeches and exhibit themes.

Aside from the national state war commemorations and memorials, many localities commemorate war events directly related to provinces and towns. Essentially these can be divided into three: memorials commemorating the return of the Americans to that particular province or town (or in some cases, the guerrillas securing a province or town prior to the U.S. landings); the guerrilla resistance forces in the area; and the civilian casualties resulting from Japanese massacres.

Many provinces celebrate the anniversary of the return of the Americans: Iloilo, Cebu, Zamboanga to name a few. Memorials have been built at the landing sites—that in Iloilo (Tigbauan beach) topped by a replica of the American cruiser which bombarded the beaches. The Cebu memorial (Tali-say beach) added larger than life statues of Americans wading ashore, similar to the beach memorial at Palo, Leyte. The monument is not authentic: the landing in Talisay was made under strong Japanese fire, and the American soldiers crouched as they landed. The Zamboanga memorial has a sculpture of a dove of peace.

Since, however, this group of memorials tended to emphasize the American return and relegated the Filipino guerrillas to the background, changes to some of the ceremonies were made to bring the Filipino role to the fore. The Iloilo ceremony, previously dubbed Liberation Day, was changed to Victory Day, giving more emphasis to the guerrillas who had retained control of most of the island during the war. The monument at the landing beach has been superseded by one with the busts of the three Filipino guerrilla leaders in the area.

Private or local government memorials to the guerrilla forces are many. The memorial in Iloilo is maintained as a national shrine by the Military Shrines Service of the Armed Forces of the Philippines, and is both a museum and a cemetery for the deceased veterans. The Veterans Federation of the Philippines put up signature markers (pylons marked with a kris) all over the country, usually with the names of local veterans inscribed.

Local governments took pride in specific historical events in their vicinity relating to the resistance. One recurring theme was in the sites where American submarines unloaded weapons and supplies to strengthen the guerrillas. Several markers exist, some placed fairly recently (in the last ten to fifteen years), by former guerrillas, submariners and the local government. One contains an anchor; another has a large replica of the submarine that landed there.

Puerto Princesa, in the island province of Palawan, commemorates not the landing of the Americans, but the end of the liberation campaign. A private museum (established by the son of the wartime guerrilla leader there) highlights the local people's participation in the resistance, and also serves as a museum of military history in the Philippines and elsewhere. It also remembers one of the war's most gruesome atrocities, the massacre of American prisoners of war within the grounds of the city.

There exist some memorials to civilian victims of battles and Japanese massacres. Some were erected in the 1950s (a statue of a beheaded man in Legazpi City; and a small marker in a Laguna town were both put up at this time), but larger ones were built much later. The memorials to the civilian victims were usually built near or at the sites where the massacres took place, such as in the city of Lipa, in Batangas Province. The civilian dead of Manila are memorialized in a pieta inside the old walled city of Intramuros, where many were killed. Some of these were erected only in the 1990s, when the survivors decried the lack of any state memorial for the non-combatant victims of the war. Painful memories had been suppressed until then. A group organized themselves into Memorare Manila 1945, whose aim is to remember the civilians of the Battle of Manila.

The local memorials and commemorations help develop local pride and awareness, and place a particular city, town or province in the national historical map. This is particularly so in the case of guerrilla victories. They also serve as tourism attractions, thus improving a locality's visibility and income.

In the Philippines, World War II state commemorations are organized and carried out by many state agencies. Among them are the National Historical Commission of the Philippines, the Department of Interior and Local Governments, and the Department of Tourism. The Department of National Defense, specifically the Philippine Veterans Affairs Office and Military Shrines Service; the Department of Foreign Affairs and the Department of Education are also actively involved.

Closely linked with the government offices are two private organizations, the Philippine Veterans Bank and the Veterans Federation of the Philippines. These are deputized agencies of the government and the Veterans Bank pays veterans' pensions. The Veterans Federation is a government-recognized aggregation of veterans' organizations and enables mobilization of veterans to participate in the various commemorative activities.

Private organizations dedicated to memorializing World War II include the Filipino-American Memorial Endowment, which is donation driven. Formed in 1986, its aim is to preserve and maintain tangible reminders of the "shared values for which Americans, Filipinos and their allies fought side-by-side in World War II."[18] Memorare Manila 1945 is an association of survivors or relatives of survivors or casualties of the Battle of Manila. Another private organization dedicated to keep the memory of World War II alive, albeit in a more limited location, is the Corregidor Foundation, founded after 1986, which seeks to preserve the remains of war in the island fortress of Corregidor.

One organization that has been very active in trying to keep the memories of World War II alive, and pass the legacy of valor to the youth, is a private group called Spyron-AV Manila, headed by Lucky Guillermo, the son of a World War II guerrilla leader. He has made it his passion to document the war in the Philippines and bring the lessons of the war and pride in its heroes to the youth. In partnership with Peter Parsons, the son of one of MacArthur's most important American intelligence agents, Guillermo's daughter and a young and talented director, Bani Lugronio, Spyron-AV Manila has produced documentaries and books to carry the message to the Filipino youth.

There are a number of Japanese organizations dedicated to keeping the memory of the war alive. One, the Philippine War Memorial Preservation Association, Inc., founded in 2005, surveys Japanese war memorials and supports their maintenance and upkeep. It is low key but tries to work for mutual understanding. More active and visible is the Bridge for Peace, an organization of young Japanese who seek to cross the divide in war memories and share them on both sides. Their stated goal is: "We record messages from war survivors and acknowledge our past through workshops. To prepare for the future, what we must do today is to build a bridge between Japan and the rest of Asia and bring together those who experienced the war with the generation of tomorrow."[19] Founded in 2004, its members come to the Philippines regularly to interview and document victims of Japanese atrocities while also interviewing Japanese soldiers and bringing their testimony to the Philippines. They are regularly invited to speak in the Memorare memorial ceremonies.

70TH ANNIVERSARY COMMEMORATIONS

The year 2015 marked seventy years since the end of World War II as well as anniversaries of many bloody battles in the liberation of the Philippines from Japanese rule. As such, it was considered by some an appropriate time to hold special commemorative events throughout the Philippines. What was obvious in the year's commemorations was the relatively low profile of the national government in these activities, and thus few major state-sponsored activities. More active players were local governments and private institutions which held exhibits, lectures, and more extravagant programs.

The state ceremonies for World War II focused on the annual Day of Valor and Veterans' Week activities, which were held almost as a matter of routine. The theme for the year's commemoration was "Transplant valor to the youth, prepare them to be the veterans of the future." Formal ceremonies were held in Mount Samat, Bataan, where fierce fighting to hold the peninsula took place in April 1942. President Benigno Aquino III led the rites, on April 9, with the U.S. and Japanese ambassadors, other foreign dignitaries and some veterans present. The speeches echoed standard themes: the futility of war, the need for friendship and good relations; homage to the veterans and Filipino valor. The national government did not hold anything in addition to the regular ceremonies: the annual rites for Veterans Week (April 5 to 11) included a sunrise ceremony at the Philippines' Libingan ng mga Bayani (Heroes Cemetery) and various activities to fete local veterans.[20]

While tales of Filipino valor were retold, it had become painfully obvious that the younger generation did not know the reason for the holiday. The week ended without much publicity with a sunset ceremony at the Heroes' Cemetery in Fort Bonifacio.

The Philippine Veterans Bank did sponsor a new way of commemorating the Bataan Death March, and gain public appeal—a marathon dubbed the

Freedom Run. Runners were invited to retrace the route of the march, with the winners receiving prizes at the finish line—the Camp O'Donnell POW camp site, now a national shrine. Reenactors dressed in World War II period costume representing American, Filipino and Japanese soldiers in authentic uniforms provided visual reminders of what the fighting men looked like.[21] But the National Historical Commission of the Philippines (NHCP), officially tasked to oversee historical commemorations, could not do more because the 70th anniversary was not part of the officially sanctioned years. Legally, the NHCP could hold special events for the 50th and 75th anniversaries, but not the 70th. Thus no funding was allotted to official World War II commemorations for 2015.[22]

The Aquino administration had very good relations with Japan at this time, and it apparently did not want to burden the friendship with old memories. President Aquino's grandfather had served as an important member of the Japanese-sponsored Philippine government during the occupation, and discussions of the occupation period tended to bring back criticisms of him as a Japanese collaborator. Keeping ceremonies commemorating World War II low key thus reduced the possibility of bringing back that controversial topic. A memorandum from the secretary of the interior urged local governments to commemorate the week with "simple but meaningful activities."[23] An attempt by the civilian survivors of the Battle of Manila (the Memorare Manila 1945 organization) to have September 2 declared a special day (but not a non-working holiday), was blocked by officials of various government agencies who cited the possible negative effect on Philippines-Japan relations. No large-scale national state commemorations were held for any of the events of 1945.[24]

The onus fell on non-government organizations or local governments to fill the gap. Schools and universities which had direct experience with the war held their own commemorations. For Metro Manila, the months of February and March proved to be the most active months. The University of Santo Tomas (UST), which had been used as an internment camp for American and allied civilians, holds annual rites commemorating the liberation of the camp in February 1945. Twenty fifteen being the 70th anniversary of that event, a large contingent of former internees and their families came on a pilgrimage to the university. The internees, mostly in their late 80s and 90s, considered this the last time they could return to the site of the camp, which was their home for three years. The university opened its doors to them and accorded the survivors special honors with a formal wreath laying, a commemorative program in the lobby of the main building, and a sumptuous lunch. Members of the Philippine Living History Society lent color to the occasion, dressed in 1945 U.S. and Japanese uniforms and as Filipino guerrillas. The UST History Department held a conference where historians explained the background of the internment camp, placing it in the perspective of World War II and the Philippine experience. Former internees shared their experiences with students, reminding them that the university site was especially historic. A photo exhibit was opened in time for the former internees to view it.[25]

The liberation of UST Internment Camp marked the beginning of the month-long Battle of Manila, in which an estimated 100,000 civilians died and much of the city was destroyed. The City of Manila holds an annual wreath-laying ceremony commemorating the liberation of Manila, in two memorial markers located on one side of Manila's City Hall. For 2015 the event was not particularly special, with the mayor delivering a speech in front of city hall employees and a handful of survivors of the battle.

Memorare Manila 1945, composed of survivors of the battle and their families, had a larger than usual program, on February 14, in front of a memorial they had built. The monument, in the form of a pieta, dedicated to the memory of the civilian victims of the Battle of Manila, is inside Intramuros, the old Spanish walled city, where much fighting had taken place. Representatives from Bridge for Peace attended, and apologized for the wartime conduct of their countrymen, vowing that it would never happen again. The guest speaker was former president Fidel V. Ramos, and he spoke about the importance of remembering the battle and its victims. But he suddenly shifted to an encounter that had occurred a few weeks earlier, where an elite team of Philippine police had been killed in Mindanao. He took off his barong Tagalog and revealed the uniform of the unit that had been ambushed, thus detracting from the purpose of the occasion. The press crowded around him afterwards asking his views on the bungled mission, and press coverage the next day focused on Ramos' comments on the Mindanao fiasco rather than the Battle of Manila survivors.[26]

Libraries, museums and schools contributed their share to commemorate the 70th anniversary of the battle—and WWII in the Philippines—even as the national government laid low. The Ayala Museum in Makati opened a special exhibit on World War II in Manila—photographs, models, artifacts and other items—and sponsored a month-long mini conference where various aspects of the war and Japanese occupation were discussed by experts and eyewitnesses. The events were entitled "Manila, My City at War!" and also included documentary film showings.[27] The weekly lectures—on varied topics not usually mentioned in standard histories—were always packed, and the audience reaction was very lively and positive.

The Ortigas Library, with many books and resources on the war, held a series of talks on the war, on a smaller and more intimate scale, wherein eyewitnesses shared their experiences to an interested audience. "Chronicles of War: The Liberation of Manila" included film showings, testimonies from eyewitnesses, and lectures by James Zobel, the archivist of the MacArthur Memorial in Norfolk. The Far Eastern University and Ateneo de Manila

University opened exhibits focused on World War II books and periodicals as well as relics and sponsored lectures. The local Filipino-Chinese community put up a special exhibit and held a series of talks on the role of Filipino-Chinese in the war in their museum (Bahay Chinoy, a museum and research center on the Filipino-Chinese) in Manila.[28]

On the occasion of the 70th anniversary of the Battle of Manila, Spyron-AV Manila released a new dynamic and vibrant documentary on the battle, entitled *Manila 1945—The Rest of the Story*. A book of the same name was launched in the premiere, in the historic National Museum building.[29] The building had formerly been the Congress of the Philippines, and had been destroyed in the fighting. It has been reconstructed to its prewar grandeur. Amidst the historical setting, the film was screened in front of a distinguished audience, which included survivors of the fighting, veterans and diplomats. Spyron-AV Manila maintains its crusade to bring the lessons of the war to young people, showing their documentaries to different schools throughout the Philippines.

Capping the ceremonies commemorating the 70th anniversary of the Battle of Manila was a special concert, dubbed "Music for Peace," by the Manila Symphony Orchestra replicating the first post-war program in 1945. The Manila Symphony Orchestra had refused to collaborate with the Japanese and had hidden their instruments rather than using them for Japanese propaganda. In 1945, during the Battle of Manila, the instruments were recovered, and a special concert (featuring Beethoven's *Eroica* Symphony and Dvorak's *New World* Symphony) was presented in the midst of the city ruins to give hope to the city's residents. The anniversary performance, in a private auditorium filled to capacity, was moving. One musician who played in 1945 attended, as well as a number of individuals who had been there seventy years earlier. A cello used in the performance was displayed. It served to connect the members of the audience and the orchestra with those events seventy years before.

Not connected with the Battle of Manila but bringing attention to World War II in the Philippines was the announcement in early March 2015 of the discovery of the wreck of the Japanese super battleship *Musashi*, which had been sunk during the Battle of Leyte Gulf in October 1944. A private remote submersible, working quietly, had found the wreck and photographed it, creating a rush in the Philippine and Japanese media to learn more about the ship and its sinking. A few Japanese survivors of the sinking were brought to the site to remember their dead comrades.[30]

Apart from the Battle of Manila, 1945 was important to many others because this was the year when they were freed from Japanese rule. Battles were fought in many cases, or destruction caused by retreating Japanese or American aerial or naval bombardment. Many cities and provinces commemorate the anniversary of their liberation annually, with the date of liberation usually a local holiday. This is so for, at least, the cities of San Fernando (La Union), Iloilo, Cebu and Baguio, the municipality of Kiangan, and the provinces of Leyte and Ilocos Norte. In these instances, the local government plays a big role.

The 70th anniversary meant more to San Fernando, La Union, which hosted a special exhibit, opened a Heroes' Wall in the city hall, and sponsored a lecture recounting the events of 1945. Surigao City commemorated the 71st anniversary of the Battle of Surigao Strait with a new monument, and a newly discovered Japanese torpedo ceremoniously added to the holdings of a museum dedicated to the battle. New memorials were unveiled in the location of a former Japanese camp, and wreaths were dropped at sea to commemorate all those who died in the naval battle. An Australian veteran who had served on a cruiser during the battle graced the occasion, as well as Filipino veterans. The City of Baguio, in addition to the annual wreath laying and tributes to veterans in the city's veterans' memorial, held a special lecture for its students and government employees so they would know more about what happened in the city during the war.[31]

One city held its commemorations for the first time, in conjunction with a tourist agency seeking to develop World War II tourism destinations as a package. Rajah Travel Corporation pulled together members of the local government, tourism officials, the academe and others sectors to celebrate the end of the military campaign in Palawan and give special honors to the province's veterans and heroes. A gala dinner was held to honor veterans and their families. This had never been done before, and was timed specifically for the 70th anniversary. It was also aimed to develop domestic tourism, in particular tourism relating to World War II sites.[32] The activities were so successful the local government has institutionalized this as an annual event, to honor veterans and their families and to instill in the local people a sense of pride.

Not to be forgotten were the Filipino comfort women, who spoke out in a public forum during Veterans Week in a historic bakery.[33] Unfortunately they have not been given significant attention by the government.

Perhaps the most significant commemoration in terms of the academic sector was the holding of a commemorative conference on World War II and the Japanese occupation at the University of the Philippines on September 3, coinciding with the day when, in 1945, the Japanese forces in the Philippines formally surrendered. The three-day conference was well attended and paper presenters included Japanese, a Frenchman, a Belgian and Filipinos from different parts of the country. The papers, covering various topics, will be published as monographs by the History Department, which organized the conference.[34]

Rounding up the ceremonies for the year was the launching of a new documentary and book on the Filipino guerrillas of World War II in November, held in a new museum in Quezon City. The book and documentary, both entitled *Unsurrendered 2* were the work of Spyron-AV Manila, which as mentioned above has dedicated itself to spreading awareness of World War II in the Philippines to the youth.

Some countries sent representatives to attend some of the commemorative events. In earlier years, the United States played a key role in World War II commemorations, usually sponsoring lectures and special exhibits. In recent years, and particularly in 2015, due to budgetary and other reasons, the U.S. role was minor. The Japanese embassy participation has almost always been low-key; for the 2015 events it remained so. Australia, on the other hand, was more visible in many of the events. Mexico attended the Memorare commemoration in February; and a representative of the Chinese embassy spoke at the opening of the exhibit sponsored by the local Filipino Chinese.

Thus, while the national government did not go out of its way to specially observe the 70th anniversary of the events of 1945—the numerous battles, the liberation of cities and towns from Japanese rule, the heroes, the dead— the local governments and non-government sectors took up the slack.

CONCLUDING REMARKS

After the Philippines marked the 70th anniversary of World War II, more lavish commemorations in the major state memorials will be held to commemorate the 75th anniversaries of the events. As the number of actual participants and eyewitnesses to the war diminish, the focus of the speeches will extoll the feats of the veterans, few as they are. But as has been noted, World War II will be interpreted differently. No longer in the framework of Philippine-American friendship, but within the larger sphere of international peace and nation building.

And yet, there are other wartime incidents which have not received sufficient attention. The Filipino comfort women have just one small, often overlooked memorial in Manila. A house in Bulacan Province which had been used to rape local women was recently torn down, despite a clamor to preserve it as a museum for the comfort women and victims of rape. There are no markers or memorials testifying to the wartime government put up by the Japanese, or to depict the issue of wartime collaboration. These are contained in textbooks, but not in the mainstream narrative presented by most of the World War II memorials.

The memorialization of World War II serves at least two purposes, one of which is strengthening the national identity and instilling greater pride. Thus the memorials to Bataan, Corregidor, the guerrillas, and the liberation sites all add to national or local identity. They extoll patriotism, valor and heroism. The other purpose, to remember the tragedy of war, its victims, and to ensure peace, is also present in these commemorations and memorials. Concerned groups (veterans, survivors of the war and their families) have been reaching out to the younger generation to get these messages across, through the monuments, the memorial rites and reaching out to schools. The impact of these efforts has not yet been studied and perhaps only time will tell whether these efforts are successful in achieving their goals.

NOTES

1. In the writing of this paper, the author consulted various commemorative booklets and programs in the author's possession. The author attended many of these ceremonies from the 1970s. The author participated in most of the 2015 commemorations cited in this paper. He has also documented most of the physical memorials and monuments mentioned.

2. Many of the U.S. Army unit histories detail the fighting in various fronts and sometimes the memorials they put up. See for example Robert F. Karolevitz, *The 25th Infantry Division and World War 2* (Baton Rouge: Army and Navy Publishing Company, 1946), 152. The 25th Division fought alongside Filipino and Chinese guerrillas, both groups of which put up their own memorials. See Ricardo Trota Jose, "War Memorials and Commemorations in the Philippines: An Exploratory Look," in Lydia N. Yu-Jose, ed., *The Past, Love, Money and Much More: Philippines-Japan Relations Since the End of the Second World War* (Quezon City: Japanese Studies Program, Ateneo de Manila University, 2008), 17–18 for further discussion on the early U.S. Army memorials.

3. The monument still stands. This was the only unit of the Mexican armed forces to ever fight outside Mexican borders. After declaring war against the Axis, the Mexican government decided to dispatch this unit to the Philippines owing to its long historical relationship with the islands.

4. Manuel Roxas, *Speeches, Addresses and Messages of President Roxas* (Manila: Bureau of Printing, 1954), 274; Elpidio Quirino, *The Quirino Way* (Manila: privately printed, 1955), 70–74.

5. Quirino, *The Quirino Way*, 67–69.

6. *Corregidor: Island of Valor, Peace and International Understanding* (Manila: Department of Tourism, 1990); *Battleground of the Brave: Bataan and Corregidor* (Manila: National Media Production Center, 1977); also see Benjamin Locsin Layug, *A Tourist Guide to Notable Philippine Historical Landmarks, Monuments and Shrines* (Quezon City: New Day, 2010), 76–82; Chuck Thompson, *The 25 Best World War II Sites – Pacific Theater* (San Francisco: Greenline Publications, 2002), 10–17.

7. There are many works on Bataan and the Philippine defense campaign. Still reliable is Louis Morton, *The Fall of the Philippines* (Washington, DC: Government Printing Office, 1953).

8. This memorial still stands, and the text remains.

9. Republic Act 3022, passed on April 6, 1961.

10. Layug, *A Tourist Guide*, 10–12; Thompson, *The 25 Best World War II Sites*, 196–203.

11. Layug, *A Tourist Guide*, 76–82; Thompson, *The 25 Best World War II Sites*, 10–17; *Corregidor: Island of Valor, Peace and International Understanding*.

12. Satoshi Nakano, "The Politics of Mourning," in Ikehata Setsuho and Lydia N. Yu-Jose, eds., *Philippines-Japan Relations* (Quezon City: Ateneo de Manila University Press, 2003), 337–376.

13. Quijano de Manila, "What Really Happened in Bataan?" *Philippines Free Press*, April 6, 1963; "Veterans Defend Bataan," *Philippines Free Press*, May 6, 1963.

14. See related chapters in Charles C. McDougald, *The Marcos File* (San Francisco: San Francisco Publications, 1987).

15. Conference on the Development of the Capas National Shrine. Quezon City: Department of National Defense, 2001. Republic Act 8221, approved on October 9, 1996.

16. Leyte Provincial Government, *Peace and Prosperity: 40th Leyte Landing Anniversary* (Tacloban: Leyte Provincial Government, 1984).

17. "MacArthur's Fall" was witnessed live on local television and proved embarrassing to the U.S. government.

18. Filipino-American Memorial Endowment brochure, revised 2015

19. Bridge for Peace information card; Bridge for Peace, *Unforgettable Voices: "Accounts of War Victims"* (Tokyo: Bridge for Peace, 2011)

20. Newspaper coverage of the events of the week: *Philippine Star* and *Philippine Daily Inquirer*, April 5–11, 2015.

21. These re-enactors belong to a group called the Philippine Living History Society, professionals who dress the part for special occasions as a hobby.

22. Interview with Alvin Alcid, chief, Research Division, National Historical Commission, January 2017. There is funding for the 75th anniversary conferences and ceremonies.

23. Secretary of the Interior Mar Roxas memorandum circular 2015–33.

24. Ambassador Juan Rocha (president of Memorare Manila 1945) to President Benigno Aquino III, correspondence. Interview with Ambassador Rocha and Ambassador Miguel Perez-Rubio.

25. The author was one of the speakers in the conference and was able to talk to some of the former internees.

26. *Philippine Daily Inquirer*, February 2015; *Philippine Star*, February 2015.

27. Programs, leaflets and invitations to the series; *Philippine Star*, February 2, 2015. The Filipinas Heritage Library located in the museum has one of the best collections of World War II publications in the Philippines.

28. Far Eastern University was the site of a Japanese Kempeitai detachment during the war; its founder and members of his family were executed by the Japanese in 1945. The honorary president, Lourdes Montinola, was the lone survivor of the family. The Ateneo de Manila Rizal Library houses the American Historical Collection, formerly the U.S. Embassy Library, and contains many rare publications relating to World War II as well as manuscripts, particularly on the UST Internment Camp.

29. Veterans Bank press release on the premiere and book launch; program. The author wrote a chapter in the book and was interviewed for the documentary.

30. *Philippine Daily Inquirer*, March 5, 2015.

31. The author was a speaker in all these events. See also invitations and programs to these events in the author's possession; Mary Jane C. Ortega, *The Men Behind the Battle of Bacsil Ridge* (San Fernando: privately printed, 2015), a comic book aimed at the young on the Filipinos who won the battle which liberated the city of San Fernando. The San Fernando activities were on March 19, 2015; Baguio's event took place on April 27; Surigao City on October 24, 2015

32. The author served as a resource person for the ceremonies. See also *A Salute to Valor: 70 Years of Freedom, April 21–23, 2015* (Puerto Princesa: City of Puerto Princesa, 2015). *Philippine Star*, April 23, 2015. The Department of Tourism and some of its local offices are also looking into developing World War II as a special tourism package.

33. This was held in the Kamuning Bakery, a pre-war Filipino-owned bakery being made a site of a regular current events forum.

34. See *Occupation and Liberation: An International Conference on the Pacific War in the Philippines: Book of Abstracts*.

Chapter Six

Singapore

Commemoration and Reconciliation

Tze M. Loo

Compared with the commemorative events by some other Asian countries, Singapore's commemoration of the 70th anniversary of the end of WWII may appear modest in scale.[1] Singapore's National Heritage Board (NHB) announced the addition of 6 new guided tours to the "Battle for Singapore" heritage project aimed at introducing visitors and locals to WWII battle sites around the island and organized an exhibition about the B and C war crimes trials.[2] On August 15—the anniversary of Japan's announcement of surrender—the Singapore Chinese Chamber of Commerce and Industry screened a Chinese-language documentary film, "Singapore 1942" on the massacre of Chinese civilians during the occupation and the activities of the Singapore Overseas Chinese Anti-Japanese Volunteer Army.[3] The NHB also organized a commemorative ceremony that was attended by 200 people; several weeks later, a "remembrance ceremony" was held at the Kranji War Cemetery. The absence of large-scale national commemorative events in Singapore may give the impression that the 70th anniversary of the end of WWII was not one of Singapore's priorities in 2015, which may seem a little surprising given that the Japanese invasion and occupation of Singapore was a brutal time during which many of the island's inhabitants suffered.[4] However, this would be a misrecognition of Singapore's substantial and sustained investment in the history of WWII. Singapore's slate of commemorative events, though modest in scale, demonstrates a radical commitment to remembering and representing the Japanese occupation on Singapore's own terms that is marked by an emphasis on reconciliation with its former wartime enemy.

The sense of reconciliation with Japan over issues of the war was especially pronounced in two of Singapore's commemorative events. The NHB-organized ceremony was held on August 27 at the former Municipal Building where Japan signed the surrender document. In his speech at the event, the minister for community, culture and the youth, Lawrence Wong, held Singapore up as:

> living proof that, with sincerity and largeness of spirit on both sides, it is possible to move on. Singapore and Japan have not let any historical grievances stand in the way of our cooperation to pursue a better quality of life for the peoples of both our nations. We have put the past behind us so that future generations can have a brighter tomorrow. So that they can enjoy peace, understanding and mutual respect—the very values that are needed to preserve harmony between nations and prevent future tragedies of war. We have embraced reconciliation; and we hope to one day see the same healing and reconciliation throughout Asia.[5]

This theme of Singapore's reconciliation with Japan took a different form several weeks later, at the Kranji War Cemetery's hour-long "End of WWII Remembrance Ceremony" on September 12.[6] Attended by representatives from 10 countries involved in the war, a highlight of the ceremony was the presence of the Japanese ambassador to Singapore, Takeuchi Haruhisa, and about 20 members of the Japanese community. The *Straits Times* reported that Takeuchi was the "first of the foreign dignitaries to lay a wreath of poppies at the foot of the Kranji War Memorial." Next to this, representatives of the Japanese community placed 1,500 origami-paper cranes, symbols of peace folded by students of Japanese schools in Singapore. Referring to the Japanese community's participation, the director of the Changi Museum, which organized the event, "called the event a 'world first' in terms of reconciling former combatants," and the guest-of-honor at the ceremony, Walter Woon, echoed this sentiment when "he hoped for a reconciliation in a similar vein for the leaders of Japan, China, and Korea."[7]

Singapore's emphasis on reconciliation with Japan during the commemoration of the 70th anniversary of the end of WWII sets it apart from those Northeast Asian countries and should be situated within the larger and longer context of the city-state's management of the history of WWII and the Japanese occupation. Many scholars have pointed to how Singapore has deployed the history of the Japanese occupation to suit its nation-building aims since the 1990s after years of amnesia, something that sets Singapore apart from its Southeast Asian neighbors.[8] Kevin Blackburn, for instance, has suggested that two patterns can be discerned in how Southeast Asian countries have dealt with the history of Japanese wartime aggression: some countries—like Singapore—deploy the history of Japanese occupation to suit the political agendas of nation-state building, while others practice a national amnesia of the war to avoid the war's overshadowing of national revolutions, or because the history of the war is too divisive for national unity in the postwar.[9] Much of this scholarship focuses on how Singapore uses the Japanese occupation to produce Singapore's national identity, but what is less noted is how a by-product of the state's strategies for managing the history of WWII emphasizes a high level of reconciliation between Singapore and its former aggressor, and this impacts how Singapore commemorated the end of WWII.

Commemorations are in general highly political acts; in East Asia, the period around the anniversary of Japan's surrender on August 15 has, for some time now, become highly politicized. It is a moment in which postwar Japan performs its attitude toward its war responsibility and aggressive acts—performances that are invariably evaluated for their sincerity, or lack thereof. At the same time, nation states who suffered Japan's wartime aggressions use the period to present *their* understanding of the history of Japan's wartime conduct and, as is often the case, to include a criticism of the perceived inadequacies of Japan's contrition. The end of the war and its commemoration in East Asia are thus, in this sense, a proxy stage on which some nation states fight the history war. Political actors were not unaware of how the commemorations in 2015 had the potential to function as a way to criticize Japan, as suggested by Taiwanese president Ma Ying-Jeou's comments in an interview with Japanese journalists about his confidence that Taiwan's commemoration of the war's end would not hurt the relationship between Taiwan and Japan.[10] Commemorations of the war in East Asia do not necessarily have to take on these meanings, but in 2015 they took on significations that exceeded their meanings for individual countries and became collectively a circuit of "commemoration as critique." Singapore however, has little use for this kind of commemoration for it sees itself as having long since achieved a reconciliation with Japan on the question of Japan's war responsibility in WWII and its conduct in Singapore, and this paper traces the history of this condition.

***

Singapore achieved independence in 1965 but the city state did not pay much attention to its history—including its history of Japan's brutal 3½ year occupation of Singapore—for almost two decades after that, considering it too divisive to be useful for producing a sense of unity and common purpose that the country needed at the time.[11] There was a concern that the separate histories of Chinese, Indian, and Malay migration that came to populate Singapore would provide little basis for their rootedness in the island. There was also the worry that these disparate histories would exacerbate communal tensions that had carried over from the period of British and Japanese rule into the postwar. The newly independent nation state had good reason to be wary: riots between Chinese and Malays had in fact broken out in 1964 and

1969 and were potent reminders of the explosiveness of issues of race in Singapore at the time.

The result was what Brenda Yeoh and Shirlena Huang call a "structural amnesia" about the island's past, but beginning in the mid-1980s, Singapore turned to history as a tool to strengthen Singaporean national identity, motivated by several anxieties that emerged and reinforced each other at that time.[12] The first was an apprehension that Singapore's rapid modernization had resulted in a level of "Westernization" that threatened its "traditional values" and "Asian roots."[13] The second was a concern with whether Singapore could continue to grow economically and remain competitive.[14] A third source of dis-ease was an anxiety about whether the younger generation of Singaporeans, who had been born into the country's relative economic prosperity and who knew little of the hardship of the early years of independence, would have the mettle to meet and overcome the challenges that Singapore now faced.

A speech by the second deputy prime minister at the time, S. Rajaratnam, offers an indication of the state's thinking of the usability of its past. Titled "The Uses and Abuses of the Past," Rajaratnam held up Poland's successful deployment of its long history that predated the twentieth-century introduction of Communism in the service of its national identity in the present as a proper use of history.[15] Regarding Singapore's own history, he signaled an expansive and accepting sense of the island's past by talking about how the city-state, in a move that "completely mystified" "many of our third world friends," declared the British colonial official, Sir Stamford Raffles, the official founder of Singapore.[16] Rajaratnam explained that this decision was simply proper history because it was a fact that Singapore was founded as a British colony and that "to pretend otherwise is to falsify history."[17] For him, Singapore's approach was not one of imperial nostalgia, nor did it allow for a whitewashing of British colonialism's excesses. Instead, it would rigorously evaluate its colonial past, discern its positive dimensions, consolidate its strengths while jettisoning its negative elements, and move on to a future that was entirely its own. While Rajaratnam did not discuss the Japanese occupation directly, his speech gave an indication of the state's highly pragmatic approach to its history. Embracing the usability of the past for its current needs allowed Singapore to master *all* aspects of its histories—even the ones imposed upon it—on its own terms for the present and future good of the nation.[18]

In November 1988, a government committee outlined which parts of the island's past would be useful for its present.[19] It recommended that Singapore "remember the lessons of our history and transmit this to new generations of Singaporeans so that they fully appreciate the factors that made for Singapore's success," and called for the opportunity to "learn from the pioneering enterprise of those who came before us so that we constantly renew work values and maintain the adaptiveness which underlies our economic success today."[20] The committee identified five different kinds of heritage that were useful for this endeavor, the first of which it called "nation building heritage" that was:

> derived from the historical events and experiences we have lived through and which have shaped our lives. Our experience of living under British colonial administration; the Japanese Occupation, the post-war struggle for independence and the struggle against Communism are some of the key events and experiences which have made us what we are today.[21]

Of the key moments in Singapore's history outlined here, the committee singled out the Japanese occupation for further elaboration. It noted that "as the trauma fades away, the lessons of the War are a valuable source of experience for Singaporeans. . . . The time may now be right for an objective account of the War to be presented to young Singaporeans who have no personal memories of the traumas and who can therefore be entirely objective."[22] In so doing, the committee effectively elevated the Japanese invasion and occupation to a central role in the cultivation of Singaporean national identity.

The use of Singapore's history took clear shape in 1997 with the introduction of "National Education" into school curriculums as a way "to develop national cohesion, cultivate the instinct for survival as a nation and instill in our students confidence in our nation's future . . . [and] a sense of belonging and emotional rootedness to Singapore."[23] At the center of National Education was an official narrative of Singapore's formation, "The Singapore Story," whose primary message was "how Singapore succeeded against the odds to become a nation."[24] Lee Hsien Loong, who was deputy prime minister of Singapore at the time, outlined the contours of this historical narrative when he launched National Education:

> As a British colony, from 1942 to 1945 for three and a half years of the Japanese Occupation we suffered a traumatic experience of cruelty, brutality, hunger, and deprivation. We lived through the post-war years of Communist-inspired unrest and upheaval. We then joined with the Federation of Malaya to form Malaysia. Despite pressure and intimidation we stood firm in Malaysia against the communalists. . . . As a result we suddenly found ourselves out on our own as an independent country, with few means to make a living or defend ourselves. Yet we developed our economy, built up the [Singapore Armed Forces], educated and housed our people, got them to work together, and gradually became one nation. Year by year we transformed Singapore into what it is today.[25]

The narrative centers on how Singapore's existence in the present is possible only because of how the island's inhabitants and its leaders overcame the repeated challenges presented to them in which the Japanese occupation is cast as the first moment of crises that impacted the island's inhabitants in two important ways. First, they acquired a resilience from having suffered and survived the Japanese occupation which formed the basis of a later Singaporean nationalism; second, they experienced the pitfalls of depending on others/foreign powers for the island's defense and security.

Almost a decade after the launch of National Education, the National Archives of Singapore opened a new museum in 2006. Called Memories of Old Ford Factory (MOFF), it was dedicated to the history of everyday life during the Japanese occupation of Singapore and was a clear articulation of the role that it played in Singapore's national history.[26] The museum's coverage of the period of the Japanese occupation left no question about the brutality of Japan's occupation of Singapore. Beginning with an account of the "Sook Ching" massacre, MOFF's narrative emphasized the brutality of the *kempeitai* (military police), highlighting the surveillance, arrest, and torture of anti-Japanese elements within the local community. It also documented the less dramatic—but no less violent—quotidian cruelties and indignities that the island's inhabitants were subjected to.[27] Importantly, while acknowledging that occupation policy to divide the island along communal lines and that the varying treatment of different ethnic groups produced the notion that the non-Chinese community enjoyed better treatment from the Japanese, MOFF's narrative emphasized that *all* communities suffered.[28] Nor were the exactions limited to bodily or psychological ones: occupation authorities' demand that Chinese communities in Singapore and Malaya "donate" $50 million to "atone" for their support of the British and mainland Chinese government's fight against Japan featured prominently.

However, Japanese brutality was only one part of MOFF's narrative. The exhibition's primary focus was on everyday life during the Japanese occupation and emphasized the canny and creative skills that *all* people who lived under Japanese rule in Singapore—local, migrant, European—used to survive, and celebrated their resilience and courage under conditions of terrible brutality and brutalization. The museum noted the relative quickness with which everyday life in Singapore reacquired a semblance of rhythm and routine as occupation authorities attempted to impose a level of stability. Two months after the cessation of hostilities, shops and businesses reopened, and banks and the postal service resumed operations. By April, primary schools throughout Malaya resumed classes; the judicial system reopened in May. But hardship and suffering were constant, and MOFF underscored the various ways that people coped, whether by growing more food in vegetable plots, finding ways to acquire necessities on the black market, or improvising with substitutes for soap, cooking oil, and flour, or turning to traditional medicines for illnesses. Woven into the narratives of resilience are also moments of joy and leisure. People celebrated marriages and holidays, restaurants continued to serve meals (granted the best restaurants were off limits to locals), and there were gatherings at teahouses for storytelling and at amusement parks for gambling.

While constantly present, Japanese brutality and the hardship of the period forms the backdrop against which the primary aspect of MOFF's narrative—the experience of living in occupied Singapore for the island's inhabitants—dominated. Indeed, the exhibition catalogue introduced its material this way:

> In [this] volume, the story continues from the fall of Singapore on 15 February 1942, focusing on daily life during the 44 months of Japanese rule. Through the realism of the story and accompanying visuals, open your eyes to life under Japanese rule and take away valuable lessons of resilience, hope, creativity and adaptability taught by our forefathers. [29]

For example, in dealing with the issue of death from malnutrition, rather than focus on Japanese mismanagement of resources or people's plight during food rationing, MOFF's narrative turns the issue into one of resilience and adaptability, as demonstrated in the museum's use of oral history from Mohinder Singh, who credited the Sikh community's ability to adapt to harsh conditions for saving many in that community from malnutrition. [30] MOFF's narrative strategy of radical localization of memory to focus on *Singapore's* experience of the war that apprehends the occupation from the perspective of the island's inhabitants rather than that of the invading Japanese had important—if unintended—effects. It takes the focus off Japanese actions and the period of the Japanese occupation is important for what the people of Singapore got out of the experience. In a sense, MOFF is an example of a mastery of the history of the war which produces an interpretation that empowers Singapore in the present.

The radical localization of the history of war was also evident in the lesson of never depending on a foreign power for the island's defense and this featured prominently in the first section of the museum. Detailing the experience of Allied Prisoners-of-War (POWs), its most arresting feature were two life-sized statues of gaunt POWs, bare from the waist up to reveal their emaciated torsos, placed on either side of a wall of stained glass panels featuring the artwork of William Haxworth, who captured the everyday life of POWs while himself a prisoner in Changi Prison. The display highlights how POWs had to "exercise considerable ingenuity to survive" the brutal conditions of their captivity, and suggests that Europeans in Singapore—both those who called it home and who fought for its defense—suffered no less than local communities during the occupation. At the same time, however, the display can also be read as having less laudatory meanings: while celebrating their courage, this presentation not only emphasized the failure of

British military power, it also stripped away any semblance of British super-iority in explicit, unequivocal ways. The figures of half-naked, emaciated POWs were especially powerful in this regard. If the fallibility of British power and its agents is taken as a framing device, then the narrative of everyday life for local communities under occupation that followed can be read as a story of how life in Singapore could continue to function without British rule, even under the most brutal of conditions.

This changed attitude toward the British was crucial to the island's politi-cal future. In his memoirs, Singapore's first prime minister, Lee Kuan Yew, was unequivocal about his "disillusionment" after realizing that Japanese occupation authorities were "more cruel, more brutal, more unjust and more vicious than the British." But he also wrote eloquently of the impact that the Japanese invasion had on his thinking about British colonials, whose coward-ly behavior in the face of the advancing Japanese forces lay waste to British claims to superiority.[31] This was important, as Lee goes on to note, because "the British had built up the myth of their inherent superiority so convincing-ly that most Asiatics thought it hopeless to challenge them. But now one Asiatic race had dared to defy them and smashed that myth." That this was one of MOFF's key messages was reflected in remarks by Singapore's then president, S.R. Nathan, in MOFF's exhibition catalogue and resource guide in which he noted that:

> Singapore paid a high price during the occupation, but arguably there were some compensations. The eclipse of our colonial masters, previously assumed to be all-powerful, meant that the journey to independence was shorter than it would have been otherwise. As a result of shared experiences, our people began to identify with Singapore, rather than seeing themselves as Chinese, Indians, or Malays owing prime allegiance to the place of their ancestors.[32]

MOFF's narrative put the war and Japanese occupation into the service of overcoming and criticizing British colonialism, casting it as a period that enabled the island's inhabitants to make the epistemological shift to a post-colonial imagination that could envision life without the British as colonial masters.

***

In MOFF's narrative, the Japanese occupation of Singapore was represented not as an open wound for the city state nor an unresolved issue between Singapore and Japan today. There was a strong sense that while deeply committed to remembering the Japanese occupation, Singapore had moved on, having achieved reconciliation of a kind with this difficult past and its former wartime enemy. Indeed, Singapore's politicians have embraced a forward-looking position when it comes to Japan's wartime aggressions in

Singapore. As early as 1969 Lee Kuan Yew noted that "my generation and that of my elders cannot forget [the Japanese occupation] as long as we live. We can forgive, but we are unlikely ever to forget. . . . Our population is by and large a hardheaded one. The policy of the government is not to allow the unhappy experiences of the past to inhibit us from a policy which can enhance our growth rates by Japanese participation in our industry," which Chin Kin Wah frames as a clear reflection of "a general tendency [in Southeast Asia] not to allow negative historical memories to cloud overall relationships."[33] Similarly in 2006, then prime minister Goh Chok Tong, in comments about the difficulties facing Sino-Japanese relations stemming from Japanese politicians' visits to the Yasukuni Shrine and the history of WWII, said that:

> Singapore too suffered under Japanese occupation during World War II. We have not forgotten the past, but we have moved on. For we believe in building a better future than be forever weighed down by the bad memories of the past.[34]

In 2015, Lee Hsien Loong commented on the 70th anniversary of the end of WWII by recognizing that war-related issues continued to reverberate throughout Asia and affected Japan's relationships with China and Korea, but suggested that it "is past the time to put this history behind us properly, just like the Europeans have done."[35] This is also reflected in how Singaporeans in general do not see Japan's wartime conduct as posing a problem for relations between Singapore and Japan today, with a majority of Singaporeans regarding Japan as a "trustworthy friend."[36] Even as Singaporeans remember the occupation's brutality and suffering, the period seems to be safely in the past and sentiments of revenge are largely absent, as is any sense that Japan still needs to do more to compensate Singapore for its aggression in WWII.

But Japan and its wartime conduct have not always enjoyed such an untroubled place in Singapore. In March 1962, the Singapore Chinese Chamber of Commerce (SCCC) called on the Singapore government to demand an apology and compensation from Japan after mass graves of Chinese victims of Japanese wartime atrocities were discovered in the eastern part of the island, and Japan remained silent on the issue.[37] On June 23, 1963—more than a year later—the UPI reported that Japan was considering offering 600 million yen as "condolence money" but Tokyo denied this. The SCCC immediately condemned Japan's "shrewd, insincere, and evasive attitude." Several days later, SCCC members met with the Japanese counsel-general, Tanaka Hirota, in what the latter described as an informal meeting, but that meeting produced no agreement.[38]

During a meeting between then prime minister Lee Kuan Yew and Tanaka on August 7, 1962, Japan proposed "technical and scientific projects and
education and scientific equipment" for Singapore's four institutions of higher learning.[39] The SCCC again rejected these proposals as "insincere" and
announced plans to organize a rally of 100,000 to press the issue. The Japanese government's next salvo was a warning from Tanaka not to jeopardize
the increasing economic cooperation between Japan and Singapore with this
demand for compensation. He went on to state that Japan was not legally
obligated to meet any demand for reparations because it had settled all such
claims with Great Britain with the signing of the San Francisco Peace Treaty.
Tanaka further noted that Japan's offer of equipment and the establishment
of a cancer research center was "a gesture of atonement . . . made on moral
grounds" and even chastised Singapore for being "improper" in its attempt to
"negotiate the terms."[40]

If Tanaka hoped that this hard line would bring about Singapore's ac-
quiescence, he was gravely mistaken. The SCCC expressed its "dissatisfac-
tion of the highest degree" with Tanaka's statements, with its president, Ko
Teck Kin—in a gesture to the multiple dimensions of accountability and
blame—pointing out that Singapore was "demanding a settlement of a 'blood
debt,' not a war debt."[41] Furthermore, Ko noted that gestures of atonement
were meaningless unless they had specific monetary value and made a claim
for $50 million.[42] He countered that Japan's offer—which Tanaka did not
specify the value for—could be well below that amount, and this was all the
more egregious because Japan had amassed a surplus in its trade with Singapore. Ko also announced that the SCCC was calling for a mass rally to "press
for a reasonable settlement" and hinted at a boycott of Japanese goods if
Japan did not meet Singapore's demands.

The rally took place on August 25 and was attended by more than
100,000 people. Speaking to the crowd, Ko cast Singapore's demands as "a
struggle between justice and foul play," and that "horrors of the Japanese
occupation endure" for the island's inhabitants "which could not be erased
without atonement."[43] Noting that "without malice we have allowed the
Japanese to come among us to trade," he pointed out that Singapore was not
seeking revenge but only wanted justice for past wrongs. As a demonstration
of the SCCC's "peaceful but insistent demand," the rally adopted three resolutions: that the people of all races in Malaya and Singapore unite to press
Japan for compensation for the atrocities against the civilian populations
during WWII; a campaign of "non-cooperation" against Japan should it fail
to settle the matter satisfactorily; and that Singapore's government not issue
any new visas to Japanese people if the issue is not settled.[44] These resolutions were not empty statements because the Singapore government threw its
full weight behind the rally in support, with Lee Kuan Yew touching on this
in his speech at the rally:

For after tonight, once the resolutions have been passed and adopted, the Government's attitude to the Japanese Government must alter. A stand once taken cannot be abandoned until a satisfactory settlement has been reached. Once these resolutions calling for non-cooperation have been passed, at all levels, amongst the people and in the Government, there must be non-cooperation, until a fair and just solution is found.[45]

To that end, Lee announced that while Japanese projects already underway in Singapore could continue, no additional visas would be issued for new Japanese commercial or industrial projects. For Singapore, which was dependent on technical and managerial skills from Japan for its industrialization, this was not a decision that the government made lightly.

The response of Japan's Foreign Office to the rally was the announcement of Japan's refusal to negotiate with Singapore as long as it "assumes a threatening attitude."[46] It added that while Singapore lacked standing to make such claims, Japan was "ready to show its 'gesture' of atonement" but it would not comply with any demand for a large amount of money.[47] On September 6, the SCCC delivered an ultimatum to Japan to settle the issue within ten days, or face economic non-cooperation. The boycott of Japanese goods and the cessation of exports to Japan began on September 16 but was suspended on September 28 after Tokyo gave assurances to a Japanese business delegation from Singapore that it would address the issue and Tengku Abdul Rahman, the prime minister of Malaysia—to which Singapore was then a part of—agreed to take up the issue with Japan. Japan and Malaysia discussed the issue several times in the next two years but saw no resolution.

However, following Singapore's full independence on August 9, 1965, after being ejected from Malaysia, the issue moved quickly toward resolution. On October 26, 1966, Singapore and Japan issued a joint communique announcing a settlement: Japan would provide $25 million in grants and another $25 million in loans to Singapore. The SCCC accepted this settlement on November 30, and the Singapore government considered the issue of Singapore's "blood debt" to be resolved.[48] With the issue behind it, Singapore welcome a new era of relations with Tokyo, which Lee Kuan Yew reflected in comments on his subsequent visit to Tokyo in 1968 this way:

My visit demonstrates officially that we are friends. The past is the past and it is the future we are interested in. I was able to pay a call on the Japanese Emperor and the Empress and I think it's a symbolic desire on both sides to begin anew.[49]

Singapore and Japan, it seemed, had successfully navigated the issue of compensation and achieved reconciliation about Japan's wartime responsibilities.

***

The process of historical reconciliation in Asia is often compared to the process in Europe, and the state of Japan's postwar relations with its neighbors compared to Germany's. However, as Gi-Wook Shin reminds us in his discussion of historical reconciliation in East Asia of the need to "continue to search for an East Asian model, while using the European experiences as a reference," Asia has "specific histories, memories, and perhaps even different cultural modes of reconciliation" that make it unreasonable to expect that Asia will simply replicate Europe's process.[50] The process by which nation states reach historical reconciliation is a highly situated one that is influenced by the specificities of place and time, and there is likely more than one path to its achievement. Shin's reminder also raises the possibility of there being more than one understanding of what reconciliation should, can, or ought to comprise of. This should not be taken to mean that, the people of Singapore for instance, have a culturally relative sense of historical wrong or a conception of redress that is different from more universally held ones; as Singapore's demand for compensation for the "blood debt" demonstrates, it had a clear anger about Japanese atrocities and a strong certainty about its right to demand that Tokyo compensate them for those wrongs.

But Singapore's example also demonstrates that the settlement of claims between nation states depends not only on the moral legitimacy of the individuals who have suffered injustice or the force of their claims, but also in large part on the national governments who undertake negotiations and who—in the final analysis—make the decision about the resolution of those claims. Kevin Blackburn and Karl Hack, who show that Singapore deftly managed this demand for compensation by moving it away from a focus on the suffering of the Chinese community toward a sense of the collective victimization of the people of Singapore as a whole during the Japanese occupation, note that:

> There was no Japanese apology, but the Singapore government chose to view the matter as closed. Lee privately slapped down Chinese Chamber of Commerce demands for more. The latter were angry that the settlement only included $25 million as a grant, not the $50 million targeted, and had been accepted without consultation with them. But they were told not to pursue the issue as it would harm much needed Japanese investment at a time when the country badly needed to accelerate economic development.[51]

Indeed, Lee sent a letter—the contents of which were not made public—to the SCCC after the latter remained undecided on the settlement, and it accepted the terms a month later.[52] While the Singapore and Japanese governments resolved the issue at the diplomatic level, it raises the question of what happens in negotiations when a state, with its own agendas and exigencies, reaches an agreement that diverges from what local or otherwise vested parties—who must depend on the state to represent them in these international negotiations—would prefer.

Blackburn and Hack's analysis raises another related issue: does the lack of an apology from Japan render the reconciliation that Singapore underscores somehow "less authentic" or "less genuine"?[53] The answer to this is inflected, at least in part, on what the political realities of the moment were thought to allow, as well as what actors considered to be the desired result of reconciliation. At the time that it was searching for a solution to the "blood debt" issue, Singapore faced serious political instability and an uncertain economic future. In a time when Singapore's political and economic survival was at stake, its leaders privileged solutions that would most benefit the country in the moment. Furthermore, Singapore was trying to seek redress from a Japan that was not only much stronger economically despite suffering devastation in the war, it was also a Japan that had shown itself to be most unwilling to address Singapore's claim for compensation, and did so only most grudgingly when it did. In remarks the day before Singapore and Japan announced the settlement, Singapore's foreign minister, S. Rajaratnam, told the visiting Japanese foreign minister Shiina Etsusaburo that, "we cannot shape a bright future in Asia solely in terms of old and unpleasant memories . . . it is good to have a long memory, but what we dig out of the past should be such as to help us advance toward a brighter and happier future," an indication of the political calculation that went into accepting Japan's offer of loans and grants, over the $50 million compensation that the SCCC originally demanded.[54]

Lee Kuan Yew elaborated on this position in a speech to the SCCC several months earlier that also casts the settlement that Singapore eventually reached with Japan in a different light. Underscoring Singapore's vulnerable political and economic situation at the time, Lee called on his audience to have the courage and "a determination to do what is fair and right by ourselves and by our neighbors, and to ensure our future in Southeast Asia."[55] This required Singaporeans not only to learn how to adapt quickly to the new situation, it also demanded that they act with caution. Without the "safety net" provided by inclusion into the British Empire or Malaysia, Singapore would have to take responsibility for each decision that it made henceforth. As such, Lee counselled that "every act—either doing or 'non-doing'—must be carefully weighed" and that in some instances, "an abstention from an act is more meaningful than the commission of an act." Lee used the "blood debt" issue to develop this point. He said:

> Let us sit back and think. What is this worth? Fifty million dollars! What percentage is this of the revenue collected last year which was $450 million? One-ninth, one-tenth. For one-tenth of the revenue, you will wash away all the

sins of the past and all is forgiven and forgotten? Is it worth the pursuing at this time? *Let us take a deep breath and re-calculate*. What is at stake in our relationship between our neighbors and ourselves—and that includes Japan— is worth more than $50 million. *And I would myself prefer to have that $50 million unpaid—unless the gesture of atonement is one accompanied by a deep and sincere regret for what has happened.* Not a cash payment to wipe off an evil they perpetrated. But I think these bones and all the sadness of the past should make us think of something even more important than a blood debt: can you be sure that this will never happen again?[56]

While Lee urged his audience to consider whether or not it was in Singapore's best interest to pursue the issue, he was also laying out a position about reconciliation with Japan. Lee was unequivocal about what he considered a proper resolution: compensation had to be "accompanied by a deep and sincere regret for what has happened" and that compensation should not be a way for Japan to escape responsibility and remorse. In the context of these remarks, the settlement reached between Singapore and Japan on the "blood debt" may have produced reconciliation at the level of diplomatic relations between the two countries, but as Lee's remarks suggest, Singapore's notion of reconciliation was much more complicated than its acceptance of the settlement with Japan would indicate at first.

Indeed, despite the sense of having been reconciled with its former wartime occupier, Singapore remains critical of Japan's current conduct and the history of Japan's past aggressions can still evoke strong animosity. Singapore's leaders have frequently called on Japan to be more forthcoming and clearer with admissions of culpability for its wartime aggressions and to rein in revisionist histories.[57] Singaporeans also continue to exhibit deep sensitivity about the Japanese occupation as a period of brutality and are critical of any attempts that might sanitize it. In February 2017, the Memories of Ford Factory (MOFF) exhibition was scheduled to be replaced by a new permanent gallery similarly dedicated to the everyday experience of the Japanese occupation and it was be named "Syonan Gallery: War and its Legacies." The gallery, however, was renamed after many Singaporeans voiced their objections to the use of the name that was imposed on Singapore by its Japanese occupiers, and cited the deep hurt to survivors of the war and their families that its use evoked.[58] Thus while Singapore's commemorations of the 70th anniversary of the end of WWII may have contained a strong sense of diplomatic reconciliation with Japan, beneath it is a deep memory of the Japanese occupation which informs the people of Singapore about what is acceptable in their nation state's quest to "move on"—and what is not.

NOTES

1. For instance, China's commemoration event on September 3, 2015, marking the end of the "Chinese People's War of Resistance Against Japanese Aggression and the World Anti-Fascist War" included a parade through Tian'anmen Square attended by world leaders which the Xinhua news agency hailed as "a glorious event that has been 70 years in the making." Taiwan's events were on a smaller scale, but its commemoration of "the 70th anniversary of the end of the War of Resistance Against Japan and the retrocession of Taiwan" was no less pronounced and deliberate. They consisted of 16 events over a 3-month period organized by Taiwan's Executive Yuan. In Great Britain, ceremonies to commemorate "Victory over Japan" Day (VJ Day) were attended by Queen Elizabeth, members of the royal family, and then prime minister David Cameron.

2. The National Heritage Board is a statutory board under the Ministry of Culture, Community, and Youth and is "responsible for telling the Singapore story, sharing the Singaporean experience and imparting our Singapore spirit." (https://www.nhb.gov.sg/about-us/overview) These new additions included a bunker in the former British naval base in Woodlands which had previously been off limits to the public. National Heritage Board, "Media Release: New World War II Tours and Exhibition on War Crimes Tribunal to Commemorate 70th Anniversary of the Liberation of Singapore," 28 January 2015. http://www.nhb.gov.sg/~/media/nhb/files/media/releases/ new%20releases/ 2015–19.pdf.

3. The film was produced by a civic group known as the WWII History Research Association and was followed by a forum, during which participants spoke of their experiences during the occupation. "Session at SCCCI auditorium tomorrow to mark end of World War II 70 years ago," *Straits Times*, 15 August 2015.

4. To be sure, Singapore's national energies were largely focused on year-long celebrations of the 50th anniversary of the island's independence. The city-state's emotional energies were also consumed by the passing of its first prime minister, Lee Kuan Yew, in March of 2015.

5. "Commemorating the 70th Anniversary of the end of World War II." Speech by Lawrence Wong, 27 August 2015. https://www.mccy.gov.sg/en/news/speeches/2015/Aug/WWII_Commemorative_Event.aspx.

6. The cemetery is the resting place for Allied military service people who lost their lives during the invasion and occupation of Singapore and is managed by the Commonwealth War Graves Commission.

7. "Marking 70th Year of End of WWII," *Straits Times*, September 13, 2015.

8. Diana Wong calls Singapore's "elaborate program of commemoration" in 1995 "one exception to the pattern of official indifference [in other parts of Southeast Asia]." Diana Wong, "Memory Suppression, Memory Production: The Japanese Occupation of Singapore," in *Perilous Memories: The Asia-Pacific War(s)* (Durham: Duke University Press, 2001), 219.

9. Kevin Blackburn, "War memory and nation-building in South East Asia," *South East Asia Research* 18: 1 (2010), 5. For an eloquent discussion of Indonesia's privileging of memories of the struggle for liberation over memories of the Japanese invasion and occupation, see Anthony Reid, "Remembering and Forgetting War and Revolution," in *Beginning to Remember: The Past in the Indonesia Present* (Singapore: Singapore University Press, 2005).

10. "Taiwan says remembering end of WWII won't hurt ties with Japan," Kyodo News, 15 April 2015. The Japanese government is also similarly aware of the power of commemorations of the war's end, with the cabinet secretary criticizing Ban Ki-moon's participation in Beijing's commemorative ceremony as contradicting the expectation of the U.N.'s neutrality in world affairs. "China Blasts Japanese Criticism of Ban's Attendance of WWII Event," *Japan Times Online*, September 1, 2015, http://www.japantimes.co.jp/news/2015/09/01/national/politics-diplomacy/china-blasts-japanese-criticism-bans-attendance-wwii-event/.

11. The island's inhabitants suffered a great deal under Japanese rule as victims of atrocities and everyday brutalities. The most well-known of the Japanese atrocities in Singapore was the massacre of Chinese in the early days of the occupation, during which some estimate 50,000 people were murdered. See "Transcript of Minister Mentor Lee Kuan Yew's interview with Mark Jacobson from National Geographic on 6 July 2009 (for National Geographic magazine Jan 2010 edition)," National Archives of Singapore, document number 20100104007. For a

discussion of the different numbers of casualties, see Hayashi Hirofumi, "The Battle of Singapore, the Massacre of Chinese and Understanding of the Issue in Postwar Japan," *Asia-Pacific Journal*, Vol. 28–4–09, July 13, 2009. Local communities were not the only victims; Japanese brutality toward European POWs in Singapore is also well-documented.

12. Brenda Yeoh and Shirlena Huang, "Strengthening the Nation's Roots? Heritage Policies in Singapore," in *Social Policy in Post-Industrial Singapore* (Leiden: Brill, 2008), 201.

13. Ibid., 202.

14. Following independence, Singapore pursued a labor-intensive economic model as a way to address the high levels of unemployment and by the 1970s had become a manufacturing hub with a highly skilled workforce. With no natural resources of its own and a limited population, Singapore's economy aimed in the 1980s to move toward service and high technology sectors. Singapore's high wage policies in the early 80s to attract highly qualified labor contributed to the country's first recession in 1985–86, and resulted in deep anxieties about Singapore's competitiveness. See *Report of the Economic Committee: The Singapore Economy: New Directions*, February 1986. Ministry of Trade and Industry, http://www.mti.gov.sg/ ResearchRoom/ Documents/ app.mti.gov.sg/data/pages/885/doc/econ.pdf.

15. S. Rajaratnam, "The Uses and Abuses of the Past," vol. 8 (Singapore: Ministry of Culture, 1984), 1–9. I also refer to Rajaratnam's speech in "Historical Reconciliation in Southeast Asia: Notes from Singapore" in Jun-Hyeok Kwak and Melissa Nobles, *Inherited Responsibility and Historical Reconciliation in East Asia* (London: Routledge, 2013).

16. Rajaratnam, "The Uses and Abuses of the Past," 5–6.

17. Rajaratnam, "The Uses and Abuses of the Past," 6. Importantly, Rajaratnam dispelled any notion that recognizing Raffles as the country's founder was something that betrayed Singapore's credentials as an independent, post-colonial state; instead this was an example of a "balanced assessment of imperialism" which, regardless of what one's personal feelings toward British colonialism might be, recognized that imperial rule had both "positive and negative aspects."

18. Rajaratnam's pragmatism echoes the guiding principle of Lee Kuan Yew's vision for Singapore during his long leadership of Singapore, a notion that continues to guide Singapore's government today. See "Keep pragmatism as guiding principle," *Straits Times*, 30 March 2015.

19. The Committee on Heritage, formed by the Advisory Council on Culture and the Arts and tasked to make "recommendations to encourage Singaporeans to be more widely informed, creative, refined in taste, gracious in lifestyle and appreciative of our collective heritage." Committee on Heritage, "The Committee on Heritage Report, November 1988," 1988, 1.

20. Ibid., 8.

21. "The Committee on Heritage Report," 27.

22. "The Committee on Heritage Report," 31.

23. Ministry of Education National Education website: http://ne.moe.edu.sg/ne/slot/u223/ ne/index.html (accessed 10 June 2015). See also Yeow Tong Chia, "History education for nation building and state formation: The case of Singapore," *Citizenship Teaching & Learning* (7:2), 191–207.

24. "Speech by B.G. Lee Hsien Loong, Deputy Prime Minister at the launch of National Education," 17 May 1997. http://www.moe.gov.sg/media/speeches/1997/170597.htm.

25. "Speech by B.G. Lee Hsien Loong, Deputy Prime Minister at the launch of National Education." National Education was not intended as a separate subject of instruction, but was rather to function as a set of ideas that infused all levels of instruction. See, Steven Tan Kwang Sen and Goh Chor Boon (eds.), *Securing Our Future: Sourcebook for Infusing National Education into the Primary School Curriculum* (Singapore: Prentice Hall, 2003).

26. The museum is located on the premises of the former Ford motor factory, which was the first motor car assembly plant in Southeast Asia and was completed only months before Japan began its invasion of Southeast Asia. Japanese imperial forces used the factory during the occupation first as their headquarters and then to manufacture trucks, but the factory is most well known as the site of the British surrender to Japan on 15 February, 1942. I also discuss MOFF in my essay, "Historical Reconciliation in Southeast Asia: Notes from Singapore." MOFF was replaced in 2017 by a new exhibition. See n. 24.

27. These issues are more fully developed in the accompanying exhibition catalogue and resource guide, Lee Geok Boi, *The Syonan Years: Singapore under Japanese Rule 1942–1945* (Singapore: National Archives of Singapore & Epigram, 2005). It documents the threat of torture at every turn (for example, for not surrendering radio sets to be set only to the occupation's Syonan Radio, 117), censorship of information (110), cultural control through things like Japanese language education and a Japanese calendar of celebrations and festivals, dire economic conditions of food rationing and shortages, and murder of the very sick (236).

28. "[I]t soon became clear to the local population that on the whole, Syonan residents suffered the same fate under Japanese rulers. No one community was completely safe from the horrors of rape, looting of assets, and beheading." Ibid., 50.

29. Ibid., 9.

30. MOFF's narrative included Mohinder Singh's words: "Why was it [referring to the relatively fewer Sikh deaths] so? It was not that we were the favorite sons of the Japanese that were given anything. No! The same rations were issued to the Sikhs, why the Indian community died so much? Why not the Sikhs? That is the real question. According to the situation we have seen, (the answer is) adaptability. We are big eaters, basically we are wheat eaters, ghee eaters . . . so immediately changed ourselves to (eat) maize, rice . . . We couldn't get any butter or ghee, we used the red palm oil. Immediately adapted . . . We told so many friends, 'Why don't you use it' [they replied that] 'it's not tasty.' Don't look after taste now. See the situation. Adapt yourself to the situation." Ibid., 235.

31. Lee wrote: "In 70 days of surprises, upsets, and stupidities [during the Japanese invasion], British colonial society was shattered, and with it all the assumptions of the Englishman's superiority. The Asiatics were supposed to panic when the firing started, yet they were the stoical ones who took the casualties and died without hysteria. It was the white civilian bosses who ducked under tables when the bombs and shells fell. It was the white civilians and government officers in Penang who, on 16 December 1941, in the quiet of the night, fled the island for the 'safety' of Singapore, abandoning the Asiatics to their fate. . . . The white in charge had gone. Stories of their scramble to save their skins led the Asiatics to see them as selfish and cowardly. . . . The whites had proved as frightened and at a loss as to what to do as the Asiatics, if not more so. The Asiatics had looked to them for leadership and they had failed them." Lee Kuan Yew, *The Singapore Story: Memoirs of Lee Kuan Yew* (Singapore: Prentice-Hall, 1998), 52–53.

32. National Archives, *Battle for Singapore: Fall of the Impregnable Fortress* (Singapore: National Archives of Singapore, 2011), 6.

33. Chin Kin Wah, "Regional Perceptions of China and Japan," in *China, India, Japan and the Security of Southeast Asia* (Singapore: Institute of Southeast Asian Studies, 1993), 11.

34. Goh Chok Tong, "Towards an East Asian Renaissance" (4th Asia-Pacific Round Table, Singapore, February 6, 2006).

35. Lee Hsien Loong, "Keynote Address" (14th Asia Security Summit, Singapore, May 29, 2015).

36. Ministry of Foreign Affairs of Japan, "2008 Opinion Poll on Japan in Six ASEAN Countries," http://www.mofa.go.jp/region/asia-paci/asean/survey/index.html.

37. "Mass War Graves," *Straits Times*, February 24, 1962; "Discovery of 40 More Mass Graves," *Straits Times*, February 27, 1962; "War Massacre of Civilians: Compensation Demand," *Straits Times*, March 1, 1962. For a history of the Chinese community's early postwar agitation for compensation, see Kevin Blackburn and Karl Hack, *War Memory and the Making of Modern Malaysia and Singapore* (NUS Press, 2012), 146–55.

38. "Atonement Talks No Agreement," *Straits Times*, July 6, 1963.

39. "War Compensation Talks Progress," *Straits Times*, August 7, 1963.

40. "Tanaka: Don't Hurt Trade Ties," *Straits Times*, August 9, 1963.

41. "Atonement Will Cost $50 Million," *Straits Times*, August 10, 1963.

42. Ko did not give a reason for this figure, but another member of the SCCC had previously noted that claims for compensation were based on "the unwarranted killing of people and the extortion of $50 million from the Chinese community." "Memorial to Jap (sic) Victims to Be Built with Our Own Money," *Straits Times*, March 15, 1963.

43. "The 'Blood Debt' Rally," *Straits Times*, September 26, 1963. Leaders of the Malay, Eurasian, Ceylonese, Sikh, and Indian communities also voiced their support for the SCCC's claims. Representing the Indian community, D.T. Assomull pointed out that while the people of Singapore had borne the past silently, "it is time the Japanese atone for their past misdeeds and become once again our brothers in Asia." Theo Leijssius affirmed that "it was proper that the memory of those who suffered under the Japanese be perpetuated by some form of atonement." "Community Leaders All Back the Demand for Proper Atonement," *Straits Times*, August 28, 1963.

44. "Government Backing for Giant 'Blood Debt' Rally on Padang," *Straits Times*, August 22, 1963.

45. Lee Kuan Yew, "Speech at the Mass Rally on the Padang" (Singapore, August 25, 1963).

46. "Japan's Reply to 'Blood Debt' Rally," *Straits Times*, August 27, 1963.

47. In August 1963, Singapore was on the cusp of merging with Malaysia to end British colonial rule and the authority to negotiate the island's foreign affairs would lie with the Malaysian federal government.

48. When asked by journalists in October 1968 at a news conference as he was about to leave for a trip that included Japan if he would "stress the need for direct war reparations to Singapore," Lee replied that, "I've just told our two correspondents from Kyodo and Jiji [news services] who asked me about the war reparations. I told them it is over and done with. It is all settled, finished, out of the way. We have to look forward to the next 25 years, not the last 25." "Transcript Of Press Conference At Singapore Airport Before The Prime Minister's Departure For Hong Kong, Japan, Canada And U.S.A.—12 October, 1968." National Archives of Singapore. lky\1968\lky1012A.doc.

49. "Transcript Of General Press Conference Given By The Prime Minister, Mr. Lee Kuan Yew, At TV Centre on Saturday, 21st December, 1968." National Archives of Singapore. lky\1968\lky1221C.doc.

50. Gi-Wook Shin, "Divided Memories and Historical Reconciliation in East Asia," in *Routledge Handbook of Memory and Reconciliation in East Asia* (New York: Routledge, 2016), 412.

51. Blackburn and Hack, *War Memory and the Making of Modern Malaysia and Singapore*, 164.

52. The SCCC was initially surprised with the settlement, complaining that the Singapore government had not consulted them before accepting Japan's offer, and it was undecided on whether to accept it. The Appeal Committee for Singapore Chinese Massacred by the Japanese went even further in its criticism. Its secretary stated that "The Singapore government has no right to not accept anything less than the $50 million which was the amount decided" upon at the 1963 mass rally. "$25m Grant $25m Loans Settle Singapore's Blood Debt," *Straits Times*, October 26, 1966. On the appeal committee, see Blackburn and Hack, *War Memory and the Making of Modern Malaysia and Singapore*, 149–50.

53. The literature on historical reconciliation and apology is extensive, and many scholars emphasize the centrality of apology to the process. See Lily Gardner Feldman, "The Principle and Practice of 'Reconciliation' in German Foreign Policy: Relations with France, Israel, Poland and the Czech Republic," *International Affairs* 75, no. 2 (April 1, 1999): 333–56; David A. Crocker, "Reckoning with Past Wrongs: A Normative Framework," *Ethics and International Affairs* 13, no. 1 (1999): 43–64; Elazar Barkan, *The Guilt of Nations: Restitution and Negotiating Historical Injustices* (Baltimore: Johns Hopkins University Press, 2001); Elazar Barkan and Alexander Karn, eds., *Taking Wrongs Seriously: Apologies and Reconciliation* (Stanford: Stanford University Press, 2006). Some scholars, however, call into question the meaning, and even the very possibility, of apology. See Elizabeth A. Cole, *Teaching the Violent Past: History Education and Reconciliation* (Lanham, MD: Rowman & Littlefield, 2007), 24–25, note 23; Michel-Rolph Trouillot, "Abortive Rituals: Historical Apologies in the Global Era," *Interventions* 2, no. 2 (January 1, 2000): 171–86.

54. "Shiina Flies in for a Two-Day Goodwill Visit," *Straits Times*, October 25, 1966.

55. Lee Kuan Yew, "Transcript of a Speech by the Prime Minister, Mr. Lee Juan Yew, at the Chinese Chamber of Commerce on 4th July, 1966," July 4, 1966, lky/1966/lky0704.doc, National Archives of Singapore.

56. Ibid. Emphasis mine.

57. In 2006, Goh Chok Tong counselled that Japanese leaders should give up visits to the Yasukuni Shrine and find some other way to honor the war dead without appearing to endorse the political message of the Yasukuni Shrine. Goh Chok Tong, "Towards an East Asian Renaissance." In 2015, Lee Hsien Loong called on Japan to give more explicit acknowledgment of its past aggressions and clearer rejection of "outrageous interpretations of history by its right wing academics and politicians." Lee Hsien Loong, "Keynote Address."

58. Not everyone agreed that the name should be changed. Singaporeans also supported the gallery's original name, citing the need to not avoid difficult parts of the country's history. "World War II Exhibition to Reopen on Feb 16 at Former Ford Factory," *Straits Times*, February 9, 2017; "The Syonan Gallery Name Change Saga: A Timeline," *Straits Times*, February 18, 2017. This is not the first time Singaporeans have spoken out on representations of the Japanese occupation. Kevin Blackburn and Edmund Lim describe how in 1989, the Singapore Tourist Promotion Board was forced to abandon plans to turn the Chureitō, a Japanese memorial to their war dead built during the occupation, into a tourist attraction after protests from Singaporeans. Kevin Blackburn and Edmund Lim, "The Japanese War Memorials of Singapore: Monuments of Commemoration and Symbols of Japanese Imperial Ideology," *South East Asia Research* 7, no. 3 (1999): 339–40.

Chapter Seven

The United States

Remembrance without Recrimination

Marc Gallicchio

FADING MEMORIES

When Americans commemorated the 70th anniversary of the end of World War II, they did so in a variety of ceremonies, most of which were character- ized by a solemn, somber tone, and a touch of nostalgia. The generation that fought the war is passing from the scene. According to some estimates, only 10 percent of the men and women in uniform then are alive today. The attendance of surviving veterans at many of the ceremonies, many of them in the veterans' home towns, made for a bittersweet atmosphere and may have inclined speakers to make the day one of thanksgiving and gratitude that was nearly devoid of political comment or controversy. The former enemy was barely mentioned except to note the marvelous transformation it had under- gone under American supervision. The allies received an obligatory nod, more when their representatives were present.[1] Otherwise, these local cere- monies were low-keyed homegrown affairs in which the sacrifice, bravery, and magnanimity of the veterans was honored.[2]

For a variety of reasons, the Pacific War remains less well-known to Americans today than the conflict that took place in Europe. There are sever- al enduring images from the Pacific, including the pictures of smoldering wrecks at Pearl Harbor and the flag raising on Iwo Jima, but the ebb and flow of the Pacific campaigns and the geography of the vast theater of action remains hazy for most. It was probably with that reality in mind, for example, that the 2008 revival of the Broadway 1949 award-winning musical *South Pacific*, featured a large map of the South Pacific in one of its three interior sets.[3]

Although the use of atomic bombs at the end of the war continues to stir controversy in academic circles, the 70th anniversary of the attacks on Hiroshima and Nagasaki did not spark another ferocious public fight over the end of the war like the 1994–1995 furor over the Smithsonian Institution's doomed *Crossroads* exhibition. History remained red meat for political animals but the columnists, bloggers and Congressmen were too busy tearing into the new AP History curriculum to pay too much attention to the scholars and peace groups who continued to question American use of nuclear weapons to end the war.[4] Gary Trudeau, the culturally pitch-perfect cartoonist of the long-running *Doonesbury* comic, used the Sunday strip closest to the unofficial V-J Day to lampoon the new history textbooks adopted by the state of Texas.

Changes in the international context also explain the more subdued atmosphere this time around. In the 1994–95 period the United States was newly triumphant in the Cold War and had driven Saddam Hussein out of Kuwait. There had been setbacks in Somalia and the war in Bosnia-Herzegovina tested American leadership, but the public debate then was over how American power should be used to reform world politics rather than if it should be used. In that setting, the triumph of America in World War II and the achievements of its postwar policies were often used by advocates of an activist policy to justify interventions after the Cold War.

In 2005, President George W. Bush commemorated the 60th anniversary of V-J Day at Naval Air Station North Island in San Diego. In a long address he compared the Pacific War to the Global War on Terror and encouraged Americans to continue the fight for the freedom won sixty years earlier.[5] That message lingers in some commemoration speeches and online posts, but in 2015 after more than a decade of two wars that were at best inconclusive, Americans were uninterested in making the anniversary of V-J Day an occasion for summoning the nation to great military endeavors.[6] Instead, those who commemorated the event were more likely to use it as a call for action at home.

In other words, the American commemoration of the 70th anniversary of the end of the 15 year, Asia-Pacific War took place in a political climate that was a far cry from the situation in Asia where political officials remained on high alert for rhetorical miscues and signs of resurgent militarism. This is not to say that American remembrances were completely devoid of social messages or political commentary. But those messages seemed less confrontational than the ones that fueled the debates of twenty years ago.

In the United States, local commemorations took place on different dates in August and September, there being no universally agreed upon date for commemoration of V-J Day. Although privately sponsored events did not differ greatly from those held under federal auspices, the failure of the government (in this case, the executive branch), either through disinterest or inability, to establish an agreed upon date for the holiday is one small way in which local groups have claimed ownership of the commemoration. President Harry S. Truman declared September 2, the day the surrender documents were signed on the battleship USS *Missouri*, as V-J Day. That is the date observed by most commemorations sponsored by the federal government. But many individuals and groups use August 14, the day when Truman announced Japan's surrender, to mark the end of the war. Although this year, because August 14 fell on a Friday, many groups held their commemorations on Saturday the 15th. Not so New Hampshire. "In New Hampshire we do things right," explained an event organizer.[7] One can only imagine General Douglas MacArthur's dismay at this slighting of September 2.[8]

MEMORY AND GENERATIONAL IDENTITY

More recently a group called "The Spirit of '45" has been in the forefront of organizing events on the second Sunday in August, which was designated by Congress in 2010 as "National Spirit of '45 Day." This day is marked out as an occasion "to say 'Thank you' to the members of the Greatest Generation, which is rapidly passing away." The Spirit of '45 organization provides an event planning kit to help local groups host their own ceremonies. These events sponsored by local affiliates of the Spirit of '45 feature veterans who live nearby and often include some form of entertainment including military displays, movies, and re-creation of USO shows.[9] Major League Baseball cooperates with the Spirit of '45 by having veterans attend games in August in which there are brief commemorative ceremonies.[10]

In addition to honoring veterans, the goal of the Spirit of '45 is "to serve as an annual call for re-dedication to their can-do spirit of courage, self-sacrifice and national unity, to help America face and solve its current and future challenges."[11] According to Warren C. Hegg, national supervisor for the Spirit of '45 project, he hopes to remind Americans:

> of a time when our country faced much more daunting threats than those we are dealing with today, [when] Americans of all ages and backgrounds were able to come together and mobilize to assure the future, not only of our country, but of the world. Unlike the legacy of service and sacrifice left by the World War II generation, the "Me" generation seems to be leaving their children and their children's children with a nation in decline. . . . Our political leadership seems to be in a state of perpetual gridlock that discourages any effort to bring people together in common cause to deal with the very real problems that face our country. . . . It is our hope that if youth have a chance to form a personal connection with these folks and learn more about what they achieved together during their lifetimes and the values that shaped their lives, they will be inspired to become the "ordinary heroes" of their generation to assure a better future for themselves and for their country.

Hegg's message is not a partisan one, but it is political. Although commemoration of the war's end served to reinforce national and racial identities elsewhere in Asia, in the United States, the divide was generational, not racial or ethnic. The paeans to the Greatest Generation were not intended to draw distinctions between Americans and others, instead, they marked supposed differences between one generation of Americans and another. In perpetuating the Greatest Generation myth, the Spirit of '45 set an impossibly high standard for civic action that must lead inevitably to disappointment or disillusionment. Indeed, even the Greatest Generation could not live up to the virtues attributed to it. The American public was far more united in World War II than in the War of 1812 or the Vietnam War, but The Spirit of '45 glosses over the political battles, strikes, black market exchanges, tax evasion, and racial divisions of the era.[12] It also ignores that one of the guiding principles of American strategy in the conflict was the belief that the public would only be able to tolerate the sacrifices of war for a limited time.[13]

Moreover, the theme of an older generation failing its successors, in this case the "Me" generation, unknowingly repeats worries voiced during World War II that what would later be called the Greatest Generation had been psychologically deformed by the "moral debauches" of the previous two decades.[14] It is easy to understand the attraction of the myth of national unity and equal sacrifice at the heart of the Greatest Generation legend. But one could argue that the nation's achievements would seem all the more remarkable and inspiring to that generation's descendants if they knew how fractious and disputatious their forbearers really were during the war. At the least, they might draw some comfort from knowing that they need not declare a moratorium on politics or live like saints in order to cope with today's problems.

COMMERCIALIZATION AND COMMEMORATION

As historian Emily Rosenberg has noted, no one owns society's memory and there is no single arbiter of what constitutes a society's memories. That has made collective memory fair game for commercialization and commodification.[15] Nevertheless, American popular culture went AWOL during the 70th anniversary celebration. Apart from locally arranged band concerts and shows, there were no big galas. There were no blockbuster films like Disney's *Pearl Harbor* timed to coincide with V-J Day. There was nothing on cable, no made-for television movies. Opportunities for marketing seem to have been almost nonexistent; no Timex watches, flight jackets, or MacArthur corn cob pipes, crushed caps, or aviator shades hit the market.

The closest thing to the *Pearl Harbor* marketing extravaganza was the publicity effort to make the famous Albert Eisenstadt *Life* magazine photograph of a sailor kissing a nurse, actually a dental assistant, in Times Square the universal symbol of V-J Day commemorations.[16] The photograph first appeared on page twenty-seven of the magazine and was republished intermittently after that. It gained its current notoriety in 1980, when the publishers mistakenly announced they had identified the nurse. The identities of the sailor and the nurse have been in dispute since then. It is only over the last several decades that the photo of the drunken sailor and the clearly startled object of his attentions has captured the public imagination. It is probably the single most famous image to capture the sense of sheer elation and joy felt by millions upon hearing the war had ended. It communicates those emotions across decades. Various groups, including the Spirit of '45 organization use illustrated versions of "the kiss" on their promotional materials.[17] Other reproductions of "the kiss" seem detached from that moment in 1945 and devoid of meaning. They exist as curiosities or publicity stunts. Examples of the former include the twenty-five-foot sculpture replicating "the kiss" in Times Square and the miniature versions used as wedding cake toppers. Every five years, including this year, the Times Square Alliance, a business improvement association, holds a reenactment of the famous event. The first two hundred couples in the square are given sailor caps and red roses and upon hearing the countdown "five, four, three, two, one, smooch," they proceed to reenact the famous scene. This year, as a part of its V-J Day celebration, the Eisenhower Presidential Library set up a photo station for couples to "recreate their own version of the famous 'kiss' between an unknown sailor and a nurse celebrating the end of World War II in New York's Times Square in 1945."[18]

OFFICIAL COMMEMORATIONS

As noted, Douglas MacArthur would be appalled at the public's use of one of several days in August to mark the end of the war. But he would almost certainly be pleased to see that animosity toward Japan has been absent from most local ceremonies. Occasionally in local commemorations, and nearly always in official government-sponsored events, speakers paid tribute to Japan's magnificent transformation, aided by America's guidance and generous assistance. Japan's role as one of America's most stalwart allies was also a common theme in these ceremonies.

Commemorations officially sponsored by an entity of the federal government displayed considerable finesse in celebrating the victory of freedom over tyranny. The etiquette of these events is in flux and, like collective memory itself, there is no single authority making up the rules. For example, how does one celebrate the crushing defeat of one's steadfast ally of the past six decades? Answers vary. In 1995, President Bill Clinton was criticized for omitting mention of V-J Day and referring only to the end of the Pacific War during his commemoration speech at Pearl Harbor. The president, according to critics, was guilty of showing too much sensitivity for Japan's feelings.[19] That seems an odd charge to bring against the president who introduced the practice of "Japan passing," into presidential trips to Asia. Moreover, the text of Clinton's speech repeatedly referred to the Japanese as the enemy in the war.[20] President George W. Bush avoided Clinton's faux pas and forthrightly celebrated V-J Day in 2005. But in 2015 Japan was often omitted from remarks or made only a cameo appearance. Participants could be forgiven if after reading the myriad statements issued by legislators and executive department officials or, after attending any of the numerous commemorative events, they came away thinking that the war was against a country called Japan that no longer exists.

On August 5, Senator Susan Collins of Maine, one of the co-sponsors of The Spirit of '45 resolution, issued a statement commemorating the anniversary of the end of the war. Largely a paean to the citizens of Maine who served in uniform or worked at the state's shipyards, the statement, which filled a full page in the *Congressional Record*, mentioned Japan only twice.[21] Senator Orrin Hatch of Utah used the occasion of a speech by the Republic of China's president to affirm in Clintonian language that "On the 70th anniversary of the end of the Second World War, our strategic partnerships in the Pacific are more critical now than ever." Although President Ma had devoted the first half of his speech to the Republic of China's fight in "the war of resistance against Japan," the only country mentioned in Senator Hatch's brief statement was North Korea.[22]

Prime Minister Abe Shinzō's April visit to the United States provided an occasion for several legislators to remember the war while highlighting the current U.S.-Japan alliance.[23] But Abe's statement on the anniversary of Japan's surrender drew a nuanced response from Congressman Matt Salmon of Arizona that was reminiscent of the carefully worded apologies issued by the Japanese government. Congressman Salmon, who is the chairman of the House subcommittee on Asia and the Pacific, wrote that:

> While it is very difficult to move beyond a history of past aggressions, I recognize Prime Minister Abe's remorseful apology to those impacted by hurtful acts during the War, and I welcome Prime Minister Abe's commitment to uphold prior Japanese cabinet statements on history. The omission of certain terminology and references did leave something to be desired, though it is my hope that our Asian neighbors can understand and appreciate fully the intentions behind Japan's regrets over its actions in the twentieth century. I hope that future generations can work toward reconciliation and toward a more prosperous and cooperative future together.[24]

On the official V-J Day, Senator John McCain indirectly referred to the history wars that still roil politics in East Asia, but he emphasized the peace motif in the commemoration and also pointed to contemporary events that posed a challenge to hopes for international tranquility. "While some have chosen to mark this anniversary by focusing on the past," McCain said in a statement issued by his office, "I view this day as an opportunity to celebrate not only the end of war in the Pacific, but all of the progress we have achieved since then. . . . And from the ashes of war was born a rules-based international order predicated on the principles of good governance and rule of law, human rights and democracy, open markets and the conviction that wars of aggression should be relegated to the bloody past." "For seven decades," he added, "the United States and its allies, including Japan, have committed our power and influence to the defense of these principles. Now as the rules-based international order confronts increasing challenges, including in the Asia-Pacific, we must recommit ourselves to the principles that have produced and extended prosperity and security across the globe."[25]

U.S. secretary of state John Kerry issued a similar statement in which he praised the bravery of the men and women who fought the war, and extolled the marvelous transformation in the region since then. Kerry also celebrated the spirit of reconciliation that had made the U.S.-Japan relationship so productive and, seemingly in response to McCain's call for a recommitment to defend the international order, he affirmed that "The United States will continue to deepen its active engagement in the region as a resident Pacific nation, working with allies and partners to strengthen the institutions, networks, rules, and good practices that promote stability and prosperity."[26] Such statements, in downplaying or ignoring the alleged inadequacy of Prime Minister Abe's remarks, were in their own way political statements indicating Washington's current concerns in the region. The emphasis on the virtues of reconciliation had broader applications as well. On August 14, the unofficial V-J Day, the secretary of state was in Havana to formally redesignate the U.S. Interests Section as the U.S. Embassy in Havana. While in Havana, he met with senior Cuban government officials as part of the process of reestablishing diplomatic relations.[27]

American officials in Asia played a minor role in the commemorations in Japan and the Philippines but the symbolism of their presence spoke volumes even when the officials themselves were silent. In recent years, commemorations of the nuclear attacks on Hiroshima and Nagasaki have occasioned calls from some Japanese groups for an American apology, similar to the ones the Japanese have made regarding the invasion of China or the attack on Pearl Harbor. No such controversy ensued in 2015, in part because the Japanese government did not wish to disturb its relations with the United States while it moved to expand its military posture in the region. On August 6, Ambassador Caroline Kennedy and Under Secretary for Arms Control and International Security Rose Gottemoeller attended the commemoration ceremony in Hiroshima's peace park. This was Kennedy's third visit and her second as ambassador. Three days later, the ambassador issued a statement on the anniversary of the attack on Nagasaki and attended a ceremony there with Under Secretary Gottemoeller. Kennedy laid a wreath at the memorial but the two diplomats did not speak at the ceremony. Nevertheless, their presence at both events demonstrated sensitivity toward Japanese concerns over nuclear weapons and symbolized the Obama administration's policy of reducing nuclear armaments.[28]

Elsewhere in the region, American diplomatic officials attended ceremonies commemorating the liberation of several of the Philippine Islands, as well as one marking the surrender of General Yamashita Tomoyuki at the former summer residence of the American ambassador in Baguio. By calling attention to America's role in the liberation of its former colony, American attendance was intended to convey support for Manila in its dispute with China over the islands in the South China Sea. Speaking at the Baguio ceremony, Ambassador Philip Goldberg, shifting from past to present, said "It was the relentless and indomitable spirit of a generation from both our nations that forged a great alliance—the U.S.-Philippine alliance—which is the oldest in the region and has helped preserve and protect the security and stability of the entire Pacific region."[29] In contrast to the ceremonies in Japan, the presence of the American ambassador to China at Beijing's military parade on September 2 was a minor snub of the Chinese who had "pressured" Western governments to send high level officials to the event.[30]

The American reaction to China's parade was a statement of disapproval of Beijing's saber rattling. But overall, as far as Americans are concerned, militaristic displays were clearly considered to be out of step with the solemnity of the year's commemorations. Speaking from the deck of the USS *Missouri*, Admiral Scott Swift, the commander of the U.S. Pacific Fleet, told his audience that the surrender ceremony that took place on the *Missouri* seventy years earlier "was not about retribution. Like today's ceremony, it was an acknowledgement that the shared losses of World War II vastly exceeded the immediate gains at the time."[31] Also in attendance was the mayor of Nagaoka City, which contributed fireworks to the commemoration. The ceremonies included presentations of chrysanthemums and paper cranes, both symbols of peace.[32]

Although most American officials successfully avoided giving offense or creating controversy, that was not possible for President Obama. On August 14, the president devoted his weekly radio remarks to the anniversary of the Ferguson, Missouri, riots. Internet critics pounced, declaring among other things that the president did not feel comfortable talking about wars that America won. Of course, the president was not ignoring V-J Day, as was alleged, he was using the official date, September 2, to issue his remarks. On that day, the White House issued an anodyne statement in which Obama honored the sacrifices of the men and women who fought and then moved on to praise the nation's valuable partnership with Japan.[33]

Surprisingly, there does not appear to have been any criticism of the president's having the White House communications office issue a statement while he was in Alaska promoting his environmental policies. Unlike presidents Clinton and Bush, Obama did not attend a ceremony at a military installation or deliver his remarks live. Perhaps that choice was a harbinger of future ceremonies. One of the president's supporters asked how long American officials will be expected to commemorate the war's end. After all, he added, Americans did not commemorate the signing of the Treaty of Paris that recognized the nation's independence. To that, one might add that we also lost Armistice Day a long time ago. That someone would raise the question of how long we must memorialize the end of the war suggests that at least some people think there should be a statute of limitations on commemorations.

ENCORE: OBAMA AND ABE'S RECONCILIATION TOUR

Nevertheless, American officials still found it useful to commemorate the war's end. In May 2016, President Obama became the first sitting U.S. president to visit Hiroshima. The president's historic visit came during an eight-day trip to Japan and Vietnam that included a meeting of the G7 summit held on Kashiko Island in Shima City, Japan. The president's team understood the controversial nature of their trip. In advance of the meeting, the White House issued statements explaining that the president would not be apologizing for the United States's having used atomic bombs in World War II. Instead, the visit would be an occasion to recognize all the innocent lives lost in the war and to re-emphasize the president's desire to reduce the threat of nuclear war. According to Ben Rhodes, the president's communications adviser on national security affairs, Obama intended to "offer a forward-looking vision focused on our shared future." Rhodes added that "The President and his team will make this visit knowing that the open recognition of history is essential to understanding our shared past, the forces that shape the world we live in today, and the future that we seek for our children and grandchildren."[34]

By this time, however, the 2016 presidential race was in full swing and the president's opponents insisted that the very act of visiting Hiroshima was tantamount to an apology. The president, according to Sarah Palin, the former Republican nominee for vice-president was "dissing our vets" by going to Hiroshima. John Bolton, a former ambassador to the United Nations under President George W. Bush, complained that the president compulsively apologized for American actions whenever he went abroad. Even if he did not say the words, Bolton argued, everyone knew that Obama's visit to Hiroshima was just another stop on his "shameful apology tour," of the world.[35]

One can only speculate as to the president's reasons for visiting Hiroshima. A fuller explanation will require access to the planning papers and communications concerning the visit. Obama's informal comments and more formal speeches surrounding his visit made it clear that the president was primarily concerned with the contemporary dangers posed by nuclear proliferation, although given the historical significance of Hiroshima, he could not ignore the past. During an impromptu press conference held the day before he went to Hiroshima the first question the president fielded asked why he had decided to go to Hiroshima when his predecessors had not. Obama declined to speculate on why previous president's had not paid their respects at Hiroshima and avoided any observations on the decision to use atomic weapons to end the war with Japan. "I can tell you how I'm thinking about it," he added, "and that is that the dropping of the atomic bomb, the ushering in of nuclear weapons was an inflection point in modern history":

> It is something that all of us have had to deal with in one way or another. Obviously, it's not as prominent in people's thinking as it was during the cold war, at a time when our parents or grandparents were huddling under desks in frequent drills. But the backdrop of a nuclear event remains something that, I think, presses on the back of our imaginations. I do think that part of the reason I'm going is because I want to once again underscore the very real risks that are out there and the sense of urgency that we all should have. So it's not only a reminder of the terrible toll of World War II and the death of innocents across continents, but it's also to remind ourselves that the job is not done in reducing conflict, building institutions of peace, and reducing the prospect of nuclear war in the future.[36]

The remainder of the questions dealt with contemporary concerns including relations with Iran and Cuba, and the presidential election.

The following day, the president signed the guest book at the Hiroshima Memorial Museum and a laid a wreath at the cenotaph in the Hiroshima Peace Memorial. Then he and Prime Minister Abe spoke about the significance of that place and the importance of remembering what happened there.[37] Both leaders spoke poignantly about the atomic bomb's devastating power, the loss of innocent lives, and the suffering of the survivors. In mourning the destruction wrought by the bomb, the president placed that apocalyptic event in the broader sweep of humanity's persistent resort to war and violence. World War II was unprecedented only in the scope of its brutality. The bomb had been made possible by a scientific revolution, noted Obama, but Hiroshima showed that what was needed now was an accompanying "moral revolution." "That is why we come to this place," he said:

We stand here in the middle of this city and force ourselves to imagine the moment the bomb fell. We force ourselves to feel the dread of children confused by what they see. We listen to a silent cry. We remember all the innocents killed across the arc of that terrible war and the wars that came before and the wars that would follow. Mere words cannot give voice to such suffering. But we have a shared responsibility to look directly into the eye of history and ask what we must do differently to curb such suffering again. Someday, the voices of the *hibakusha* will no longer be with us to bear witness. But the memory of the morning of August 6, 1945, must never fade. That memory allows us to fight complacency. It fuels our moral imagination. It allows us to change.[38]

It was a moving tribute to the victims of the bomb, but in broadening the scope of his remarks while at the same time confining them to the victims, as opposed to perpetrators, the president avoided addressing the entire controversy over the bomb's use. By generalizing about the horrors of war, even as he spoke movingly about the victims of Hiroshima, the president made the future avoidance of conflict through the building of strong international institutions, the main lesson of Hiroshima. This relentlessly forward looking approach, tinged with hope, was a hallmark of the president's rhetorical style.

The president's remarks were generally well-received in Japan but he provoked sharper commentary at home. Dean Cheng, a specialist on Asia and national security at the conservative Heritage Foundation, complained that even if he did not apologize, the president "created the optics of an apology" that would complicate the U.S. alliance with Japan. "The first problem is, do the Japanese now owe the United States an apology for Pearl Harbor?" Were the Chinese now expecting Abe to visit Nanjing to offer an apology for the Japanese army's 1937 massacre of Chinese civilians? Cheng correctly predicted the immediate reactions to Obama's visit both in China and in the United States. Almost immediately, the Chinese government declared that if the president of the United States could visit Hiroshima, then surely the Japanese prime minister was obligated to visit Nanjing to apologize for the atrocities committed there. The state news agency also warned that Japan had a "covert agenda" in welcoming Obama to Hiroshima. "The Japanese government is trying to use the historic visit to highlight Japan's image of a 'war victim' while downplaying its role as an aggressor in WWII," Xinhua declared.[39] In the United States, presidential candidate Donald Trump dismissed the significance of Obama's visit and asked why the president never mentioned Pearl Harbor when he was in Japan.[40]

The prolonged commemoration of the end of the war that began with Obama's visit to Hiroshima, concluded in December 2016 with Prime Minister Abe's visit to Pearl Harbor, where the American part of the war began. Technically, Abe's visit commemorated the seventy-fifth anniversary of the

Pearl Harbor attack, but observers saw it as a ceremonial bookend to Obama's trip to Hiroshima earlier that year. Abe was the first prime minister to *publicly* visit the memorial; apparently Yoshida Shigeru had gone there in 1951 while on a stopover in Hawaii. Some commentators saw Abe's public visit to the memorial as a gesture of friendship toward the outgoing president, with whom he had become close after an early period of strained personal relations. But he may have also viewed it as an opportunity to shore up the bilateral relationship following the victory of Donald Trump in the 2016 presidential election. In addition to criticizing Obama for not mentioning Pearl Harbor when he was in Japan, Trump had repeatedly criticized Japan for engaging in unfair trade practices and for not paying its fair share for its own defense. Trump's verbal sallies against Japan were part of the candidate's broader campaign strategy summarized in such slogans as "America First" and "Make America Great Again." Although "America First" recalled the pre-Pearl Harbor non-interventionist movement in the United States, it appears that Trump intended the slogan to signify that in contrast to proponents of multilateralism, he would always place Americans' interests first in international affairs.[41]

Nevertheless, it seems possible that there was at least a tenuous connection between Trump's slogans and the nostalgic sensibility present in the 70th anniversary commemorations, particularly the Spirit of '45 events. In a manner reminiscent of the 70th anniversary events, the presidential candidate's rhetoric tapped into the public's desire for a time when Americans pulled together and overcame challenges. The staid and mostly apolitical V-J Day commemorations had, however, largely ignored the former enemy; they told a story of heroes but left out the villains. In contrast, Trump's rhetoric invariably shifted from nostalgic references to American greatness to scathing denunciations of those at home and abroad whom he believed had undermined America's greatness.

Japan was not the only ally to be singled out for Trump's criticisms but his verbal sallies were particularly disturbing in Tokyo because they recalled the difficult period of the 1980s and 1990s when trade friction strained the relationship between the United States and Japan. Trump's remarks alarmed American supporters of the alliance as well, but observers on both sides of the Pacific were also perplexed by the candidate's outdated depiction of Japan as an economic juggernaut that threatened U.S. primacy.[42]

In the end, Abe's visit came off without causing undue controversy in the United States or Japan. The Pearl Harbor visit and an earlier trip to New York to meet the president-elect, most likely helped smooth the way for the prime minister's February 2017 meeting with President Trump at the latter's Florida resort. For his part, the newly sworn-in president proved willing to reaffirm the strength of the U.S.-Japan relationship, although American withdrawal from the Trans-Pacific Partnership indicated that differences remained on the economic front.[43] The U.S.-Japan relationship had made it through another round of anniversaries and an election cycle. The past had been present throughout those occasions but the role of collective memory in the formation of American attitudes toward Japan was clearly changing.

Those changes had been in the making for some time. The clearest indication of them was the growing tendency of Americans to question the use of the atomic bombs to end World War II. By 2015, 56 percent of Americans believed that the United States was justified in using the bombs and 34 percent believed it was not. In 1991, the numbers had been 63 percent and 29 percent respectively. In 1945, shortly after V-J Day, 85 percent of Americans viewed the bombs as justified. In short, although a majority still believed the bombs were justified, opinion was gradually moving toward the opposite conclusion. That trend was made even more apparent considering the generational split in opinion. 70 percent of respondents over 65 believed the bombs were necessary, but only 47 percent of those 18–29 agreed.[44] In light of the polling data, it is easy to see why conservatives were so alarmed by the president's trip to Hiroshima. Twenty years earlier, conservatives had been among the main victors in the battle over the *Enola Gay* exhibit. It now appeared that although they had won that skirmish in the culture wars, the victory had been fleeting.

Conservative critics of President Obama need not have been so worried about the political impact of historical revisionism in the AP curriculum or Obama's alleged predisposition to apologize for America's actions. Other factors were at work in this transformation of attitudes. One was the mounting distance between the present and the end of the war. Despite its continuing presence in popular culture, for many Americans, World War II was entering the realm of ancient history. Younger Americans' questioning of the bombs' use was not so much a critique of Truman's decisions as it was evidence of a new, more positive, image of Japan taking hold in the American imagination. Support for this conclusion could be found in research that showed that despite their growing disapproval of the use of atomic bombs against Japan, a majority of Americans were not opposed to using atomic weapons against other enemies in the twenty-first century.[45]

In short, the passage of time and the durability of the U.S.-Japan relationship in the seventy years since the end of the war may have more to do with changing American attitudes about Hiroshima and Nagasaki than any historical critiques of those events. Certainly, the tenor of the seventieth anniversary commemorations suggests as much. As Seiko Mimaki has noted "Japan-US reconciliation has been supported by 'another past' that took place after World War II." When asked to pick from a list of the most important events in U.S.-Japan relations over the preceding seventy-five years, 31 percent of respondents said World War II. But the same percentage chose the Great East Japan Earthquake of 2011. Thirty-six percent of Japanese respondents chose the alliance, 20 percent chose the earthquake, and only 17 percent picked World War II. Professor Mimaki, who has written extensively on the process of reconciliation in international relations also observed that "It is not possible to erase war memories, but it is possible to relativize [them] and to build another past with a fresh perspective. Some have criticized Obama's visit to Hiroshima and the visit of both heads of state to Pearl Harbor as empty political performance setting the stage for 'reconciliation,' but their actions should be viewed as a symbolic endorsement of the well-established historical reconciliation between the United States and Japan."[46] Jennifer Lind, the author of a book on the role of official apologies in international affairs agrees. On the eve of Abe's visit to Pearl Harbor, Lind observed that "These visits don't cause reconciliation. It is the exact opposite. Reconciliation causes these visits."[47]

In the future, new international circumstances may create conditions where once again, war remembrance has the potential to disrupt U.S.-Japan relations, as it did in the 1980s. But for now, reconciliation has trumped recrimination. Within the United States, unofficial and local commemorations of the 70th anniversary of the war's end were resolutely inward looking, praising a passing generation of citizens, summoning a new one to challenges at home, and, occasionally, inviting Americans to engage in frivolous celebrations. Are we approaching the statute of limitations on commemoration of V-J Day? Perhaps, but although first-hand memory of the war is fading, and other pasts are shaping American attitudes about the war and its aftermath, it seems doubtful that we will see an end to commemorations of the war's end any time soon. Until that time arrives, individuals, civic groups and politicians in the United States will continue to memorialize the end of the Asia-Pacific War in ways they find personally meaningful and useful. And, one should add, they probably will not agree on what day they should do it.

NOTES

1. The Australian ambassador to the United States was a speaker at the National World War II Museum in New Orleans. The museum was designated by Congress as the "official World War II museum of the United States" but it is not run by the National Parks Service and appears to be a private entity. Commemorating the 70th Anniversary of V-J Day, http://nw2m.convio.net/site/Calendar/852424676?view=Detail&id=119202.

2. James A. Jones, Jr., "End of World War II 70 Years ago remembered in Bradenton and Sarasota," *Bradenton Herald*, August 12, 2015, http://www.bradenton.com/2015/08/12/5937150_end-of-world-war-ii-70–years-ago.html?rh=1; Peggy Lee, "Berwick Celebrates 70th Anniversary of V-J Day, Its Role in WWII." *WNEP*, September 2, 2015, http://wnep.com/2015/09/02/berwick-celebrates-70th-anniversary-of-vj-day-its-role-in-wwii/; Joan Hellyer, "VFW Post in Lower Makefield Celebrates 70th Anniversary of V-J Day." *Bucks County Courier Times*, September 3, 2015, http://www.buckscountycouriertimes.com/news/communities/yardley/vfw-post-in-lower-makefield-celebrates-th-anniversary-of-v/article_276d4afa-51c0–11e5–ad7d-7bfe0886cfa1.html.

3. For instructive comparison of American memories of the European and Pacific Wars see Daqing Yang, "Entangled Memories: China in American and Japanese Remembrances of World War II, in Marc Gallicchio, ed., *The Unpredictability of the Past: Memories of the Asia-Pacific War in U.S.-East Asian Relations* (Durham: Duke University Press, 2007), 287–318, especially pages 288–89; and Richard Frank, "An Overdue Pacific War Perspective," *Naval History Magazine* (April 2010), 24:2, https://www.usni.org/magazines/navalhistory/2010–04/overdue-pacific-war-perspective.

4. Cheryl Carlesimo, "Hiroshima and Nagasaki," August 10, 2015, *World Post*, http://www.huffingtonpost.com/cheryl-carlesimo/hiroshima-and-nagasaki_b_7962388.html; Judith Mohling, "Peace Train 70th Anniversary of Hiroshima/Nagasaki bombings." Colorado Coalition, July 24, 2015, http://thecoloradocoalition.org/2015/08/peace-train-70th-anniversary-of-hiroshimanagasaki-bombings/; "PSR-LA Commemorates the 70th Anniversary of Hiroshima and Nagasaki Atomic Bombings." Physicians for Social Responsibility. August 9, 2015, http://www.psr-la.org/psr-la-commemorates-the-70th-anniversary-of-hiroshima-and-nagasaki-atomic-bombings/. For the continuing scholarly debate over the use of the atomic bombs see the two articles by D.M. Giangreco and J. Samuel Walker posted on the History News Network (HNN), Giangreco: http://historynewsnetwork.org/article/159960, Walker: http://historynewsnetwork.org/article/159959.

5. President Bush Commemorates 60th Anniversary of VJ Day, August 30, 2005, http://georgewbush-whitehouse.archives.gov/news/releases/2005/08/20050830–1.html.

6. For examples see, John Daniel Davidson, "70 Years Later, We Can Still Learn From V-J Day," *Federalist*, August 15, 2015, http://thefederalist.com/2015/08/15/70–years-later-we-can-still-learn-from-v-j-day/; Warren Kozak, "The Liberators of World War II," *Philadelphia Inquirer*, August 28, 2015, A17. Kozak's article first appeared in the conservative journal, *The Weekly Standard* on August 17.

7. In holding the event on August 14, New Hampshire also bucked the preferences of the Spirit of '45 organization which was a sponsor. Dan Seufert, "NH remembers 70th anniversary of the end of World War II," *New Hampshire Union Leader*, August 15, 2015, http://www.unionleader.com/article/20150816/NEWS18/150819457&source=RSS#sthash.jqh6NHjh.dpuf. Sunday, August 16, also seemed like an appropriate day for commemoration in 2015. "Quantico ceremony part of global tribute marking 70th anniversary of World War II's end," *Fredericksburg.com*, http://www.fredericksburg.com/features/people_and_places/quantico-ceremony-part-of-global-tribute-marking-th-anniversary-of/article_6ae1c0a9–9eda-5935–b9c1–7e8f042c7214.html. (This was a privately organized event.)

8. San Diego held a commemorative celebration on August 15 on board the USS *Midway*. This followed a Spirit of '45 event held at the Veterans Museum in San Diego on August 9. The festivities sponsored by the *Midway* museum included a recreation of a USO show. http://www.midway.org/WWII-Event.

9. For examples see: The Spirit of '45 Events Calendar at http://sof45–calendar.org/events/map/?home=yes; For a sample of events see also "Marion, VA host Spirit of '45 Celebration, http://wjhl.com/2015/08/09/marion-va-host-the-spirit-of-45–celebration/; Spirit of '45 Celebration, *La Junta Tribune-Democrat*, http://www.lajuntatribunedemocrat.com/article/20150820/NEWS/150819831; Spirit of '45 Celebration, Travelers Rest Historical Society, Travelers Rest, SC; http://travelersresthistoricalsociety.org/index.php/about/spirit-of-45; Spirit of '45 70th Anniversary Celebration (105.1 The River), radio advertisement for ceremony at the Mississippi Veteran's Memorial Cemetery in Newtown, MS, http://www.1051theriver.com/calendar/august-16–2015/spirit-of-45–70th-anniversary-celebration-463955/; "Spirit of '45 Day Remembrance Celebration," Veterans Museum and Memorial Center, Balboa Park, San Diego, CA, http://www.veteranmuseum.org/.

10. In another Spirit of '45 event coordinated with the National Parks Service, one thousand "Rosies," women and girls dressed in blue overalls and red bandannas attended an event in Richmond, California. The event, which was not specifically about V-J Day, maintained the Spirit of '45's theme of renewal with the slogan "We've done it before. We can do it again." The original Rosie poster bore the motto "We Can Do It." http://www.spiritof45.org/new_page_test1.aspx; "Major League Baseball Steps Up to Celebrate Spirit of '45 Day,"http://www.spiritof45.org/major_league_baseball1.aspx.

11. Vision Statement, 70th Anniversary, http://spiritof45conference.org/vision-statement/; Background, http://spiritof45conference.org/spirit-of-45/.

12. On June 1, 1945, President Harry S. Truman announced that the Internal Revenue Service would be employing 10,000 more agents to help catch black marketers and tax cheats. The President's News Conference, 1 June 1945, *Public Papers of the Presidents: Harry S. Truman, 1945–1953,* http://www.trumanlibrary.org/publicpapers/index.php?pid=51&st= Japan&st1=.

13. This is the thesis of Charles F. Brower, *Defeating Japan: The Joint Chiefs of Staff and Strategy in the Pacific War, 1943–1945* (2012). See also Ronald Spector, "The Pacific War and the Fourth Dimension of Strategy," in Gunter Bischof and Robert L. Dupont, eds., *The Pacific War Revisited* (Baton Rouge, 1997), 40–55.

14. The quote is from anthropologist Margret Mead. For Mead's statement and other expression of generational weakness see Spector, "The Fourth Dimension," 43. Philip Wylie's *Generation of Vipers*, a scathing indictment of American society and of the culture of "Momism" was published in 1942.

15. Emily Rosenberg, *A Date Which Will Live Pearl Harbor in American Memory* (Durham, NC, 2003), 5–6, 63–173.

16. Karen Matthews, "Couples gather in Times Square to re-enact V-J Day kiss," *Navy Times,* August 14, 2015, http://www.navytimes.com/story/military/2015/08/14/couples-gather-times-square-re-enact-v-j-day-kiss/31730137/; "Remembering the iconic V-J Day kissing photograph," CBS News, August 15, 2015, http://www.cbsnews.com/news/remembering-the-iconic-vj-day-kissing-photograph/; Maureen Callahan, "The True Story behind the Iconic VJ Day Sailor and 'nurse' Smooch," *New York Post,* June 17, 2012, http://nypost.com/2012/06/17/the-true-story-behind-the-iconic-v-j-day-sailor-and-nurse-smooch/; Sarah Zang, "The Unromantic Truth Behind the VJ Day Kiss Photo," *Mother Jones,* October 10, 2006, http://www.motherjones.com/mixed-media/2012/10/unromantic-truth-vj-kiss-photo.

17. The Norwayne Community Citizens Council and the City of Westland, MI, also illustrated its announcements with a version of "the kiss." http://yankeeairmuseum.org/homefront/pages/friday.php.

18. Eisenhower Presidential Library to Commemorate V-J Day 70th Anniversary, http://www.salinakansas.org/events/Eisenhower-Presidential-Library-to-Commemorate-VJ-Day-70th-Anniversary-8223/details.

19. V-J Day, http://www.history.com/topics/world-war-ii/v-j-day.

20. Remarks at a Wreath-Laying Ceremony Aboard the USS *Carl Vinson* in Pearl Harbor, Hawaii, September 2, 1995, http://www.gpo.gov/fdsys/pkg/PPP-1995-book2/html/PPP-1995-book2-doc-pg1284.htm.

21. "Recognizing the 70th Anniversary of the End of World War II," *Congressional Record,* August 5, 2015, S6371–S6372, http://www.collins.senate.gov/public/_cache/files/dda9f91b-5dd9–45ed-906f-e854a1c32d56/Collins-King%20WWII%20Statement.pdf.

22. President Ma's Speech at the Videoconference with Stanford University, August 5, 2016, http://english.president.gov.tw/Default.aspx?tabid=491&itemid=34848&rmid=2355; Hatch Comments on Taiwan President Ma's Remarks at Stanford University Event, June 9, 2015, http://www.hatch.senate.gov/public/index.cfm/2015/6/senator-hatch-responds-to-taiwan-president-ma-s.

23. Referring to Abe's visit and his historic address to both chambers of Congress, Senator Marco Rubio of Florida and Congressman Joaquin Castro of Texas noted that it came in the year in which the world commemorated the 70th anniversary of the end of World War II. Both legislators emphasized the peace that had prevailed between the two countries since 1945 and affirmed the importance of the U.S.-Japan alliance in economic and military affairs in the Asia-Pacific region. Rubio, Marco. "Asia Needs a Strong U.S.-Japan Alliance." *Wall Street Journal,* April 29, 2015, http://www.rubio.senate.gov/public/index.cfm/2015/4/asia-needs-a-strong-u-s-japan-alliance; "Castro Statement on Japanese Prime Minister Abe's Visit to Washington." Congressman Joaquin Castro, April 28, 2015, http://castro.house.gov/media-center/press-releases/castro-statement-on-japanese-prime-minister-abes-visit-to-washington.

24. "Chairman Salmon Statement on Prime Minister Abe's WWII Anniversary Statement." Congressman Matt Salmon, August 19, 2015, https://salmon.house.gov/media-center/press-releases/chairman-salmon-statement-prime-minister-abe-s-wwii-anniversary.

25. "Statement by Senator John McCain Marking the 70th Anniversary of Official End of World War II." September 2, 2015, http://www.mccain.senate.gov/public/index.cfm/press-releases?ID=acfd6588–01e5–45c1–a738–6c3abf8f8a8f.

26. "On the 70th Anniversary of the End of World War II in the Pacific." September 2, 2015. Accessed September 3, 2015, http://www.state.gov/secretary/remarks/2015/09/246573.htm.

27. Travel to Cuba, http://www.state.gov/secretary/travel/2015/t17/index.htm.

28. Kennedy also visited Hiroshima on the anniversary of the attack in 2014. Kennedy To Visit Hiroshima, Nagasaki, August 4, 2015, *Japan Bullet,* http://www.japanbullet.com/news/kennedy-to-visit-hiroshima-nagasaki; Ambassador Kennedy and Under Secretary Gottemoeller Represent the United States at the 2015 Nagasaki Peace Memorial Ceremony, August 9, 2015, http://japan.usembassy.gov/e/p/tp-20150809–01.html.

29. The ceremony was held on September 3. "In Baguio, remembering the Japanese forces' World War II surrender," Rappler.com, September 5, 2015, http://www.rappler.com/nation/104781-baguio-japanese-surrender-ww2.

30. Edward Wong, Jane Perlez and Chris Buckley, "China Announces Cuts of 300,000 Troops at Military Parade Showing Its Might," *New York Times,* September 2, 2015, http://www.nytimes.com/2015/09/03/world/asia/beijing-turns-into-ghost-town-as-it-gears-up-for-military-parade.html?_r=0.

31. "US officials mark 70th anniversary of WWII's official end," *Washington Post,* September 2, 2015, http://www.washingtonpost.com/national/us-officials-mark-70th-anniversary-of-wwiis-official-end/2015/09/02/ed026dce-51e6–11e5–b225–90edbd49f362_story.html.

32. "Peace in the Pacific," *Baltimore Sun, The Darkroom,* August 16, 2015, http://darkroom.baltimoresun.com/2015/08/peace-in-the-pacific/#15.

33. "Statement by the President on the 70th Anniversary Commemorating the End of World War II in the Pacific." September 2, 2015, https://www.whitehouse.gov/the-press-office/2015/09/02/statement-president-70th-anniversary-commemorating-end-world-war-ii. For online criticism see https://groups.google.com/forum/#!topic/alt.politics/VGzh74pPMSM and Kim Quade, "Obama Ignores V-J Day," *Victory Girls,* August 15, 2015, http://victorygirlsblog.com/obama-ignores-v-j-day-remembrance/; "Queen risks life to mark V-J Day; Obama ignores event," http://sportshoop.la/threads/queen-risks-life-to-mark-v-j-day-obama-ignores-event.187370/page-6.

34. Barack Obama to visit Hiroshima on Japan and Vietnam trip, May 10, 2016, http://www.bbc.com/news/world-asia-36258866.

35. John Bolton, "Obama's shameful apology tour lands in Hiroshima," May 26, 2016, *New York Post,* http://nypost.com/2016/05/26/obamas-shameful-apology-tour-lands-in-hiroshima/ Palin quoted in, Sophie Tatum, "Trump asks why Obama didn't mention Pearl Harbor during Japan trip," CNN, May 29, 2016; http://www.cnn.com/2016/05/28/politics/donald-trump-criticizes-barack-obama-pearl-harbor/index.html.

36. Barack Obama, "Remarks and a Question-and-Answer Session With Reporters in Shima City, Japan," May 26, 2016. Online by Gerhard Peters and John T. Woolley, *American Presidency Project,* http://www.presidency.ucsb.edu/ws/?pid=117896.

37. President Obama Visits Hiroshima, Live Coverage, *New York Times,* May 27, 2016, https://www.nytimes.com/live/president-obama-hiroshima-japan/; "Remarks With Prime Minister Shinzō Abe of Japan at Hiroshima Peace Memorial Park in Hiroshima, Japan," May 27, 2016. Online by Gerhard Peters and John T. Woolley, *American Presidency Project,* http://www.presidency.ucsb.edu/ws/index.php?pid=117688&st=&st1=.

38. Ibid.

39. "Opinion: Obama's Hiroshima trip no occasion to whitewash Japan's WWII atrocities," May 27, 2016, *New China,* http://news.xinhuanet.com/english/2016–05/27/c_135393117.htm.

40. Sophie Tatum, "Trump asks why Obama didn't mention Pearl Harbor during Japan trip;" CNN, May 29, 2016; http://www.cnn.com/2016/05/28/politics/donald-trump-criticizes-barack-obama-pearl-harbor/index.html.

41. Jonah Goldberg, "What Trump means When he Says 'America First,'" *Los Angeles Times*, January 24, 2017, http://www.latimes.com/opinion/op-ed/la-oe-goldberg-america-first-20170124-story.html.

42. Motoko Rich and Gardner Harris, "In Pearl Harbor Visit, a Symbol of Reconciliation in Japan," *New York Times*, December 24, 2016, https://www.nytimes.com/2016/12/24/world/asia/pearl-harbor-japan-shinzo-abe.html?_r=0; Jonathan Soble and Keith B. Radsher, *New York Times*, March 7, 2016, https://www.nytimes.com/2016/03/08/business/international/unease-after-trump-depicts-tokyo-as-an-economic-rival.html?_r=0; Barney Henderson, "Donald Trump savages Japan, saying all they will do is 'watch Sony TVs' if US is attacked and threatening to walk' away from treaty," *Telegraph*, August 6, 2016, http://www.telegraph.co.uk/news/2016/08/05/donald-trump-savages-japan-saying-all-they-will-do-is-watch-sony/.

43. "The President's News Conference With Prime Minister Shinzō Abe of Japan," February 10, 2017, http://www.presidency.ucsb.edu/ws/index.php?pid=123196&st=&st1; "Joint Statement by President Trump and Prime Minister Shinzō Abe of Japan," February 10, 2017, http://www.presidency.ucsb.edu/ws/index.php?pid=123192&st=&st1; "Remarks With Prime Minister Shinzō Abe of Japan to Reporters in Palm Beach, Florida," February 11, 2017, http://www.presidency.ucsb.edu/ws/index.php?pid=123404&st=&st1; Motoko Rich, "Relief in Japan After Abe Visit with Trump," *New York Times*, February 13, 2017, https://www.nytimes.com/2017/02/13/world/asia/trump-japan-shinzo-abe.html?mcubz=0.

44. Bruce Stokes, "70 years after Hiroshima, opinions have shifted on use of atomic bomb," Pew Research Center, August 4, 2015, http://www.pewresearch.org/fact-tank/2015/08/04/70-years-after-hiroshima-opinions-have-shifted-on-use-of-atomic-bomb/.

45. Adam Taylor, "More and More Americans Question the Hiroshima Bombing. But Would they do it Again?" *Washington Post*, May 26, 2016, https://www.washingtonpost.com/news/worldviews/wp/2016/05/26/more-and-more-americans-question-the-hiroshima-bombing-but-they-would-they-do-it-again-maybe/?tid=a_inl&utm_term=.c9a32744a7ef.

46. Dr. Mimaki has written extensively on the process of reconciliation in international affairs. Seiko Mimaki, "The Significance of Abe's Pearl Harbor Visit: The Japanese prime minister's visit shows that liberals don't have the monopoly on reconciliation." January 25, 2017, *Diplomat*, http://thediplomat.com/2017/01/the-significance-of-abes-pearl-harbor-visit/ See also, https://www.washingtonpost.com/news/worldviews/wp/2015/08/06/how-the-hiroshima-bombing-is-taught-around-the-world/?utm_term=.6cb26ec65387.

47. Motoko Rich and Gardner Harris, "In Pearl Harbor Visit, a Symbol of Reconciliation in Japan," *New York Times*, December 24, 2016, https://www.nytimes.com/2016/12/24/world/asia/pearl-harbor-japan-shinzo-abe.html?_r=0.

Chapter Eight

Looking West more than East

Russia's World War II Commemorations

Marlene Laruelle

Russia marks the end of World War II on May 9, commemorating the signing of the German act of capitulation to the Allies in Berlin on May 9, 1945, at midnight Moscow time. The event has been *the* major secular holiday in Russia since the 1960s. The military parade in Red Square allows the country to demonstrate its status as a world power, while the grassroots festivities honoring veterans—seen as living icons of the people's heroism—make it a genuinely popular celebration. The memory of World War II, known as the "Great Patriotic War" (*Velikaia otechestvennaia voina*) in Russia, plays a critical role in fostering popular support for the regime. In recent years, it has provided a relatively unique moment of harmony between the Kremlin and the Russian public,[1] with some notable exceptions such as the annexation of Crimea in March 2014. In Russian collective memory, the war is, above all, a battle against "German aggression": its international aspect as a world war is secondary, as is the Nazi extermination of Jews and other groups of people. For the Russian side, the war began with the German invasion in June 1941. The two previous years are conveniently omitted from the official memory, so that the Kremlin does not have to justify the Molotov-Ribbentrop non-aggression pact of 1939. The Asian side of the war is almost totally absent from public mourning and memory, as I explain below.

The 2015 commemoration was exceptional, not only because it was the 70th anniversary, but also because of the tension with the West, especially the United States, over Ukraine. It was the largest commemoration ever, displaying a large number of Russian troops and ultra-modern military equipment, as well as 1,300 troops from ten foreign countries, mostly former Soviet republics, who had also played a critical role in the war. For the first time, troops from China, India, Serbia and Mongolia paraded on Red Square. More than 50,000 civilians marched through central Moscow, and thanks to the festivities organized across Russia—more than 20 cities had their own parades—about 12 million people participated nationwide. While most Western countries boycotted the festivities or sent only second-rank political personnel, the parade featured many of Russia's new and old friends on the international scene. Participants included Chinese president Xi Jinping, Indian president Pranad Mukherjee, Palestinian leader Mahmoud Abbas, South Africa's Jacob Zuma, Serbian leader Tomislav Mikolic, Mongolia's Tsarkhiargijn Elbegdori, the Vietnamese leader Trương Tấn Sang, Cuban president Raul Castro, Venezuela's Nicolas Maduro, Egyptian president General Abdel Fattah el-Sisi, UN Secretary-General Ban Ki-moon, and several presidents of post-Soviet republics. Some Western veterans, including former American and British soldiers, also attended.

The Ukrainian crisis accelerated the ongoing politicization of history in Russia and the Central European countries that were occupied by both Nazi Germany and the Soviet Union—the Baltic states, Poland, and Ukraine. For the Kremlin, as well as large parts of Russian society, the 2015 commemorations thus sought not only to project domestic consensus, but also to brand Russia as the "savior of Europe" and the leader of the global fight against Nazism and neo-Nazism. They also offered a prime occasion for Moscow to display its strategic honeymoon with China and to reinforce its stance toward Japan over the contested Kuril Islands/Northern Territories.

DOMESTIC CONCERNS DRIVE COMMEMORATIONS

Contemporary Russia is a fragmented society in terms of living standards, international contacts, access to information, and political and identity perceptions. It has very few elements that could create an overarching social bond or civic consensus. Since he came to power in 2000, President Vladimir Putin has been building a new political vocabulary to underpin his so-called elective authoritarian regime, based not only on the high popularity of its president—approval ratings hover around 80 percent—but also on citizens' deep distrust of post-Soviet political institutions and the market economy. One major element of the post-Soviet social consensus between the authorities and the society is the positive reassessment of the Soviet past, rehabilitated in the symbols of the Russian state (national anthem, coat of arms, etc.), official commemorations, and public discourses.[2] While *perestroika* thrived on contradictory debates about the Soviet past, in the 2000s the emphasis was placed on victory in the Second World War; and Stalin's repression campaigns were discreetly set aside. In 2005, a few days before the 60th anniversary of V-E Day, Putin put into words the feelings of most Russians, namely that "the collapse of the Soviet Union was the greatest geopolitical catastrophe of the century."[3] Popular attitudes toward the Great Patriotic War are based on the notion that war provides a unique moment during which the strength of the nation is revealed to its people and to the world.

In the postwar period, after the cycles of massive repression ended, the Soviet Communist Party sought to consolidate its authority by mythologizing the Great Patriotic War, which it claimed confirmed the soundness of the Socialist system. Paradoxically, Stalin and Khrushchev were not particularly interested in cultivating the memory of the victory—it was too 'fresh' for the current generations and the Soviet leadership was not interested in being questioned on its mismanagement of the first months of the war. It was only under Brezhnev, after 1965, that the war became the focal point of Soviet history and May 9 the most important state holiday, eventually surpassing November 7—the anniversary of the Bolshevik Revolution.[4] A well-crafted and unassailable narrative emerged, emphasizing that only the Red Army had been able to defeat Fascism. In the 1990s, when many elements of Soviet culture were sharply questioned or became obsolete, the image of the Great Patriotic War managed to survive contextual changes. Major criticisms of how the war had been fought, prevalent during the *perestroika* period, stopped with the fiftieth anniversary in 1995.[5]

All surveys confirm that about 90 percent of Russian citizens regard the Great Patriotic War as *the* most important event in the whole of Russian history.[6] Even if the young are less well versed in historical details,[7] the Russian population at large sees the war as the primary event of national history, regardless of social class or age. Given the unity created by the war, other major historical moments seem to fade precisely due to their non-consensual nature. In sociological surveys asking about the ten major dates in the nation's history, not a single reference is made to the pre-revolutionary past, which is too distant and arouses mixed feelings. The conflicts of the late twentieth century have also gradually disappeared. The putsch of August 1991, which featured prominently in polls in the 1990s, is no longer mentioned as a top ten historical reference, absent along with *perestroika* and even the collapse of the Soviet Union. The only date to have moved up the list over the years is the space flight of Yuri Gagarin in 1961, due to the feeling of returning to Cold War-era technological competition with the United States.[8]

Today, the Great Patriotic War is described in terms that are increasingly nationalist. The war's international context has been partially erased, such that not only are references to the Western Allies less explicit, but the idea that the Soviet Union could have won the war without outside help is on the rise. The victory is also transformed into a strictly Russian event: the role of the other Soviet peoples is increasingly marginalized. The Jewish Holocaust occupies a minor position in the narrative, which focuses instead on the massive Soviet losses (about 27 million people). The loss of lives allegedly reflects the heroism of the Russian people, who exult in the massive number despite the human suffering involved. As the director of the Levada Center, sociologist Lev Gudkov, explains, the Great Patriotic War allows individuals to talk about the nation without referring to the state or the authorities, institutions that are perceived negatively today. The dominant feeling is that, unlike the peoples of Western Europe, Russians reveal their true character in times of hardship, conflict, and suffering.[9] This directly corroborates their own version of Russian identity, whose features include patience, resistance to life's difficulties, spirituality, collectivism, and hospitality.[10]

The extent of the casualties during the Second World War is seldom blamed on Soviet mismanagement or Stalin's lack of military preparation, but rather on Russia's being surprised by "German aggression."[11] This version of events supports the commonly held view of Russia as a victim country. A large number of the population had not heard of the Molotov-Ribbentrop pact and its secret clauses that allowed Moscow to invade Finland, the Baltic countries, and Poland. Among those with knowledge of this historic document, many believe that it was propaganda, a fake text or one of Hitler's tactics; alternatively, they accept the Soviet-era explanation that in order to better prepare for war, the Soviet Union had no choice but to grant this concession.[12]

Nationalist perceptions of the Great Patriotic War have become even more pronounced with the Ukrainian crisis of 2014. The whole state media machine, which controls television, the main radio channels, and newspapers, has directed its energy toward highlighting supposed historical parallels between the current tensions between Moscow and Kyiv and the fight against Fascism in World War II. The Euromaidan protests have been presented as dominated by Ukrainian far-right parties and movements calling for the rehabilitation of locals who collaborated with Nazi Germany, such as Stepan Bandera; the new Poroshenko regime has been painted as a "Fascist junta."[13] In the face of this threat, Russia supposedly stands as the last vanguard against the resurgent Fascist flame in Europe, and the Donbas secessionist authorities in Donetsk and Luhansk as the heirs of the Soviet heroes of the Great Patriotic War. This heavy media campaign has deeply affected the meaning of World War II commemorations for both the Kremlin and the Russian population.[14] For example, World War II-era symbols have reappeared in everyday life: the St. George Ribbon, a black and orange pattern used in many military decorations, is now displayed in Russia as a patriotic symbol of loyalty toward the Kremlin,[15] while in Ukraine it is associated with Russian nationalism and Donbas separatism.[16]

RUSSIA'S BELONGING TO EUROPE AT THE CORE
OF THE WORLD WAR II DEBATE

The emphasis on World War II commemorations in Russia is not only linked to the Kremlin's need for domestic support and loyalty, but also underpins Russia's strategies toward Europe. Since the second half of the 2000s, political tension around historical memory questions and their valence in relations between post-communist states has heightened, particularly in terms of Russia's relations with Ukraine, the Baltic States, and Poland—a region that faced both high levels of violence and extermination during the war *and* the brutal (re)Sovietization that followed. The memory policies implemented in the countries of Central Europe directly attack the Soviet narrative as well as the Western one. The interpretation of World War II has, in fact, become one of the identity matrices of the Central European members of the European Union, who have sought for some years to redirect the West European-centered interpretation of World War II that regards Russia as an ally and does not debate the region's transition from Nazi to Communist totalitarianism. A discursive escalation among all actors has intensified the new interpretation of some of the notions espoused by Central European regimes and has transformed the debate into a component of foreign policy strategies. [17]

In the early 1990s, the new democratic regimes in Czechoslovakia and Poland adopted lustration policies, purging their respective administrations of figures considered too closely tied to the Communist regime and especially its repressive structures. [18] The progressive criminalization of the Soviet legacy deeply shocked Russian public opinion, which was by no means prepared for such polemics. The memory wars grew in magnitude when Central European countries were admitted into the European Union: they often linked the assertion of their European identity with an official narrative denouncing Nazism and Communism as equal totalitarian regimes. [19] In 2004 for instance, the governments of Estonia and Latvia made an official request to Moscow for damages of several hundred million dollars for what they defined as the Soviet occupation, while the Estonian and Lithuanian presidents refused to participate in commemorations of the victory in Moscow on May 9, 2005. [20] In the same year, the Estonian State Commission published a White Paper, "Examination of the Policies of Repression," and then in 2007, the Polish Minister of Culture proposed removing all statues tied to World War II that were erected during the Soviet period. The official remembrances of the anti-Soviet resistance movements, even those that fought in German uniforms, have also risen in number. Lastly, Ukraine tried to have the Holodomor (the Ukrainian famine of 1932–1933) recognized internationally as not only a crime against humanity but a genocide. [21]

The controversy around the Bronze Soldier statue in Tallinn in 2007 has played a leading role in the rise of Russian concerns about the interpretation of World War II abroad. The Estonian authorities, as well as Estonian nationalist associations, have undertaken a long process of reinterpretation of history, calling for active remembrance of their countrymen who took up arms against Soviet troops during the war. In 2002, a monument built to the Estonians who, in Nazi uniforms, fought for the liberation of their country, was erected in Pärnu, then taken down and moved to Lihula, where, after an international outcry, the authorities ended up removing it. In 2007, the Estonian government decided to relocate the Bronze Soldier, symbolic of the Soviet fighter, from the center of Tallinn to a more peripheral military cemetery. Estonia's Russian community came out in droves, claiming one could not celebrate those who fought under German uniforms against the Red Army.[22]

This interpretation was given new force with the Ukrainian crisis of 2014, and the decision by the Ukrainian authorities, in May 2015, a few days before the 70th anniversary, to ban the use of any Soviet symbols as well as Nazi ones, making them equal—an equation that already exists in the Baltic states. The law also makes it a criminal offense to deny the "criminal character of the communist totalitarian regime of 1917–1991 in Ukraine." This was accompanied by a second, even more controversial law that declared that the nationalist credentials of Ukrainian "independence fighters" cannot be questioned, even if they collaborated with the Nazis.[23] From Russia's vantage point, this was interpreted as proof that the negation of the Soviet role in the 1945 victory had become part of the post-Euromaidan Ukrainian government's policy.[24]

Seen from the Russian perspective, the Baltic States' and Ukraine's strategies aim at negating the Soviet Union's role as a liberator of Europe in order to delegitimize modern Russia's right to participate in the affairs of the continent. On the contrary, in Russia, the cult of World War II is understood as the major legitimacy tool the country cultivates to brand itself as a legitimate actor in the contemporary European political landscape.

RUSSIA'S AMBIVALENT POSITIONING IN ASIA

The role of World War II commemorations in displaying Russia's place in Asia is more ambivalent. In 1881, Fyodor Dostoevsky brilliantly expressed the essence of Russia's position toward Asia at the time: "In Europe we were Tatars, but in Asia we too are Europeans."[25] Today, the context has totally changed: for the first time in the history of modern Russia, Asia is no longer regarded as a barbarous and backward place that needs Moscow to bring the European Enlightenment to it. The Asia paradigm in Russia's national identity framework has, therefore, been deeply modified: Russia wishes to continue to be an indispensable partner of the West on the key questions of

Northeast Asian security and hopes to benefit from the economic dynamism of the Asia-Pacific region.[26]

China's position on Russia's radar is ambivalent. Since he returned to the presidency in May 2012, Putin has praised the Russia-China partnership, insisting that both countries share a similar will to transform the world order and international institutions, and that both have built a successful economic and strategic partnership. Tensions inherited from the Sino-Soviet dispute have disappeared,[27] border issues have been resolved, and Russo-Chinese cooperation has developed within, among others, the Shanghai Cooperation Organization.[28] China became Russia's primary trading partner in 2009; trade figures show Russia's focus on primary resources and China's role as a supplier of finished products.[29] In 2014, the two countries signed the "deal of the century," a reported $400 billion 30-year agreement that China would buy natural gas from fields in eastern Siberia. However, the economic slow-down of 2015 darkened the prospects for economic cooperation.[30]

The Russia-China strategic alliance has been reinforced since the Ukrainian crisis. Even if Chinese authorities were deeply concerned by Moscow's violation of international law and its lack of respect for territorial integrity,[31] the sanctions imposed on Russia by the international community strengthened Moscow's links with Beijing. Though China is now in the process of developing an indigenous, high-tech defense industry, the bilateral arms trade was reinvigorated in 2015 with a new $3 billion deal for long-range S-400 surface-to-air missile (SAM) systems.[32] The agreement is the largest Chinese-Russian arms deal in over a decade and will impact regional security, as China's improved air defense capabilities could help secure its claims on the South China Sea.

Yet Russia's attitude toward China has to be understood in light of several glaring oversights. The 2009 National Security Strategy failed to mention any security risk in the Far East, revealing Russia's reluctance to raise the Chinese question in leadership circles.[33] But Russian elites are not at all prepared to accept China as a political or cultural power at the highest level, become Beijing's satellite, or accept the Sinification of Russia's Far East.

To avoid being trapped in a bilateral relation in which China may one day be the dominant power, Russia needs to develop strong partnerships with other Asian nations. Japan comes to mind first, and bilateral economic cooperation has been growing. Russia is increasingly targeting the Japanese energy market, and Putin ordered the acceleration of the Sakhalin-3 LNG project to meet shortfalls in Japan's energy supply after the Fukushima catastrophe of March 2011. However, the relationship is still impeded by the World War II-era question of the Southern Kuril Islands/Northern Territories.[34] Both the Russian and Japanese leaderships have their hands tied by public opinion and intransigent nationalist lobbies. Putin would have to make a rhetorical "about-face" to give back territories seized from Japan at the end of World

War II, so untouchable is the image of the victory of 1945, and this has been made even more complicated after winning Crimea back. While Moscow did not join Beijing in harshly condemning Prime Minister Abe Shinzō's controversial visit to the Yasukuni Shrine in 2014, the Russian Foreign Ministry was critical of this "different assessment of the outcome of World War II," and there was talk of Moscow growing more assertive in denying Japanese claims to be the victim on the territorial question.[35] Abe's obsession with history and boosting national identity inevitably clashes with Putin's efforts to strengthen pride in Soviet history, especially related to World War II. Russia for instance reacted negatively to Japan submitting records of repatriation of former POWs from the USSR to UNESCO's Memory of the World Register in 2015.

Broadly speaking, memory issues related to Asia are largely neglected in Russia. The memory of the Russo-Japanese War of 1905, still mentioned in Russian nationalist narratives as having paved the way for the collapse of the Tsarist regime during World War I and the two subsequent revolutions of February and October 1917,[36] is very distant. The fact that casualties in the 1905 war were minimal by comparison—about 10,000 Russian soldiers died[37] —minimizes popular mourning. However, residents of the Russian Far East have not forgotten. In Vladivostok and Khabarovsk, for instance, local historians and specialists on Asian history do research on the memory of the 1905 conflict, but this has no impact on a national scale.[38] The violent border clashes with China, in 1969, over the Zhenbao/Damanskii Island, are considered off limits. Given the official honeymoon between Moscow and Beijing, no one is trying to break the official silence to develop a memory work.

THE 2015 COMMEMORATIONS AND THE ASIAN SIDE OF RUSSIAN MEMORY

Russia's special relationship with China was prominently featured during the May 9, 2015, commemorations. Chinese president Xi Jinping received high honors, including being seated immediately to the right of President Putin— yet this was probably because almost no Western leaders, cooled by Crimea's annexation and the war in eastern Ukraine, wanted to attend the event. The PLA's Chinese Honor Guard, the largest of the ten foreign groups, paraded and sang the Russian wartime song *Katyusha* in both Russian and Chinese.[39] Commemorations organized in the cities of the Russian Far East were also given a special importance. Yet in contrast with Moscow celebrations, Chinese representatives or troops were completely absent from the commemorations in the Far East, a fact that is probably indicative of cautious local sentiments toward China. Commemorations in Vladivostok were particularly festive, with about 50,000 spectators, and for the first time the Victory Parade there contained a naval section, with the Pacific fleet involved.[40] On September 3, Russian troops paid a reciprocal visit to Tiananmen Square, where they participated in a Chinese military parade that, for the first time in history, involved foreign troops, as well as veterans who fought in World War II under the Chinese Nationalists.[41]

But the Asian side of World War II is seldom mentioned. Under President Medvedev, China and Russia signed a joint document "defending the truth about World War II" but this did not develop into anything meaningful. The dominant Russian narrative of a "patriotic war" against the "German enemy" tends to obscure depictions of the war as being worldwide. Moreover, the Soviet Union was at war with Japan for less than a month, between August 8 and September 2; Soviet engagement was decided at Yalta and the Soviet-Japanese Neutrality Pact of April 1941 only then repudiated. There are few Russian veterans—the compass of Russia's memory policy—of the Asian campaign compared to the tens of millions who fought in the European theater. Only 36,000 Soviet soldiers, mostly from the Siberian brigades and the Pacific fleet, died on the Asian front. Last but not least, the difficult negotiations between the Soviet Union and Japan over the fate of half a million Japanese POWs who were sentenced to forced labor for decades,[42] which resulted in official apologies by presidents Mikhail Gorbachev and Boris Yeltsin in 1990–1992, did not have public resonance in Russia. The story of one POW who returned to Japan only in 1998 triggered popular sentiment in Japan, but not in Russia.[43]

Moreover, it is difficult to celebrate the end of the Asian war, as Moscow has no peace treaty with Japan or a powerful visual element such as the Soviet flag flying over the Reichstag to symbolize the victory on the Asian front. The Russian narrative of the victory over Japan is therefore very neutral, with little to no pathos compared with the narrative about Germany. Debates over the nature of Japanese "imperialism" at that time have not been generated for public consumption and are limited to the professional historian community. More importantly, in Russian public discourse, Japan surrendered to the United States, not the USSR: the memory of Japan's defeat is associated with the atomic bombs on Hiroshima and Nagasaki, and therefore with the Cold War period and the technological competition between the two superpowers, rather than with the end of the Nazi-Japanese alliance.

Given the ambiguous circumstances of the war with Japan, Russia does not commemorate September 2 or 3. In 1945, the president of the USSR Supreme Soviet proclaimed September 2 a federal holiday marking "The Victory over Militaristic Japan"—a phrase still used in school textbooks— but it was celebrated only twice, in 1945 and 1946. Although the Supreme Soviet decree was never abolished, the date has stopped being celebrated or even mentioned in official documents, including in the list published with the law "On the Days of Military Glory of Russia" in 1995. In the 2000s, September 3 became the "Day of Solidarity with Victims of Terrorism" after the bloody hostage crisis at the Beslan school in 2004, leaving no room for a memory toward Japan.

However, the debate about the need for a new holiday, or at least an official date, resurfaces at regular intervals. The parliaments of the Far Eastern regions, especially Sakhalin, submitted bills to the Federal Duma in 2000, 2002, and 2003 in the hope of having September 2 or 3 recognized as a national holiday. In 2004, while preparing for the 60th anniversary of the end of the war in 2005, the Federal Duma rejected a new holiday initiative under the pretext that there would be associated costs to be paid by the federal budget. The Sakhalin local authorities insist that if September 2 or 3 does not become a recognized holiday, there is a risk of seeing the Kuril Islands returned to Japan in the future. Creating a formal day of commemoration would therefore be understood as "sanctifying" Russian sovereignty over the territories won from Japan.[44] The Sakhalin perspective is supported by Russian nationalist groups and the Communist Party of the Russian Federation, and it has been discussed online on several occasions, including in 2015, with supporters arguing that Russia should celebrate more vividly its important role in liberating Manchuria/northeast China and north Korea from Japanese domination.[45]

In a nod toward marking the Asian side of World War II commemorations, in 2015 Putin stopped in Chita, capital of the Baikal region, on his way to China for the city's September 2 commemorations, and placed flowers at the local Memorial to Military and Labor Glory.[46] Yet this remains a very timid acknowledgment. The state media agency Russia Today also released several multimedia war-related articles between May 9 and September 2.[47] In a more provocative act, Prime Minister Dmitri Medvedev visited the disputed Kuril Islands on August 22—an indirect tribute to the brief time the Soviet Union was at war with Japan—prompting the Japanese Foreign Ministry to lodge an official complaint. The situation intensified when Deputy Prime Minister Dmitri Rogozin, a former Russian ambassador to NATO and well-known for his nationalist stance, dismissed the Japanese reaction by inviting them to commit *harakiri*—ritualistic suicide for Japanese samurai—in protest.[48]

CONCLUSION

World War II commemorations, used as an important opportunity to display social consensus under the Soviet regime, have become in today's Russia a "holy day" that cannot be questioned, neither in their state-centric aspect—the military parade and Russia's quest for international status—nor in their genuinely popular character. Vladimir Putin himself has contributed to the sanctification of the Great Patriotic War's memory and the symbols associated with it. The Russian establishment and a large part of Russian society regard the ongoing politicization of memory in Central Europe as an unacceptable questioning of the legitimacy of Russia as the savior of Europe against Fascism. In such a heavily politicized context, Russia will continue to differentiate the "Great Patriotic War" from World War II for both domestic and external audiences. It will specify the unique, Russia-centered reading of it, and marginalize its international aspects, as well as the Holocaust. Contemporary Russian academic scholarship does explore difficult pages of Soviet history—the initial relationship with Nazi Germany, collaboration in occupied territories and the so-called 'Holocaust by bullets' that happened on Soviet-occupied territories—but this does not reach the level of general public opinion, which remains focused on the veneration of veterans and fallen soldiers and the exceptional heroism of Russians.

Paradoxically, the progressive internationalization of the Russian memory of the war may be driven from Asia. Indeed, moving from the *Great Patriotic War* to *World War II* on the European side would mean acknowledging the role of the United States in fighting Fascism and the right of Central Europe to its own memory of the war, which equates the Soviet Union with Nazi Germany. On the Asian side, the memory stakes are less contradictory and do not challenge Russia's international status and legitimacy. Indirectly, the Kremlin's willingness to cooperate more closely with China and to display shared strategies toward the United States and the so-called liberal world order pushes Moscow to accommodate the Chinese reading of World War II, and therefore to move the pendulum toward the Asia-Pacific side. It is possible that, in the years to come, Russia may decide to declare a national anniversary on September 2 or 3 in order to boost synergies with Asia. Promoting this Asian side of World War II memory would pave new roads for demonstrating the Russian partnership with China, but would also mean insisting on Japanese defeat—and therefore refusing to discuss the status of the Kuril Islands/Northern Territories. However, at the same time, the widespread Russian narrative about Japanese defeat already being part of the Cold War period and the nuclear competition, rather than the war itself, it avoids confronting Japan's memory too directly and portraying it as Russia's enemy. As always, memory tells us more about the present than about the past.

NOTES

1. Elizabeth Wood, "Performing Memory: Vladimir Putin and the Celebration of World War II in Russia," *Soviet and Post-Soviet Review* 38 (2011): 172–200.

2. See Stephen White, "Soviet nostalgia and Russian politics," *Journal of Eurasian Studies* 1 no. 1 (2010): 1–9; and Charles Sullivan, "Motherland: Soviet Nostalgia in Post-Soviet Russia" (PhD dissertation, George Washington University, 2014). See also Marlene Laruelle, *In the Name of the Nation: Nationalism and Politics in Contemporary Russia* (New York: Palgrave Macmillan, 2009), 120–125.

3. Vladimir V. Putin, "Poslanie Federal'nomu Sobraniiu Rossiiskoi Federatsii," *Kremlin.ru*, April 25, 2005, http://www.kremlin.ru/appears/2005/04/25/1223_ type63372type63374type82634_87049.shtml.

4. Nina Tumarkin, *The Living and the Dead: The Rise and Fall of the Cult of World War II in Russia* (New York: Basic Books, 1995).

5. Kathleen Smith, *Mythmaking in the New Russia* (Ithaca, NY: Cornell University Press, 2002).

6. Lev Gudkov, "Istoriia v soznanii nashikh grazhdan ostaetsia sovetskoi," *Novye izvestiia*, October 19, 2010, accessed January 14, 2011, http://www.newizv.ru/news/2010–10–19/ 135152/.

7. A. Petrova, "22 iiunia—nachalo voiny," *Fond obshchestvennogo mneniia*, June 26, 2002.

8. L.D. Gudkov, "Pobeda v voine: k sotsiologii odnogo natsional'nogo simvola," in L. D. Gudkov, *Negativnaia identichnost.' Stati 1997–2002 gg.* (Moscow: NLO, 2004), 21.

9. Ibid, 39.

10. L.D. Gudkov, "Struktura i kharakter natsional'noi identichnosti v Rossii," in Gudkov, *Negativnaia identichnost,* 135.

11. Gudkov, "Pobeda v voine: k sotsiologii odnogo natsional'nogo simvola," 41.

12. L.D. Gudkov, "'Pamiat' o voine i massovaia identichnost' rossiian," *Pamiat' o voine 60 let spustia. Rossiia, Germaniia, Evropa* (Moscow: NLO, 2005), 102.

13. See Robert Orttung et al., "War of words: the impact of Russian state television on the Russian Internet," *Nationalities Papers* 43, no. 4 (2015) : 533–555.

14. See Elizabeth Wood, "Putin's war of words, decoded," *Monkey Cage*, February 26, 2015, https://www.washingtonpost.com/blogs/monkey-cage/wp/2015/02/26/the-military-medal-race-in-russia-and-ukraine-a-symbolic-competition/.

15. Vitaly Shevchenko, "Russia awash with symbols of WW2 victory," *BBC*, May 8, 2015, http://www.bbc.com/news/world-europe-32650024.

16. "Kyiv Ditches Separatist-Linked Ribbon As World War II Symbol," *RFE/RL*, May 6, 2015, http://www.rferl.org/content/russia-ukraine-st-george-ribbon-wwii-commemoration/ 25375013.html.

17. See for instance the special issue "Historical Memory and the Great Patriotic War," *Canadian Slavonic Papers: Revue Canadienne des Slavistes* 54: 3–4 (2012). See also Małgorzata Pakier and Bo Stråth, eds., *A European Memory? Contested Histories and Politics of Remembrance* (New York: Bergham Books, 2010).

18. Roman David, "Lustration Laws in Action: The Motives and Evaluation of Lustration Policy in Czech Republic and Poland (1989–2001)," *Law & Social Inquiry* 28, no. 2 (2003): 387–439.

19. On the Letton case, see Eva-Clarita Onken, "Ot istorii osvobozhdeniia k istorii okkupatsii. Vospriatie Vtoroi mirovoi voiny i pamiat' o nee v Latvii posle 1945 goda," in *Pamiat' o voine 60 let spustia. Rossiia, Germaniia, Evropa*, 436–451.

20. Eva-Clarita Onken, "The Baltic States and Moscow's 9 May Commemoration: Analysing Memory Politics in Europe," *Europe-Asia Studies* 59, no. 1 (2007): 23–46.

21. The crime against humanity was accepted by the European Parliament, the Parliamentary Assembly of the Council of Europe, the OSCE and the UN General Assembly, but the accusation of genocide was rejected by the majority of states and international bodies, and only a dozen countries recognized it, including Georgia.

22. Heiko Pääbo, "War of Memories: Explaining 'Memorials War' in Estonia," *Baltic Security & Defence Review* 10 (2008): 5–28.

23. Alec Luhn, "Ukraine bans Soviet symbols and criminalises sympathy for communism," *Guardian*, May 21, 2015,http://www.theguardian.com/world/2015/may/21/ukraine-bans-soviet-symbols-criminalises-sympathy-for-communism.

24. Robert Horvath, "The Euromaidan and the crisis of Russian nationalism," *Nationalities Papers* 43:6 (2015): 819–839.

25. F. Dostoevskii, *Sobranie sochinenii v 15–i tomakh. Dnevnik pisatelia, 1881* (Moscow: Nauka, 1995), Vol. 14, 509.

26. Rensselaer Lee and Artyom Lukin , *Russia's Far East: New Dynamics in Asia Pacific and Beyond* (Boulder, CO: Lynne Rienner Publishers, 2015).

27. Elizabeth Wishnick, *Mending Fences with China: The Evolution of Moscow's China Policy, 1969–99* (Seattle: University of Washington Press, 2001).

28. R.E. Bedetski and N. Swanström, eds., *Eurasia's Ascent in Energy and Geopolitics. Rivalry or partnership for China, Russia, and Central Asia?* (London: Routledge, 2012). See also Marcin Kaczmarski, *Russia-China Relations in the Post-Crisis International Order* (London: Routledge, 2015).

29. Mark A. Smith, *The Russo-Chinese Energy Relationship* (Shrivenham, UK: Defence Academy of the United Kingdom, Oct. 2010); Igor Danchenko, Erica S. Downs, and Fiona Hill, "One Step Forward, Two Steps Back? The Realities of a Rising China and Implications for Russia's Energy Ambitions," *Brookings Policy Paper* 22, August 2010.

30. Shannon Tiezzi, "China, Russia Try to Brave Economic Headwinds," *Diplomat*, December 18, 2015, http://thediplomat.com/2015/12/china-russia-try-to-brave-economic-headwinds/.

31. Zhang Lihua, "Explaining China's Position on the Crimea Referendum," *Carnegie Endowment for International Peace*, April 1, 2014, http://carnegieendowment.org/2015/04/01/explaining-china-s-position-on-crimea-referendum.

32. Benjamin David Baker, "Russian Arms Sales in Asia May Be Poised for Trouble," *Diplomat*, November 10, 2015, http://thediplomat.com/2015/11/russian-arms-sales-in-asia-may-be-poised-for-trouble/.

33. John W. Parker, "Russia's Revival: Ambitions, Limitations, and Opportunities for the United States," *INSS Strategic Perspectives* 3 (2011).

34. Alexander Bukh, *Japan's National Identity and Foreign Policy: Russia as Japan's 'Other'* (London: Routledge, 2011).

35. "Russia to Argue 'Historical Legitimacy' in Northern Territories Dispute," *Asahi shimbun*, January 6, 2014.

36. See Marlene Laruelle, "Moscow's China Dilemma: Evolving Perceptions of Russian Security in Eurasia and Asia," in Bedetski and Swanström, eds., *Eurasia's Ascent in Energy and Geopolitics. Rivalry or partnership for China, Russia, and Central Asia?*, 76–91.

37. See Rotem Kowner, *The Impact of the Russo-Japanese War* (London: Routledge, 2007).

38. See for instance "Exhibition Devoted to 105th Russian-Japanese War Anniversary Opens in Vladivostok," *Vladivostok Times*, January 27, 2009, http://vladivostoktimes.com/show/?id=34416.

39. Chang Meng, "PLA Honor Guard performs at Moscow World War II victory parade," *Global Times*, May 9, 2015, http://www.globaltimes.cn/content/920699.shtml.

40. See for instance "Po glavnoi ulitse Vladivostoka proshel iubileinyi Parad Pobedy," *Vostokmedia*, May 9, 2015, http://www.vostokmedia.com/n236858.html, and "Iubilei velikoi pobedy byl omechen vo Vladivostoke s nebyvalym razmakhom," *Vlad.mk.ru*, May 9, 2015, http://vlad.mk.ru/articles/2015/05/13/yubiley-velikoy-pobedy-byl-otmechen-vo-vladivoke-s-nebyvalym-razmakhom.html.

41. "Russian Troops Arrive in China for 'Unprecedented' Parade," *Sputnik*, August 19, 2015, http://sputniknews.com/asia/20150819/1025915692/china-russia-troops-beijing-parade.html#ixzz3z73pMyaX.

42. "On June 20, 1990, academics and Red Cross officials from the Soviet Union found that the USSR detained more than 594,000 Japanese for forced labor after World War II, among this number, 546,000 were taken to camps and about 50,000 died." More at http://www.gwu.edu/~memory/data/government/russia_pow.html.

43. Nicholas D. Kristof, "Japan's Blossoms Soothe a P.O.W. Lost in Siberia," *New York Times*, April 12, 1998, http://www.nytimes.com/1998/04/12/world/japan-s-blossoms-soothe-a-pow-lost-in-siberia.html.

44. Alisa Bedenskav, "Podzabytoe torzhestvo," *Nezavisimaia gazeta*, March 26, 2010, http://www.ng.ru/politics/2010–03–26/3_holiday.html.

45. See for instance "Den' pobedy nad militaristkoi Iaponei—konets Vtoroi Mirovoi Voiny!," *Rusmi.news*, September 2015, http://rusmi.su/news/09–2015/news4682.html, "Za Pobedy nad Iaponiei," *Pravoslavie*, 2014, http://www.pravoslavie.ru/73300.html, and http://www.pravoslavie.ru/73328.html.

46. "Putin lays flowers to Memorial to military and labor glory in Chita," *TASS*, September 2, 2015, http://tass.ru/en/russia/818088.

47. "Russia Launches Multimedia Campaign to Commemorate World War II Victory," *Sputnik*, March 19, 2015, http://in.sputniknews.com/russia/20150319/1013810101.html#ixzz3koHSbncF.

48. "Rogozin Tells Japanese To Commit Ritualistic Suicide Amid Kuril Island Spat," *Moscow Times*, August 24, 2015, http://www.themoscowtimes.com/news/article/rogozin-tells-japanese-to-commit-ritualistic-suicide-amid-kuril-island-spat/528514.html.

Chapter Nine

Commemoration in Comparison

Germany's Comprehensive and Complex "Culture of Remembrance"

Lily Gardner Feldman

"[R]emembrance of the victims of the Nazi regime has become an integral part of our self-perception," President Joachim Gauck, on the Day of Remembrance for the Victims of National Socialism, January 27, 2015.

"Crimes against humanity are not time-barred. We will always have the responsibility of ensuring that the knowledge of these atrocities is passed on, and of keeping the memories alive," Chancellor Angela Merkel on the 70th anniversary of the liberation of Auschwitz, January 27, 2015.

"Memory has no expiry date," Foreign Minister Frank-Walter Steinmeier on the 70th anniversary of the liberation of the Sachsenhausen concentration camp, April 19, 2015.

These statements by German leaders sum up Germany's distinctive "culture of remembrance," an eternal commitment as a nation to acknowledge what happened during the Third Reich, World War II and the Holocaust; to remember the victims; and to transmit that knowledge and empathy to new generations. Remembrance and commemoration of World War II and the Holocaust are essential components of West Germany's post-war identity and are seared into its DNA. Those words—and other statements by the same three leaders—provide a useful focal point for comparison with Asia's practice of commemoration as expressed in the 70th anniversary year.[1] When comparing Asian and European experiences regarding the narrow concept of commemoration and the broad notion of remembrance, there is a tendency to view the Asian process as inherently complex and the European practice as basically straightforward. However, for comparison to be useful and yield practicable lessons, we should recognize that the German and European path has been anything but simple. Indeed, "the path was strewn with many stones."[2]

Germany's confrontation since 1949 with its dark past has been early (e.g., Chancellor Adenauer's September 1951 Bundestag statement toward Israel; the December 1970 German-Polish "normalization" treaty and Chancellor Brandt's genuflection in Warsaw) and consistent (many hundreds of examples over seventy years). It is part of a larger reconciliation strategy; and accompanied by apologies and other actions (including compensation, preferential policies, and friendship and education initiatives with victim countries). Commemoration has also involved the victims as co-actors; has been carried out by both government and civil society; has been highly institutionalized; and possesses its own, official websites.[3] However, commemoration and remembrance have also been late, for the internal process began fully only in the late 1950s with domestic trials, and some important commemorative events have taken place only in the last twenty years (e.g., the Day of Remembrance for the Victims of National Socialism was inaugurated only in 1996; the Berlin Memorial to the Murdered Jews of Europe was opened only in 2005; Chancellor Merkel was the first German head of government to visit Dachau—in August 2013). Moreover, facing history has been contested (e.g., the 1952 reparations agreement with Israel; the 1997 German-Czech "reconciliation" declaration).[4]

Prime Minister Abe's 70th anniversary commemoration statement (August 14, 2015)—and his related speeches to the Australian parliament (July 8, 2014) and at Pearl Harbor (December 27, 2016)—is narrower, less comprehensive and consistent, and more contested and solitary than the German initiatives.[5] Abe's words, however, bear some similarities to German statements by emphasizing Japan's post-war commitment to peace, by drawing on emotions, and by reflecting both personal and official capacities.

Comparison of commemoration and remembrance against the backdrop of the preceding chapters regarding the Asia Pacific can be organized around four main themes: scope; content; purpose; and context.

SCOPE

Even though "commemoration" and "the seventieth anniversary" are inevitably limited topics against the plethora of remembrance activities of the preceding seven decades in the Federal Republic, they have still been broadly conceived in Germany. As foci, there is World War II—its outbreak, its duration and its end; the Holocaust—the inhumanity in individual concentration camps and their ultimate liberation; and specific acts of barbarity—June

1942, the massacre in Lidice, Czechoslovakia; April–May 1943, the Warsaw ghetto massacre, Poland; June 1944, the massacre at Oradour-sur-Glane, France; August 1944, the punitive defeat of the Warsaw Uprising, Poland. German leaders have identified a range of victims: Jews, Roma, Sinti, political prisoners, homosexuals, mentally and physically challenged individuals, slave and forced laborers, civilian populations, prisoners of war. Of all the emphases, the Holocaust has been the priority for commemoration and remembrance, suggesting a hierarchy of victims, especially in 2015 when the 50th anniversary of German-Israeli diplomatic relations also took place.

Rather than offering a series of commemoration speeches involving different official representatives, Japan's remembrance of World War II has focused on a few statements, with Abe's words of August 14, 2015, being the focal point. It was occasioned by the 70th anniversary of the end of World War II whereas his later visit to Pearl Harbor marked the beginning of the war between Japan and the United States.[6]

CONTENT

German commemoration has been expressed in statements, speeches, and visits to sites of barbarity,[7] as well as in exhibitions and concerts.[8] While commemoration has a long history in post-war Germany, the 70th anniversary of the end of World War II and the Holocaust was underscored by leaders because of a dwindling generation of witnesses. Foreign Minister Steinmeier, for example, observed at the anniversary of the liberation of Sachsenhausen: "[I]t is getting ever more difficult to keep this memory [of the Holocaust] alive as, unfortunately, ever fewer survivors of the National Socialist terror remain to recount their experiences themselves."[9]

The agents of official commemoration have spanned the government landscape: head of state; head of government; foreign minister; and both legislative bodies (the Bundestag and the Bundesrat). The words have been uttered and the acts undertaken as representatives of the German government but also as highly personal initiatives that combine a moral tone with an emotional response, as demonstrated in President Gauck's long speech for International Holocaust Remembrance Day on January 27, 2015: "For as long as I live, the fact that the German nation, despite its admirable culture, was capable of the most horrific crimes against humanity will cause me suffering."[10]

Four areas emerge as the content of Germany's commemorative narrative: fundamental acceptance of historical facts and Germany's role as perpetrator; the suffering of the victims; the relationship between past and future; and the role of young people.

Acknowledgment

Foreign Minister Steinmeier's language of acknowledgment was stark and detailed at Sachsenhausen:

> The plans for Sachsenhausen themselves make us shudder. Here, the aim was to achieve "functionality," as well as the best architecture for realizing barbarous objectives. Symmetrically designed prison huts and watchtowers aimed to achieve total control and surveillance. A novel topography of terror was thus created. And it was from here, from Sachsenhausen, that the terror was directed bureaucratically as this became the hub of the entire concentration camp system from 1938. This place . . . bears witness to the terror of a machinery in which inhumane crimes were planned and routinely administered according to functional criteria.

President Gauck was equally graphic in describing the fate of Soviet prisoners of war in Germany:

> We have gathered here today in Schloß Holte-Stukenbrock to recall one of the worst crimes of the war—the deaths of millions of Red Army soldiers in German prisoner-of-war camps. They died in agony without medical care, starved to death or were murdered. Millions of prisoners of war for whose care the German Wehrmacht was responsible under the law of war and international agreements. [11]

At Auschwitz, the universal symbol for horror and inhumanity, Chancellor Merkel used fewer words, but they were just as incisive: "We remember all those who were persecuted, tortured, tormented, expelled and murdered by Germans during National Socialism." [12]

In his August 14, 2015, speech, Prime Minister Abe centered first, and extensively, not on the crimes Japan committed, but on the rationale for going to war that found its roots in the pre-war international system and its transformation, rather than in Japanese society and Japanese politics. Only after this recitation did he address the war itself. In Australia a year earlier, Abe omitted references to the rationale for going to war and started by referencing Kokoda and Sandakan. In both speeches and at Pearl Harbor, he offered "condolences" to all those who perished, but neither an explicit reference to Japanese agency, nor a formal new apology, nor details of the crimes.

Victims

German speeches and statements highlighted the victims in three ways: explicit recounting of what happened to the victims; inclusion of surviving victims in the commemorative ceremonies; and embrace of Germans as victims. So, for example, the German foreign minister read to an audience of survivors from the diary of a young inmate at Sachsenhausen and described the medical experiments perpetrated on the young. Again to personalize and reinstitute the dignity of the victims, President Gauck recounted on International Holocaust Remembrance Day the experience of a witness who did not survive. And at Dachau in May 2015, Angela Merkel addressed first the survivors and then recited the details of what occurred at Dachau in facts and figures. She stressed the centrality of the victims' depictions and memories:

> It is extremely fortunate that people like you are willing to share your life stories with us. The boundless suffering inflicted on you by Germany during the Nazi era is essentially beyond comprehension. Your stories are, then, even more important, because they make possible an approximation of what actually happened. [13]

Representatives of victim countries have also participated in commemorations, for example the then Polish president Bronislaw Komorowski spoke in the Bundestag in September 2014 for the 75th anniversary of the outbreak of World War II, continuing a long tradition of giving voice in Germany's national legislative body to victim country leaders such as Vaclav Havel, François Mitterrand, Shimon Peres.

In their commemorative statements, German leaders have thanked these victim countries and individual survivors for the outstretched hands that made post-war reconciliation possible. In general during Germany's extensive history of commemoration and remembrance, victim nations have been magnanimous (and sometimes forgiving) rather than shaming; and have engaged in joint, and not merely solitary, remembrance activity (e.g., the November 1989 German-Polish mass). Victim representatives have also responded physically by shaking hands, holding hands (e.g., between France and Germany in September 1984 at Verdun) and embracing (e.g., between Germany and Poland in November 1989 at Krzyżowa).[14] Yet, outward signs of friendship were not always immediate: for example, on the occasion of the 1952 signing of the reparations agreement with Israel, there were neither handshakes nor speeches from Jewish and Israeli representatives; and France invited Germany to the D-Day anniversary for the first time only in 2004, sixty years after the event.

A third pattern in commemorative activities has emerged more recently. Rather than relativizing the victims outlined above by also noting the suffering of German victims, German representatives have remembered their compatriots in separate ceremonies. There have been commemorations for three sets of German victims: victims of all wars and dictatorships involving Germany; the expellees, who by sanction of the 1945 Potsdam conference were forced to leave parts of Czechoslovakia and reconstituted Poland after the war; and victims of the Allied bombing of Dresden.

Most generally, there is the National Day of Mourning, occurring two Sundays before Advent in the fall. It includes wreath-laying at the Central Memorial of the Federal Republic of Germany in Berlin for the Victims of War and Dictatorship, attended by federal ministers and the German president, and speeches in the Bundestag. Both occasions constitute important expressions of German national identity. Another element of national identity in the form of collective remembrance is the annual commemoration by German government representatives of German resistance fighters at Plötzensee (a prison and execution ground in the Third Reich) on July 20, marking their attempted assassination of Hitler.

More specifically, the plight of expellees is recognized by German officials at the annual conference of the Federation of Expellees and also, since 2015, at the Remembrance Day for the Victims of Flight and Expulsion. At the annual conference in 2015, Chancellor Merkel made a promise: "From generation to generation, your history will be remembered."[15] On Remembrance Day, President Gauck intoned: "[T]he flight and expulsion of Germans are becoming established in the entire nation's historical awareness."[16] That process was accompanied by a protracted and heated political debate that led to the government's commitment to establishing a permanent home for the remembrance of expellees in a Documentation Center.[17]

Speaking on the 70th anniversary of the bombing of Dresden, President Gauck noted that "February 13, 1945, has burned itself into the memory of the survivors." For Gauck, remembering the bombing of Dresden and its victims did not invalidate or diminish the reality that it was Germany which started the "murderous war": "We do not forget [the victims of a German-led war] when we remember today the German victims."[18] Thousands of Dresdeners commemorated the victims by forming a human chain of peace and reconciliation. Others, marching under the aegis of the right-wing Pegida movement, used the occasion to make a political statement of neo-Nazism and xenophobia.

On August 14, 2015, Prime Minister Abe first identified "[m]ore than three million of our compatriots [who] lost their lives during the war." Understandably, he included the victims of Hiroshima and Nagasaki and the fire-bombing of Tokyo. Only then are non-Japanese countries and victims mentioned, but without numbers or names or a detailed description of the "immeasurable damage and suffering" Japan inflicted. In Australia and at Pearl Harbor, the prime minister did personalize the suffering with names, but only of Japanese individuals. In all three statements, the prime minister did recognize the forbearance of victim countries, "their manifestation of tolerance" that permitted Japan's return to the international community after the war, and thanked them for making "every effort for reconciliation." On August 14, he seemed to be referring, euphemistically, to female sexual slaves as victims when he noted that "there were women behind battlefields whose honour and dignity were severely injured." The statement lacked graphic description of their plight and personal identification.

Past, Present and Future

For German leaders, the imprint of the past is indelible and a guide for the present and future; commemoration is a collective, national effort linking past and future. Referencing his predecessor in the presidency, on January 27, 2015, Joachim Gauck intoned: "Roman Herzog . . . insisted that remembrance had to continue forever. Without remembrance, he said, evil could not be overcome and no lessons could be learned for the future." Gauck suggested the service the past could provide: "Remembrance days bring a society together in reflection on the shared past. For whether we like it now or not, formative experiences leave their traces—in the actors and in the witnesses, but also in future generations." At Auschwitz, Chancellor Merkel offered a similar perspective on the inextricable connection between past and future and a sense of responsibility: "[M]emory remains alive across generations . . . from it we can draw lessons for the future . . . for we must not forget. . . . We owe [this] to the many millions of victims." Invoking President von Weizsäcker's iconic speech thirty years earlier, at Sachsenhausen Foreign Minister Steinmeier specifically linked May 8, 1945, to the present and future: "And so May 8, 1945, does not stand for the liberation of Germans from the past, but rather it is a liberation that helps us face up to the past and learn from it. So that we can shoulder responsibility, consciously aware of our past."

Without specifics, Prime Minister Abe did allude on August 14 to Japan's "responsibility to inherit the past, in all its humbleness, and pass it on to the future." At Pearl Harbor, he indicated that the strong friendship with the United States, despite the past, would guide the alliance into the future. The past and the future, in his formulation, are connected less by the lessons of history and more by Japan's post-war commitment to democracy, freedom and the rule of law.

For German leaders, the past enables the present and the future, is a complement to later developments, whereas for current Japanese leaders the present is antithetical to a past that has to be overcome and relegated, rather than being made the centerpiece of national identity and purpose. Because of Germany's fundamental belief in the past's long, shaping shadow and concomitant actions of remembrance and commemoration, German leaders' periodic criticism of victim nations—as of Israel over its settlement policies—or occasional insensitivity to history do not impair the Federal Republic's credibility nor derail relations, as frequently happens in East Asia.

The Young

In his May 1985 speech on the 40th anniversary of the end of World War II, President von Weizsäcker articulated an important understanding of how Germany viewed young people's role in confronting the past, a notion that would remain as an assumption in the next thirty years:

> The vast majority of today's population were either children then or had not been born. They cannot profess a guilt of their own for crimes that they did not commit. No discerning person can expect them to wear a penitential robe simply because they are Germans. But their forefathers have left them a grave legacy. All of us, whether guilty or not, whether old or young, must accept the past. We are all affected by its consequences and liable for it. [19]

This combination of placing responsibility, not guilt, on the young, and preferring the notion of legacy over burden is evident in President Gauck's words on January 27, 2015:

> Future generations will certainly seek new forms of commemoration. And while the Holocaust will not necessarily be among the central components of German identity for everyone in our country, it will still hold true that there is no German identity without Auschwitz. It is part and parcel of our country's history.

The importance of maintaining places of barbarity as memorials and registering victims' memories as an obligation to the young was foremost in Chancellor Merkel's observations at Dachau:

> [Victims'] indelible and moving descriptions are of particular help to young people to allow them to connect bare facts and figures to faces, to names and to individual life stories. . . . Places of memory like this [concentration camp] are so important. . . . As places of learning for future generations, they carry the responsibility to keep alive and convey the knowledge of what happened— especially when the time comes that there are no witnesses, no survivors of National Socialism. . . . We will always remember—for the sake of the victims, for our sake and for the sake of future generations.

And, on the 75th anniversary of the outbreak of World War II in Poland, Foreign Minister Steinmeier demonstrated Germany's commitment to current and future younger generations on the victims' side by speaking at the first ordination of rabbis (trained in Potsdam) in Wroclaw since World War II:

> Dear graduates, for us, your trust is at the same time a blessing and a responsibility. When you will go on to guide communities following your ordination, you are most cordially welcome. You will shape Jewish life, life which is an

integral part of our shared European culture and identity. We will not leave you to do so alone. We do not want Jewish communities to be sheltered minorities in need of protection, we want them to be part of everyday life at the heart of our society.[20]

On August 14, 2015, Prime Minister Abe's message to the young was mixed. One the one hand, and first, he wanted to limit their involvement in dealing with the past: "We must not let our children, grandchildren, and even further generations to come, who have nothing to do with that war, be pre-destined to apologize." On the other hand, he accepts, secondly, that "even so, we Japanese, across generations, must squarely face the history of the past." At Pearl Harbor, it is the reality of Japanese-American friendship after the war that should be remembered by the young: "It is my wish that Japa-nese children and . . . American children, and, indeed, their children and grandchildren . . . will continue to remember Pearl Harbor as a symbol of reconciliation."

PURPOSE

German commemorations have devoted much time and space, as indicated above, to the principal lesson of confronting the past: to avoid a repetition of history through acknowledgment, memory and understanding, summed up in "Never again war, never again Auschwitz" (Nie wieder Krieg, nie wieder Auschwitz).[21] This fundamental goal has given rise to several related, practi-cal purposes at home and abroad.

President Gauck referred on January 27, 2015, to his country's "credo," which Germany "[affirms] today when we stand up against every form of exclusion and violence and when we offer a safe home to those who are fleeing persecution, war and terror . . . [W]e in Germany must work to reach a new understanding of the coexistence of different religious and cultural traditions." Foreign Minister Steinmeier asked at Sachsenhausen in April 2015: "[W]hat does this responsibility mean in practice?" And he answered: "[I]t means standing up to injustice, to all forms of xenophobia and discrimi-nation." He also identified an international purpose related to peace: "Our foreign policy commitment to tackle [global] crises and to work to achieve an international order in which rules of the game foster peace and under-standing also stems from the awareness of our German past." At Auschwitz and Dachau Chancellor Merkel drew the same lessons of promoting toler-ance as the essence of democracy and international cooperation as the life-blood of the global arena.

In Australia, on August 14, 2015, and at Pearl Harbor Prime Minister Abe made a similar argument for Japan's commitment to peace and diplomacy as a response to conflict. The statements reflected a desire to express gratitude to other countries for allowing Japan's return to the international community. He also sought to characterize the relationships with the United States and Australia, as "reconciliation" and a "special relationship" respectively.

At Sachsenhausen in 2015, Foreign Minister Steinmeier noted the framework of Europe that enabled this German post-war path—a context to be nurtured and not forgotten, as the chancellor and president had already indicated in 2014 at the anniversaries of D-Day in France and of World War II's outbreak in Poland.

CONTEXT

The context of the European Community/European Union was crucial for Germany's policy of confronting the past, of which remembrance and commemoration have been the central core. The EC/EU—where former enemies could not avoid each other or tough issues that separated them and where Germany could act as a structural and philosophical equal—facilitated reconciliation between France and Germany. It performed the same function for Germany after Poland and the Czech Republic became members of the EU in 2004. Furthermore, the values of tolerance and peace Germany promoted in and through its policies concerning history were the foundational values of the European project, values in jeopardy today throughout much of Europe, as German leaders frequently note.

The EU itself has used commemorations to highlight its identity as a peace community. The EU heads of state and government commemorated the 100th anniversary of the outbreak of World War I by gathering in Ypres, Belgium, for a memorial service and a meeting of the European Council, indicating simultaneously the horrors of war and the antidote of reconciliation. Chancellor Merkel underscored the EU's significance: "I believe that this once again shows us how lucky we are to live today—thanks to the European Union and thanks to the fact that we have learned from history."[22]

The 70th anniversary of World War II prompted an EU statement at the UN, signaling the collective nature of the organization in the international arena: "The European Union and its Member States believe that an honest and thorough debate on history will facilitate reconciliation based on truth and remembrance. . . . We therefore appreciate this [UN] resolution as it contributes to preserving the memory of the victims of one of the darkest episodes of our history."[23]

Commemorative statements can be a call to identity, but so can structures. In numerous ways, the EU has sought to forge an EU identity, so far with limited success given EU-antipathy and EU-fatigue in a number of member states. One recent institutional effort to forge a collective memory is the 2017 establishment in Brussels of the House of European History that centers on

European history since 1789, with the main focus on twentieth-century history and the process of European integration.

Beyond the EU, the larger international context has also provided a stimulus to remembrance and commemoration. One of Germany's first statements recalling the horrific details of the past and committing to practical responsibility—Adenauer's September 27, 1951, statement in the Bundestag—happened in part due to U.S. pressure.[24] Since many decades, Germany has internalized the value of commemoration and has not required encouragement, although on occasion its pro-action has caused controversy. In May 1985, trying to repeat the success of the 1984 Franco-German reconciliation handshake at Verdun, Chancellor Kohl persuaded President Reagan to visit the cemetery in Bitburg where SS officers were buried, causing an uproar in the United States, especially among Jewish groups and veterans. President von Weizsäcker's landmark speech of May 8, 1985, was a response to Kohl's missteps.

The manner of Germany's commemorations in 2015 had an obvious Russian dimension. Despite the war in Ukraine and the downturn in Russo-German relations, German leaders chose to honor the Russian victims, suffering and sacrifices of World War II. Chancellor Merkel forewent the big celebrations in Moscow on May 9, but she did, together with President Putin, place a wreath on the Tomb of the Unknown Soldier one day later and proclaimed: "In this way I would like to say to the people of Russia, as German chancellor I bow down before the millions of victims of war, which was unleashed by National Socialist Germany."[25] Together with the Russian foreign minister, Foreign Minister Steinmeier also laid a wreath, this time at the site of the battle of Stalingrad, and once more offered a counterpoint to tensions over Ukraine: "For me, because of the crisis in Ukraine, it was especially important to come here as a sign of reconciliation and understanding. As complicated as things have been, as different as our opinions are on different issues, faced with the memory of Stalingrad we have to try as much as we can to resolve the conflict in Ukraine."[26]

The reality of tension and contestation combining with commemoration and remembrance has also been evident in German domestic politics. Regarding one of the first acts of Germany facing its past—the 1952 Reparations Agreement with Israel—44 percent of German respondents at the time deemed it unnecessary and only 35 percent provided positive responses. Some German politicians were equally as negative, with Chancellor Adenauer forced to rely on the Social Democratic Party opposition to achieve ratification of the treaty in 1954. His own finance minister voted against the agreement. Adenauer's September 1951 Bundestag statement, well-received in parliament, that led to the negotiations and the agreement had declared:

> The federal government and with it the great majority of the German people are aware of the immeasurable suffering that was bought on the Jews in Germany and the occupied territories during the time of national Socialism . . . unspeakable crimes have been committed in the name of the German people, calling for moral and material indemnity.[27]

Another treaty premised on remembrance of World War II and National Socialism's inhumanity, the 1970 "normalization" treaty with Poland, was also not uniformly popular. Only a plurality of 43 percent endorsed the treaty, and only 18 percent of respondents saw Poles in a favorable light. The December 1970 treaty, which recognized Poland as "the first victim" of a murderous World War II, engendered much debate and opposition in the parliament before finally being ratified in 1972. In both the September 1951 Adenauer statement to Israel and world Jewry and the Polish treaty, for fear of domestic opposition, German leaders rejected the victim nations' calls for an explicit reference to collective guilt and responsibility.[28]

In the 1997 German-Czech declaration, which included statements of mutual regret about the past and a German acknowledgment that its actions in the 1938 Munich Agreement set in train a path of occupation, war and destruction, the German government faced down domestic opposition from the expellee community. Rejecting the declaration as unacceptable, Sudeten German leaders appropriated the term "genocide" to describe their expulsion and painted a picture of Germans as victims.

German public opinion has a long history of being ambivalent concerning reconciliation and drawing lessons from the past.[29] In a 2014 survey by the Bertelsmann Stiftung, on the question of "putting the past behind us," 55 percent of Germans agreed with the statement, with 42 percent disagreeing (interestingly the numbers for 1991, were 60 percent agreeing and 20 percent disagreeing). The discrepancy between leaders analyzed in this chapter and some segments of society seems clear in 2015–2016 in public responses to the influx of refugees as a result of policies developed as a counterpoint to the exclusions and persecutions of the Third Reich. In their reactions to the human crisis, Germans have been both welcoming—continuing a tradition of civil society organizations promoting tolerance and international reconciliation—and ugly—demonstrating an apparent inability to learn from the past.

One of the missing ingredients for a practicable trajectory for reconciliation in East Asia is a vibrant regional organization that can bind and embed the parties while providing institutional and psychological symmetry and equal rights and responsibilities. The larger global context of U.S. pressure, and the related Japanese awareness of an American audience, do seem to have been heavily present in the tone and language of the prime minister. Abe's speeches also have to be seen in their domestic context. The heated political debate over the last five years about how Japan should remember the past (and which history should be commemorated) militated in favor of a via media approach—neither an excessive nor a belabored apology.

Such a cautious approach was evident also in the December 2015 Japanese-Korean agreement on the so-called "comfort women," which was heavily criticized in parts of the Japanese polity. Japan's insistence that there be no more talk of the issue and that the "comfort woman" statue be removed from outside the Japanese embassy in Seoul stands in contrast to Germany's approach over slave and forced labor. Even though Germany was tardy in resolving this issue—only in 2000—and even though it insisted on legal peace and legal closure, it nonetheless committed the foundation it created (Foundation Remembrance, Responsibility and the Future) to educational activities and dialogues about the past. In terms of greater understanding and knowledge, settlement opened the door to exploring the past rather than closing it.

CONCLUSION

German official commemorations of World War II and the Holocaust have been plentiful, prioritized the victims, detailed the crimes, and perpetuated a long tradition of remembrance in emotion and policy. German officials have demonstrated leadership in using the past to draw explicit lessons for the present and future, whether of tolerance or of reconciliation, and in so doing have run into contestation both domestically and internationally. Germany's tradition of commemoration as part of a broader "culture of remembrance" has been both comprehensive and complex. Japan's unsteady path of commemoration was stabilized by the middle-of-the-road approach in the last few years, but the way ahead will not be easy, neither at home nor abroad.

The robustness of remembrance and commemoration will be tested by generational change as the witness generation disappears and the younger generation is confronted by new challenges in a transformed international system. Can young people make twentieth-century lessons relevant for the twenty-first century? Reconciliation in Europe and in East Asia will depend on their answers.

NOTES

1. For German commemorative practices between 2012 and 2015, see: http://www.aicgs. org/mercator/. The link also provides information on comparative experience with commemoration in former Yugoslavia and Turkey. For a specific comparison of Germany's relations with Poland and Japan's relations with Korea, see: Olga Barbasiewicz, "Different Anniversaries, Same Purpose: War Memory and Reconciliation in Central Europe and East Asia (2014–2015)," American Institute for Contemporary German Studies website at: http://www. aicgs.org/by-author/olga-barbasiewicz/.

2. This is the English translation of the title of the memoir by Erich Lüth, one of the chief activists in German-Israeli reconciliation: *Viele Steine lagen am Weg* (Hamburg: Marion von Schröder, 1966).

3. "Remembrance and Commemoration" at: http://www.bundesregierung.de/Webs/Breg/EN/Issues/Gedenken_en/_node.html; and "Sites of remembrance 1933–1945" at: http://www.orte-der-erinnerung.de/fileadmin/public/site/ausstellungen/2012/Bro_OdE_2011_en_Web.pdf. The analysis in this chapter will largely be confined to official commemoration.

4. For details of Germany's complex remembrance practices, see: Corine Defrance and Ulrich Pfeil (eds.), *Verständigung und Versöhnung* (Peter Lang, 2016); Eric Langenbacher, Bill Niven, Ruth Wittlinger (eds), *Dynamics of Memory and Identity in Contemporary Europe* (New York and Oxford: Berghahn, 2013); Birgit Schwelling (ed.), *Reconciliation, Civil Society, and the Politics of Memory* (Bielefeld, Germany: Transcript-Verlag, 2012); Lily Gardner Feldman, *Germany's Foreign Policy of Reconciliation: From Enmity to Amity* (Lanham, MD: Rowman & Littlefield, 2012); Jeffrey Herf, *Divided Memory: The Nazi Past in the Two Germanys* (Cambridge, MA: Harvard University Press, 1997).

5. Prime Minister of Japan, "Statement by Prime Minister Shinzō Abe," August 14, 2015, at: http://japan.kantei.go.jp/97_abe/statement/201508/0814statement.html; Prime Minister of Japan, "Remarks by Prime Minister Abe to the Australian Parliament," July 8, 2014, at: http://japan.kantei.go.jp/96_abe/statement/201407/0708article1.html; The White House, "Remarks by President Obama and Prime Minister Abe of Japan," December 27, 2016, at: https://obamawhitehouse.archives.gov/the-press-office/2016/12/28/remarks-president-obama-and-prime-minister-abe-japan-pearl-harbor.

6. Emperor Akihito's 70th anniversary statements suggest an exception to the singular person of Abe as representative of Japan. For the emperor's New Year greeting, see: http://www.kunaicho.go.jp/e-okotoba/01/gokanso/shinnen-h27.html. For his statement on the anniversary of the war's end, see: *Japan Times*, August 15, 2015.

7. See: http://www.aicgs.org/mercator/.

8. Examples are the summer 2014 exhibition on the Warsaw Uprising at the Topography of Terror museum in Berlin; and the January 2015 "Violins of Hope" (belonging to persecuted and murdered Jewish musicians) concert for the International Holocaust Remembrance Day.

9. Federal Foreign Office, "Speech by Foreign Minister Frank-Walter Steinmeier on the 70th anniversary of the liberation of the Sachsenhausen concentration camp," April 19, 2015, at: http://www.auswaertiges-amt.de/EN/Infoservice/Presse/Reden/2015/150419_Sachsenhausen.html.

10. Bundespräsidialamt, "Federal President Joachim Gauck on the Day of Remembrance of the Victims of National Socialism on 27 January 2015 in Berlin," at: http://www.bundespraesident.de/SharedDocs/Downloads/DE/Reden/2015/01/150127–Gedenken-Holocaust-englisch.pdf.

11. Der Bundespräsident, "Commemoration of the end of the Second World War," Schloß Holte-Stukenbrock, 6 May 2015, at: http://www.bundespraesident.de/SharedDocs/Reden/EN/JoachimGauck/Reden/2015/150506–Holte-Stukenbrock.html.

12. Die Bundeskanzlerin, "Rede von Bundeskanzlerin Merkel anlässlich der Gedenkveranstaltung des Internationalen Auschwitz-Komitees zum 70. Jahrestag der Befreiung des Konzentrationslagers Auschwitz-Birkenau am 26. Januar 2015," at: http://www.bundeskanzlerin.de/Content/DE/Rede/2015/01/2015–01–26–merkel-auschwitz.html.

13. Die Bundesregierung, "Rede von Bundeskanzlerin Merkel bei der Gedenkveranstaltung zum 70. Jahrestag der Befreiung des KZ Dachau am 3. Mai 2015," at: http://www.bundesregierung.de/Content/DE/Rede/2015/05/2015–05–04–merkel-dachau.html.

14. For a sample listing of Germany's commemorative and remembrance "symbolic events" with other countries, see: Gardner Feldman, *Germany's Foreign Policy of Reconciliation*, 87–90, 146–48, 216–18, 278–79.

15. Die Bundesregierung, "Rede von Bundeskanzlerin Dr. Angela Merkel beim Jahresempfang des Bundes der Vertriebenen am 5. Mai 2015 in Berlin," May 5, 2015, at: https://www.bundesregierung.de/Content/DE/Bulletin/2010–2015/2015/05/59–2–bk-jahresempfang.html.

16. Office of the Federal President, "Speech by Federal President Joachim Gauck to mark the first Day of Remembrance for Refugees and Expellees, Berlin 20 June, 2015," Berlin, June

20, 2015, at: https://www.bundespraesident.de/SharedDocs/Downloads/DE/Reden/2015/06/150620–Gedenktag-Flucht-Vertreibung-englisch.pdf?__blob=publicationFile.

17. Alexander Wochnik, "Non-State Actors, Political Opportunity Structures and Foreign Relations: The Case of Germany's Federation of Expellees and the 'Foundation Flight, Expulsion and Reconciliation,'" *German Politics*, 23, no. 3, (2014): 213–230.

18. Bundespräsidialamt, "Bundespräsident Joachim Gauck bei der Gedenkveranstaltung des 70. Jahrestages der Zerstörung Dresdens am 13. Februar 2015 in Dresden," Dresden, February 13, 2015, at: http://www.bundespraesident.de/SharedDocs/Reden/DE/Joachim-Gauck/Reden/2015/02/150213–Dresden.html.

19. The English version, a translation by the German Foreign Office, is available at: http://www.lmz-bw.de/fileadmin/user_upload/Medienbildung_MCO/fileadmin/bibliothek/weizsaecker_speech_may85/weizsaecker_speech_may85.pdf.

20. Auswärtiges Amt, "Rede von Außenminister Frank-Walter Steinmeier bei der Ordinationsfeier des Abraham-Geiger-Kollegs in Breslau," September 2, 2014, at: http://www.auswaertiges-amt.de/DE/Infoservice/Presse/Reden/2014/140902–BM_Geiger_Kolleg.html.

21. As a slogan, this phrase was articulated by then foreign minister Fischer in April 1999 concerning Germany's decision to participate in the war against Serbia. See: Nico Fried, "Ich habe gelernt: Nie wieder Auschwitz," May 19, 2010, at http://www.sueddeutsche.de/politik/fischer-ich-habe-gelernt-nie-wieder-auschwitz-1.915701.

22. The Federal Government, "European Council in Ypres. EU Heads remember the World War," June 26, 2014, at: https://www.bundesregierung.de/Content/EN/Reiseberichte/2014/2014–06–26–er-ypern_en.html.

23. European Union Delegation to the United Nations—New York, "EU Statement—United Nations General Assembly: 70th Anniversary of the End of World War II," February 26, 2015, at: http://eu-un.europa.eu/eu-statement-united-nations-general-assembly-70th-anniversary-of-the-end-of-world-war-ii/.

24. For details, see: Lily Gardner Feldman, *The Special Relationship between West Germany and Israel* (Boston: Allen & Unwin, 1984).

25. The Federal Chancellor, "Remembering World War Victims Together," May 10, 2015, at: http://www.bundeskanzlerin.de/Content/EN/Reiseberichte/2015/2015–10–05–bkin-zu-gedenken-min-moskau.html.

26. "German Foreign Minister Frank-Walter Steinmeier Marks WWII Anniversary at Site of Stalingrad Battle," NDTV, May 8, 2015, at: http://www.ndtv.com/world-news/german-foreign-minister-frank-walter-steinmeier-marks-wwii-anniversary-at-site-of-stalingrad-battle-761348.

27. Quoted in Gardner Feldman, *The Special Relationship*, 40.

28. On Israel, see: Gardner Feldman, *The Special Relationship*, 83, fn. 1. On Poland, see: Adam Bromke and Harald von Riekhoff, "The West German-Polish Treaty, *World Today*, 27, No. 3 (March 1971): 124.

29. For an analysis of German public opinion on reconciliation and the past, see: Gardner Feldman, *Germany's Foreign Policy of Reconciliation*, chapter 2.

Index

About the Contributors

Lily Gardner Feldman is currently the Harry & Helen Gray Senior Fellow at the American Institute for Contemporary German Studies at Johns Hopkins University. She has published widely in the United States and Europe on German foreign policy, German-Jewish relations, international reconciliation, non-state entities as foreign policy players and the EU as an international actor. She is the author of *Germany's Foreign Policy of Reconciliation: From Enmity to Amity* (2012). Her work on Germany's foreign policy of reconciliation has led to lecture tours in Japan and South Korea.

Marc Gallicchio is professor of history at Villanova University. He specializes in U.S.-East Asia relations and modern U.S. history. His publications include *The Scramble for Asia: U.S. Military Power in the Aftermath of the Pacific War* (2008), and *The African American Encounter with Japan and China: Black Internationalism in Asia, 1895–1945* (2000).

Akira Iriye is Charles Warren Professor of American History emeritus, Harvard University. Born in Japan, Iriye graduated from Haverford College and obtained his Ph.D. at Harvard University. He is a past president for the American Historical Association as well as the Society for Historians of American Foreign Relations. His numerous publications include *Global and Transnational History: The Past, Present, and Future* (2012); *Global Community: the Role of International Organizations in the Making of the Contemporary World* (2002); *Cultural Internationalism and World Order* (1997); *The Origins of the Second World War in Asia and the Pacific* (1987). Among the books he has edited or co-edited are: *Global Interdependence: The World After 1945* (2014); *The Palgrave Dictionary of Transnational History* (2009); *The New Cambridge History of American Foreign Relations*

(2015); *American, Chinese, and Japanese Perspectives on Wartime Asia, 1931–1949* (1990).

Ricardo T. Jose is professor of history at the University of Philippines Diliman. His interests include diplomatic and military history, particularly that of the Philippines and Japan. His research takes a multi-perspectival approach to the experience of war, seeking to grasp the experiences of Japanese civilians and soldiers, as well as Filipinos, and others from areas throughout the Philippines. He has therefore worked with various veterans' groups, radio and TV programs (local and international).

Christine Kim is visiting assistant professor in the Asian Studies Program of Georgetown University. She teaches modern Korean history and other topics in East Asian history, including courses on comparative colonialism, twentieth-century conflicts, and political symbolism. Her research and writing have focused on national identity, material culture, and political movements. Her forthcoming book, *The King Is Dead*, explores the ways in which colonization and modernization influenced Korean polity and identity during the late nineteenth and early twentieth centuries.

Marlene Laruelle is research professor of international affairs at GWU's Elliott School, director of the Central Asia Program, as well as associate director of the Institute for European, Russian and Eurasian Studies. She focuses on Russia and Central Asia, exploring post-Soviet political, social and cultural changes through the prism of nationhood and nationalism. She is the editor in chief of *Central Asian Affairs* and a member of the executive editorial board of *Demokratizatsiya, The Journal of Post-Soviet Democratization*.

Tze M. Loo is associate professor of history and international studies at the University of Richmond. Her research concentrates on the colonial dimensions of the modern Japanese nation state, in both its prewar and wartime imperial expansion, and on the functions of colonialism itself in the making of modern Japan. Her book *Heritage Politics: Shuri Castle and Okinawa's Incorporation into Modern Japan, 1879–2000* (2014) examines how Japan, Okinawan people and America during its 27-year rule of the islands, have used Okinawa's cultural heritage—particularly its iconic Shuri Castle—to negotiate and articulate the islands' relationship to the Japanese mainland.

Mike Mochizuki holds the Japan-U.S. Relations Chair in Memory of Gaston Sigur at the Elliott School of International Affairs in George Washington University. Professor Mochizuki was associate dean for academic programs at the Elliott School from 2010 to 2014 and director of the Sigur Center for

Asian Studies from 2001 to 2005. He co-directs the Rising Powers Initiative and the Memory and Reconciliation in the Asia-Pacific research and policy project of the Sigur Center. Previously he was a Senior Fellow at the Brookings Institution. He received his Ph.D. in political science from Harvard University.

Robert Sutter is professor of practice of international affairs at the Elliott School of George Washington University. His areas of expertise include contemporary U.S. policy toward Asia and the Pacific –especially China and Taiwan, and the making of U.S. foreign policy including the roles of Congress and the Intelligence Community. He has taught at Georgetown, Johns Hopkins and the University of Virginia, and has had a three decades-long governmental career with a focus on Asian and Pacific affairs. A prolific writer, he has published 20 books, over 200 articles and several hundred government reports dealing with contemporary East Asian and Pacific countries and their relations with the United States. His most recent book is *Foreign Relations of the PRC: The Legacies and Constraints of China's International Politics since 1949.*

Daqing Yang is an associate professor of history and international affairs at George Washington University, where he teaches modern Japanese history. He is a founding co-director of the Memory and Reconciliation in the Asia Pacific program. A native of Nanjing, China, he received his PhD at Harvard University and has taught in Japan and Korea. His research interests are the Japanese empire, the history and memory of the Asia-Pacific War, and historical reconciliation. His book *Technology of Empire* examines telecommunications networks in prewar and wartime Japanese expansion. He is a co-editor of *Rethinking Historical Injustice and Reconciliation* and *Toward a History Beyond Borders: Contentious Issues in Sino-Japanese Relations.*

CPSIA information can be obtained
at www.ICGtesting.com
Printed in the USA
FSHW010501100220
66987FS

9 781498 567718